Mergers and
Acquisitions Basics

Mergers and Acquisitions Basics

The Key Steps of Acquisitions, Divestitures, and Investments

MICHAEL E. S. FRANKEL

WILEY

John Wiley & Sons, Inc.

This book is printed on acid-free paper. ∞

Copyright © 2005 by John Wiley & Sons. All rights reserved.

Published by John Wiley & Sons, Inc., Hoboken, New Jersey.
Published simultaneously in Canada.

For general information on our other products and services, or technical support, please contact our Customer Care Department within the United States at 800-762-2974, outside the United States at 317-572-3993 or fax 317-572-4002.

Wiley also publishes its books in a variety of electronic formats. Some content that appears in print may not be available in electronic books.

For more information about Wiley products, visit our Web site at *www.wiley.com*.

Library of Congress Cataloging-in-Publication Data:
Frankel, Michael E. S.
    Mergers and acquisitions basics : the key steps of acquisitions, divestitures, and investments / Michael E. S. Frankel.
        p. cm.
    Includes index.
    ISBN-10: 0-471-67518-0 (cloth)
    ISBN-13: 978-0-471-67518-1
    1. Consolidation and merger of corporations.   2. Corporations—Finance.   I. Title.
HG4028.M4F73 2005
658.1'6— dc22

                                                                    2005002062

Printed in the United States of America.

10 9 8 7 6 5 4 3 2 1

contents

The nature of business is a moving target. The way markets and businesses operate is constantly evolving, changing, and developing. For those who study business this is a source of new data, and for those who conduct business it is a source of a constant stream of new challenges and opportunities. Transactions, deals, agreements, or contracts are as old as commerce itself. However, in recent decades, a variety of transactions involving control of business entities themselves have become far more common.

Mergers, acquisitions, divestitures, equity, and venture investments are all forms of what I refer to in this book as Strategic Transactions. Strategic Transactions are unique in several respects. Unlike other commercial contracts and agreements, Strategic Transactions are dramatic events for companies and often represent either the end to a company as an independent business, or at least a dramatic change in its management, ownership, or fate.

Since the 1970s, Strategic Transactions have evolved from rare events to a common business practice. Today, most large companies have an active ongoing acquisition effort and most small and private companies consider being acquired a possible and sometimes likely end-game. Strategic Transactions, in the form of private equity and venture capital investments, also represent a large and increasing source of capital for new and growing businesses.

As Strategic Transactions have become a common and popular business tool, a new class of business professionals has emerged to manage and execute these deals. While professional advisors like investment bankers, lawyers, and consultants have long been expert at structuring and executing Strategic Transactions, today this segment of the advisor community is larger than ever.

More important, a class of business professionals has emerged within companies, who are experts in doing Strategic Transactions. Some of these corporate development professionals learn their craft as bankers or lawyers while others are developed within a company. What is clear is that doing deals has become a defined and recognized business specialty like marketing, finance, and operations. We may even suppose that this is a virtuous cycle where the increasing population of deal experts will lead to an increasing use of Strategic Transactions as a business tool, in turn leading to the development of more deal experts.

In addition to the growing population of professionals both inside and outside of companies who make a career of deals, there is a growing legion of business executives who are involved in Strategic Transactions. It is rare to find a manager or executive who has not found herself involved at least tangentially in an acquisition, divestiture, or other Strategic Transaction.

The goal of this book is not to provide an all-encompassing and definitive treatise on Strategic Transactions. Many books have been written by legal, finance, and accounting experts delving into tremendous detail on the mechanics and features of Strategic Transactions. The goal of this book is to provide the reader with a basic primer and overview of the key steps and features of most deals.

I hope that this book will be read by both young professionals starting to develop an expertise in Strategic Transactions, and also by a wider range of business executives who find themselves involved in deals. For the young investment banker, lawyer, or consultant, this book can provide a foundation for understanding deals, on which they can build a deep expertise and specialty. For business executives and managers, the book can hopefully provide a complete and easy-to-read overview to help them navigate a deal and their role in it.

I have sought to balance the need for detail with ease of understanding, and to add a measure of fun and humor to a serious and complex topic. As the reader navigates this book, and then a career with some or perhaps many deals, I hope they will not only learn vital lessons to ensure their success but also share some of the huge enjoyment I have found in the infinite challenge and complexity of doing deals and building businesses.

acknowledgments

This book is the result of months of writing, but also of years of work and dozens of deals. The knowledge I try to share comes from more than a decade of work with a myriad of smart, accomplished, talented, and kind professionals. I owe a debt of gratitude to my colleagues, clients, and friends from GE, VeriSign, Merrill Lynch, Skadden, Arps, and the Chicago Mercantile Exchange for their guidance, wisdom, and mentoring.

I could not have written this book without the help and wisdom of Shayna Klopott and the invaluable assistance of Gail Nurnberger. I also need to thank my family, including Ernst, Tamar, Ray, Inna, John, Betsy, Patty, Joan, and Anat. Their kindness and intelligence also run through this book as with every part of my life.

Of course, while any wisdom or insight can be attributed to my time with these people, any errors or mistakes are entirely my own.

CHAPTER 1

Introduction

M&A, deals, buyouts, LBOs, MBOs, private equity, venture capital, corporate development, and a myriad of other terms are used to describe large transactions that fundamentally change the nature or course, and control, of a company. While there are many differences among these different types of deals, a common thread runs through all of them. They are all Strategic Transactions that involve a change or shift in control of a company and usually a corresponding shift in strategic direction.

There are many different types of transactions done by a company during its life cycle. Companies execute agreements with suppliers, customers, partners, regulators, and financiers almost constantly. A lawyer would argue that running a business is really a long series of contractual obligations, entered into, complied with, and terminated. At any given time, most companies are entering into new agreements and consummating new transactions on a daily, even hourly, basis.

Strategic Transactions are different. They are the seismic life-changing events that fundamentally alter a company. They usually change not only who controls the company but also the strategic direction the business will take. They sometimes take a public company private or make an independent company into a small subsidiary. While full acquisitions are the most commonly known Strategic Transactions, there are many variations on the theme. However, all Strategic Transactions have a lot in common. They all involve a substantial or total change in control and a large amount of money (or other form of payment) changing hands. They all involve a Buyer, who will want to learn a tremendous amount about the business and understand it deeply. Finally, they all involve a Seller, who is trying to maximize the value of its business but also often has other interests, including the long-term partnership it may be entering into with the Buyer and the fate not only of its business but also of its employees.

Over the past few decades, Strategic Transactions have played an increasingly important role in business. From the growth of private equity investments in a variety of forms to the increasing use of acquisitions as a growth tool by large, and even midsized, companies, Strategic Transactions have become a standard and common part of the business landscape, fueling the growth of large and small companies. There is a long-term upward trend in both the volume and average deal size of acquisitions in the United States. Exhibit 1.1 shows that even after a downturn during the collapse of the "tech bubble," M&A remains on a substantial upward trend over the past two decades.

While part of the explanation for the increased deal size is inflation, the increase in volume is a clear indication that Strategic Transactions are not only a core tool of growth for the large traditional acquirers but also becoming a standard growth strategy for small and midsized companies. This is also evidenced by the large number of smaller deals being done. For example, in 2002, 67% of the acquisitions reported had a purchase price of less than $100 million, and nearly 15% were between $5 and $10 million.[1]

Many of the largest technology companies in the United States today received their early funding from venture capital and private equity investments, and many of the largest and most established names in business, including IBM, General Electric, and Pepsi, as well as newer stars, such as Tyco and Cisco, drove a significant part of their growth through acquisitions. The last two decades have witnessed a dramatic and sustained jump

EXHIBIT 1.1   Historical U.S. M&A Activity

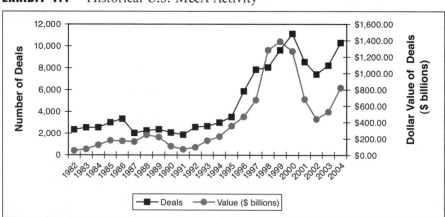

Source: M&A Activity U.S. and U.S. Cross-Border Transactions, Mergerstat (2004), *www.mergerstat.com/new/free_reports_m_and_a_activity.asp.*

in the volume of both venture capital and corporate venture capital (e.g., venture capital funds run by corporations rather than as private independent funds) investments, as shown in Exhibits 1.2 and 1.3.

However, Strategic Transactions are not a riskless exercise; far from it. While they can be a source of dramatic and quick growth when they are successful, they can be a huge drain on a business when they fail to deliver. In what is often known as the "winners curse" many studies find that most of the value derived from many deals ends up in the hands of the Seller rather than the Buyer.[2] Often, this failure is the result of a gap

EXHIBIT 1.2   Venture Capital Commitments

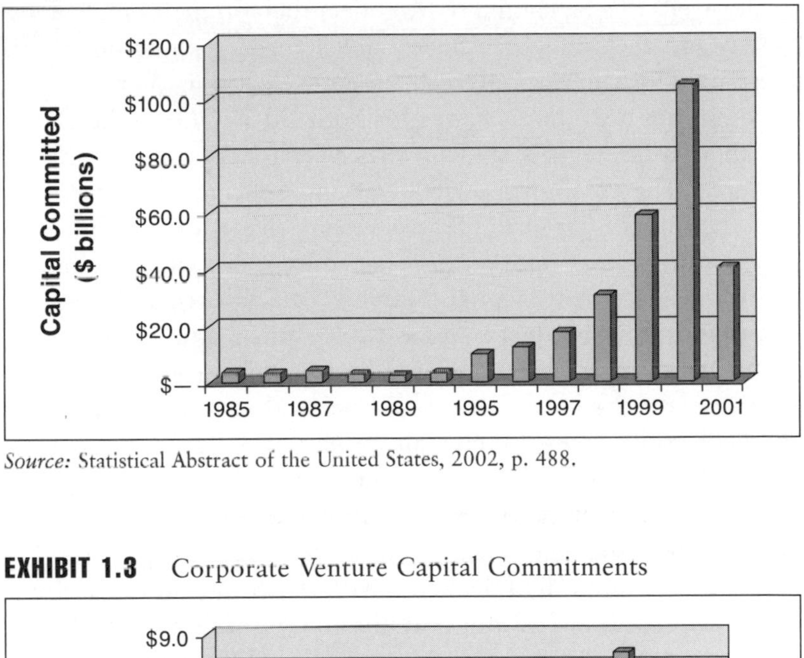

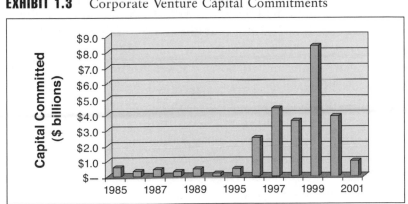

Source: Statistical Abstract of the United States, 2002, p. 488.

EXHIBIT 1.3   Corporate Venture Capital Commitments

Source: Statistical Abstract of the United States, 2002, p. 488.

between the cost and revenue synergies expected and actually found. In some cases, this is the result of optimistic expectations and in others, of a failure to execute effectively on integration plans.[3] One study found 64% of the deals studied destroyed value for the Buyers shareholders.[4]

This book will provide an overview of all the key steps in a Strategic Transaction and try to provide the reader with not only an overview of how the process works but also key lessons for how to approach and execute a deal effectively and efficiently. Many sections, will discuss each side—Buyer and Seller—individually; however, it is important for any participant in a Strategic Transaction to understand both sides. Too often, a Strategic Transaction falters, or the parties do not reach the optimal terms because one side fails to understand the other. Buyers need to understand the needs of a Seller and try to reflect them in their bid. Sellers need to understand the goals of a Buyer and manage their business to meet those goals. This can not only help to get a deal done but also in many cases result in a deal that is better for both sides. One of the interesting things about a Strategic Transaction is the potential for one plus one to equal three. The combination of Buyer and Seller can create additional value to be shared. For example, a company that is undercapitalized can actually return dramatically better results once it is owned by a larger parent with more access to capital. Similarly, a small technology company with an innovative product may be worth much more when combined with the marketing power of a large branded electronics manufacturer. In each case, the Strategic Transaction itself unlocks additional value that neither side could access individually. One of the keys to unlocking this value is a clear understanding of the other party's goals, challenges, and processes. Understanding the Buyer will make you a more effective and successful Seller, and vice versa.[5]

Chapter 2 reviews all of the key players in a Strategic Transaction. The goal here will be to discuss not only the role of each party but also their motivations and goals. This chapter will also differentiate between the goals of organizations and the individuals who run and represent them. Chapter 3 discusses the decision to buy or sell. Many of the terms, as well as the nature of the process of a transaction, will be driven by the underlying decision made by Buyer and Seller to do a deal. Chapters 4 and 5 discuss first the Buyer's preparation and then the Seller's preparation for a deal. Investing time and resources in preparing for a Strategic Transaction can yield dramatic returns. Given the large dollar amounts at stake, proper preparation is always a worthwhile investment. Chapter 6 discusses the deal process. Given the complexity of a Strategic Transaction, how the process is crafted can actually contribute to the success of the deal. Chapter 7 will focus on the core of a Strategic Transaction—due diligence. This is the period during which the Buyer tries, in a relatively short period of time, to get a sufficiently detailed understanding of the business for sale to have comfort that its price is reasonable and its plans for growing, expanding, or otherwise improving the business are feasible. This is also an opportunity for the Seller to further pitch the value of the asset and to try to allay any concerns that the Buyer may have. Effective due diligence is the key to avoiding nasty surprises after a deal is done, and failure to do proper due diligence can leave a Buyer owning a business much less attractive, less profitable, or simply much different from what the Buyer thought it was buying.

Chapter 8 will discuss valuation, arguably the core of a Strategic Transaction. The fact that a valuation is expressed in terms of a single or small range of numbers belies the fact that the process, part art and part science, of reaching this number is complex and unclear. Chapter 9 will review the often ignored issue of integration planning. For most Buyers, effective integration planning can be the difference between success and failure in a Strategic Transaction. While actual integration takes place after a deal is done, integration planning is an essential part of the transaction itself, since it both informs the other parts just mentioned (valuation, due diligence, and even the decision to buy) and helps to ensure that the actual integration can occur quickly and efficiently after the deal is closed. Financing issues that the Buyer may face will also be touched upon. While some Buyers have sufficient capital on hand to do a Strategic Transaction, such large and relatively rare deals often require outside financing, and this has an impact on both the Buyer and the Seller. Chapter 10 will also discuss such financing issues. Finally, Chapter 11 will discuss some of the mechanics of actually closing a deal and some of the "tail" issues that remain after a deal is closed. Every deal is unique and, by definition, requires a tailored set of documents. That said, some standards, forms, and checklists can be a valuable starting point. In the appendices, some examples of reports, checklists, process maps, and term sheets are provided that can help the reader flesh out the deal process.

The key steps, challenges, and processes in all Strategic Transactions are very similar. While this book will focus on the most common, the acquisition of an entire company, most of the lessons are equally applicable to transactions involving the acquisition of a strategic stake in a company as well.

NOTES

1. *M&A Journal,* vol., 38 no. 2 (2003), p. 25.
2. Scott Christofferson, Robert McNish, and Diane Sias, "Where Mergers Go Wrong," *McKinsey Quarterly,* no. 2 (2004), p. 2.
3. One McKinsey study found that in 70% of the deals studied, the Buyer failed to achieve the expected levels of revenue synergies, and in 25% of the deals the Buyer substantially overestimated cost synergies. Ibid.
4. "Of 277 big M&A deals in America between 1985 and 2000, 64% destroyed value for the acquirers' shareholders. Interestingly, mergers in recessions or periods of low growth from 1985–2000 did better than mergers consummated in good times." "The Return of the Deal," *The Economist,* vol. 368, issue 8332 (July 10, 2003), p. 57.
5. For a much more detailed discussion of this topic, see Michael E. S. Frankel, *Deal Teams: The Roles and Motivations of Management Team Members, Investment Bankers, Venture Capitalists and Lawyers in Negotiations, Mergers, Acquisitions and Equity Investments* (Boston: Aspatore, 2004).

CHAPTER 2

The Players

Y ou cannot understand a Strategic Transaction without understanding the players involved, their roles, their motivations, and the way transactions are managed. Beyond the Buyer and the Seller, there are many entities that participate in a Strategic Transaction. Beyond the entities, it is as important, if not more important, to consider the individuals. In many cases, individuals within an entity and the motivations that drive them can have a substantial impact on a deal. This chapter will review the major players in a Strategic Transaction. It will discuss what role they play, how they are motivated, and how they are managed.[1]

THE BUYER

In this book, the "Buyer" is the entity rather than the individuals who may represent it. Subsequent sections will briefly talk about the individuals who may be sitting across the table from you in a negotiation. In theory, people who work for an entity should exactly represent its best interests, but in practice this is not always the case. In this section, think of the Buyer as a corporate entity maximizing its and its shareholders' best interests.

Buyers come in many forms with different goals and motivations. When negotiating with a Buyer, it is essential to understand the Buyer's business model and priorities. Similarly, as a Buyer, it is important to first establish what your priorities are to ensure that a Strategic Transaction meets your company's specific goals.

Strategic Buyers

When people refer to strategic Buyers, they are usually referring to corporations that are making an acquisition to bolster their poor business.

A better and broader definition might be that a strategic Buyer is an entity making a purchase that it intends to somehow consolidate, link, or integrate with other operations that it owns. Strategic Buyers will be differentiated from financial Buyers shortly. Strategic Buyers generally view an acquisition in terms of the impact that it will have on the Buyer's existing business and the impact that the Buyer's existing business can have on the acquired business. These can be defined broadly as synergies. Chapter 8 will discuss synergies in detail, but for the moment suffice it to say that synergies are the exercise of making $1 + 1 = 3$. To the extent that a strategic Buyer can recognize synergies through an acquisition, it has an inherent advantage. In effect, it can buy something for $10 but by virtue of buying it and integrating it effectively, can make it worth $11. However, as will be discussed below, synergies presume an effective and efficient integration. This is a far, far more daunting task than most acquirers expect.

Strategic acquirers have an additional advantage. Unless they are looking to acquire a business in a wholly new area, a strategic acquirer will have a fairly deep understanding and knowledge of the business, operations, and customers of an acquisition Target. A strategic acquirer will also be able to call on its own staff to provide detailed expertise when reviewing an acquisition and considering the challenges of integration.

Repeat Players

For many companies, acquisition has become a standard business tool. Companies like Cisco and Tyco drove growth through acquisition and effective integration. During the year and a half between 2000 and mid-2002, Mergerstat reported that 13 U.S. companies closed more than 15 acquisitions each (see Exhibit 2.1).[2]

Repeat players have several distinct advantages even over other strategic Buyers. The most obvious and powerful is that they have learned through experience and through trial and error. Repeat players have honed their ability to evaluate, negotiate, close, and integrate Strategic Transactions. They have learned what they do well and what they do not do well. In terms of governance, repeat players have learned how to quickly and efficiently navigate their own internal approval processes for Strategic Transactions, which inevitably attract senior management's attention and scrutiny. Part of this is that the senior management and boards of repeat players have gotten more comfortable with the inherent risk and volatility of Strategic Transactions. Repeat players have also developed dedicated expertise in their staff to do these deals. Repeat players usually have dedicated deal teams and standardized procedures, documents, and

EXHIBIT 2.1 Top Acquirers 2000–2002

Company	Total Acquisitions	Total Value ($ millions)
General Electric Co.	71	$19,725.0
Brown & Brown Inc.	42	N/A
Cendant Corp.	33	$ 3,797.8
BB&T Corp.	23	$ 3,098.7
Black Box Corp.	23	N/A
Arthur J. Gallagher & Co.	23	N/A
divine Inc.	20	$ 429.0
The First American Corp.	20	$ 45.3
Tyco International Ltd.	19	$16,882.2
Citigroup Inc.	18	$21,350.5
General Motors Corp.	18	$ 175.5
Omnicom Group Inc.	18	$ 100.1
TMP Worldwide Inc.	16	$ 348.0

models. More broadly, repeat players usually develop a general understanding among their broader management and employee base of the role and purpose of strategic acquisitions. This makes both drawing resources to do a deal and the process of integrating a deal less traumatic for the organization and its employees.

Newbies and One-Timers

Like anything else in life, there is always a first time for doing deals. For some companies, a first Strategic Transaction is the first step in becoming a repeat Buyer—a serial acquirer. For other companies a Strategic Transaction may be an aberration or a one-time event, which is unlikely to be repeated. There is also the third category—occasional Buyers. While occasional Buyers are not as unsophisticated or unprepared as first-time Buyers, they do not have the same infrastructure, experience, and capabilities that a repeat Buyer does.

For first-time Buyers, a Strategic Transaction is far more frightening and far more risky than for a repeat Buyer. It is also far more expensive in terms of dollars spent, but more important in terms of resources that must be devoted and the distraction to senior management and the board of directors. Much of the rest of this book will be devoted to discussing the various parts of a Strategic Transaction and the capabilities that a Buyer or Seller needs to do one. First-time Buyers usually lack most, if not all, of these capabilities and skill sets. Part of the challenge for any first-time Buyer is overcoming the "speed bump" of developing the capabilities to do a deal. A first-time Buyer must also overcome the fear and uncertainty associated with such a dramatic change to its core business: placing one very large debt in a game with which they are not particularly familiar. For many companies the speed bump of building a capability and getting comfortable with the risks of a deal overcome the appeal of doing a deal.

If a first-time Buyer does decide to pursue a Strategic Transaction, it is crucial that the company approach the deal with caution, preparation, and a sufficient awareness among senior management and the board of directors of the inherent risks and volatility in this particular tool for growth.

First-time Buyers can often draw on internal expertise doing a deal. Even if a company has never done a Strategic Transaction, many of its managers and senior executives may have deal experience from prior roles in other companies. This said, first-time Buyers usually find Strategic Transactions to be painful and unnerving. Senior management and the board of directors really find the inherent risk hard to accept, and employees find the uncertainty created during the deal and subsequent integration to be unnerving. While repeat players will usually act decisively and efficiently in assessing transactions, first-time Buyers are often slow to make a decision and hesitant to make a bid. It is not uncommon to see first-time Buyers review a large number of deals for a long period of time before becoming comfortable with actually executing one.

Financial Buyers

Strategic Buyers look at a Target and see a component to be added to their current business. By contrast, financial Buyers look at a Target as something they can maintain as a stand-alone company, but improve, revitalize, or recapitalize and eventually sell at a substantial gain. The notable exception here is for financial Buyers, who will undertake in a roll-up, where they plan to acquire multiple businesses that can be combined and integrated. There are a variety of types of financial Buyers, who focus on different sizes of transactions, different transaction structures, and different industry sectors. Broadly speaking, all financial Buyers use some form of investor capital to acquire control of Target companies with the eventual goal of selling the company for a profit.[3]

Fundamentally, financial Buyers face two significant challenges in doing deals versus strategic Buyers. First, investors and financial Buyers generally expect a significant return on investment. "Significant" usually means well in excess of what they could realize by making investments in similar companies on the open market. Second, in most cases, financial Buyers will not be able to realize the synergies that strategic Buyers will, in an acquisition. When bidding against strategic Buyers, this puts them at a significant disadvantage. Now, the various types of financial Buyers will briefly be discussed.

Private Equity Firms

There are a variety of types of private equity firms. As a general matter, private equity firms are firms that collect a pool of capital from large institutional and private investors and then make selective investments in a portfolio of companies. While some private equity firms take small minority interests in these private companies, many acquire control, or effective control, in their portfolio companies. There are many "flavors" of private equity firms. Some private equity firms focus on making the large investments in large established businesses. Other "venture capital" firms focus on acquiring an interest in earlier-stage companies. Another variation is leveraged buyout (LBO) funds, which acquire companies with strong cash flow characteristics, where they are able to borrow money for a significant portion of the purchase price (that is, a "leveraged transaction").

Management Buyers

In some cases, a private equity firm will partner with a management team to acquire a company. This could be a public company that it takes private, effectively buying the company from the public market. This could also be a division of a public or private company that the management team, when partnered with a private equity firm, acquires from the parent company and runs on its own. In either case, the result is a company that is acquired by a combination of a private equity firm and a management team. Unlike a traditional private equity transaction, where the management team may get little equity, in a management buyout (MBO), the management team will likely get a significant chunk of the equity of the company in the acquisition.

THE SELLER

By contrast to Buyers, who often pursue Strategic Transactions repeatedly, by definition Sellers are one-time participants. With some notable exceptions, the decision to sell is a singular and final decision of the corporation.

In effect, selling a corporation is the final endgame for the shareholders. Once a company is sold, it loses the distinct nature of a separate entity and becomes a subsidiary of another company or is even subsumed in whole into an existing business. In any case, it loses many of the characteristics of a stand-alone company. From a financial point of view, the sale of the company is a true endgame for stockholders. If they receive cash, they have entirely severed their relationship with the company. Even if they receive stock, they are usually relatively uninvolved minority equity holders in a much larger company. The notable exception to this last item is a situation in which the selling stockholders receive a significant portion of the resulting parent company. This situation will be discussed further when talking about the currency of transactions in Chapter 8. The other notable exception is the case of partial Sellers. Let us discuss Sellers in three categories: (1) partial Sellers, (2) full Sellers, and (3) unwilling Sellers.

Partial Sellers

Many Strategic Transactions may involve the sale of a part, but less than all, of a company. In some cases, this is the first in a series of transactions that will eventually end in a complete sale of the company. In other cases, the Buyer will never acquire the whole company but only a minority stake. For the Seller, partial sale is thus either a prelude to a complete sale or an end in and of itself. In this vein, a partial sale can be used as a financing mechanism. Rather than trying to sell shares on the open market, in the case of a public company, or to a large number of investors, in the case of a private company, a partial Seller can get capital by selling a chunk of itself to a single counterparty. For the partial Seller, this provides capital that can be used to grow the business, or it can provide a liquidity event for some of the existing shareholders of the partial Seller. The partial Seller may also be seeking to solidify a relationship with the partial Buyer. One good example of this would be a small manufacturing company that is trying to solidify its relationship with a large retailer that it uses as its main channel of sale. By having the retailer make an investment and own a chunk of the manufacturer, the manufacturer can create a powerful incentive for the retailer to continue to sell its products. Thus, in addition to the cash from the sale, a partial Seller may use the transaction to build a relationship with the Buyer.

In most cases, partial Sellers will be private companies. Private companies have limited access to the public markets for debt and no access to the public markets for equity. A partial sale to a single large Buyer can be an attractive funding mechanism for private companies. In some cases, public companies may also choose a partial sale. In recent years, Private Investment in Public Equities (PIPES) deals have become very popular. In a PIPEs deal, a public company makes a prearranged sale of a minority interest to a single Buyer. The key issue to remember with all partial Sellers is that, unlike a full Seller, the transaction does not spell the end of the corporate entity. The company will continue to operate, albeit with a new large and potentially influential shareholder.

Full Sellers

The term "full Seller" is used in this book to refer to the traditional Seller of a company. In this situation the company is being sold in toto. This is truly the endgame for shareholders and often for senior management of the Seller. The decision to sell will be discussed in more detail below, but it is important to remember that for the Seller, this will be the first and last of this transaction. As such, the Seller usually goes through a complex and detailed process of deciding to make a sale. For reasons that will be discussed below, the Seller, its management, and its board of directors have decided that shareholders' value can be maximized by selling the company at this time.

Unwilling Sellers

This last category is a rare, but important, group of Sellers. In most cases, Strategic Transactions occur at the instigation, or at least with the enthusiastic support of, the management of the Seller. However, in some cases, a Strategic Transaction will be "thrust upon" a Seller—the hostile deal. In a hostile deal, a Buyer will bypass the management and board of directors of a Seller and appeal directly to the shareholders of the Seller to sell their shares. In most cases, the Buyer will first approach the Seller's management or board and only bypass them after being rebuffed. In either case, in a hostile transaction, the management and board of directors of the Seller are actually fighting to avoid a transaction and battling the company's shareholders for their "hearts and minds." As discussed below, unwilling Sellers behave dramatically differently from willing Sellers. In many ways, hostile deals bear little resemblance to other Strategic Transactions. There is a rich and deep literature that discusses these strategies and processes of hostile deals.[4] This book will focus largely on "friendly" deals, but it is important to remember the hostile category of deals and the category of unwilling Sellers.

INVESTORS/OWNERS

So far this book has referred to Buyers and Sellers, the two entities involved in a transaction. The remainder of this section will talk about the entities and individuals who are part of the Buyer or Seller, or who surround them during a Strategic Transaction. At this point, it is useful to review the difference between a legal entity and a person. Corporations may be legal entities that take "actions," but at the end of the day they are made up of, and advised by, a number of different groups of individuals. The way that Buyers and Sellers act during Strategic Transactions is largely driven by the motivations, interests, and views of those individuals and other entities.[5] There are several types of investors or owners of companies. Think of them in the context of the evolution of a company from its initial conception and founding through its early stage growth to its later stage growth and finally to going public and becoming a publicly held company. This section will discuss the various investors and owners along that same lifeline.

Entrepreneurs/Founders

Like fires, every company starts with a spark. That initial spark is sometimes an idea or a product or a concept or even a theme.[6] Founders are the people who take that initial spark and turn it into a concrete plan and then begin to execute it. In some cases, founders will step aside once the business starts to become successful, ceding control to "professional management." In other cases, founders will continue at the helm for years or even decades throughout the entire life cycle and growth cycle of a company. In the middle case, founders may seed the top spot to professional managers, while retaining a role on the management team, such as "chief strategy officer." By definition, founders start out owning 100% of the company. Of course, in this early stage, that means they own 100% of effectively nothing. But as a company matures and begins to have value, and even as it is diluted down by the addition of funding from other investors, founders usually retain a significant ownership stake in their companies (for example, Bill Gates who even today owns approximately 10% of Microsoft). As a result, even in large well-established companies, founders can play a significant role and have a large say in whether or when the company does a Strategic Transaction. Through both their equity ownership and their historical and continuing role in the company, founders usually have a seat at the table.

When considering the role of founders in Strategic Transactions, it is important to remember the variety of motivations at play. Certainly, as large equity holders, founders seek to maximize their personal wealth. However, founders are also driven by personal motivations. Like watching a child grow up, a founder watches the growth and progression of a company with significant emotion. A founder may be swayed for or against the Strategic Transaction based on how it will affect the company that he or she has created. For example, the founder of a company who is considering selling itself to a large competitor may have mixed feelings. Even if she is sure that this deal will maximize the value of the company, she will hate to see the business she helped build be subsumed into a larger entity whom she may have spent a large part of her career battling. In many cases, founders believe that they have built the unique corporate culture or philosophy and will be hesitant to see that diluted or destroyed by a Strategic Transaction. A founder may also consider how a Strategic Transaction will affect him or her personally on a day-to-day basis. For many founders, the company is not only a job and an asset but also a home and a family. When a company is acquired, the founder may lose her role and even her office. Similarly, when a company acquires other companies, the founder gets to watch her child grow. Acquisitions that make the company larger may be especially personally rewarding for a founder because his ego and self-worth may be closely tied to the success and perhaps the pure size of the company.[7]

When dealing with founders, it is essential to keep in mind these non-financial motivations that in some cases may even outstrip financial interests. For example, the commitment to a founder that the corporate culture she has built, or perhaps her personal role as a strategic leader, will be left intact after an acquisition may be more important to her than maximizing the purchase price for a company. Similarly, tainting an acquisition as a significant step toward demonstrating that a founder's strategy, approach, or product is superior may be a more powerful motivator than showing that the acquisition will have short-term financial benefits. This is not to say that founders are irrational, but simply that as individuals, like all of us, they can be swayed by personal as well as financial goals and preferences.

Private Equity

At a certain stage in its development, almost every company has the need for outside capital. In many cases, companies start out being funded by their founders, and in some rare cases the business grows quickly enough to fund its own growth. However, in most cases, particularly for larger, faster-growing businesses, an infusion of capital is needed relatively early in the development of the business. In the evolution of a business, there is a large space between initial founding and eventual access to public markets. When a business has grown too large to be funded by its founders, and is far too small to be taken public, it is funded by private equity and sometimes debt. Here the term "private equity" is used in its broadest sense, simply to refer to investments made outside the realm of the public markets. These private equity investors can be separated into four broad categories:[8] (1) angels, (2) venture capital, (3) traditional private equity, and (4) LBO/MBO investors.

Angels

Early in the development of a business, in some cases before the business is even launched, a founder will need to look outside of her own resources. In some cases, this is because the founder does not have the money, and in other cases, the founder is simply seeking to avoid putting her entire life savings into a risky early-stage business venture. In either case, a founder will often start by looking to people she already knows. Broadly defined, angel investors are individuals (usually with a personal relationship directly or indirectly to the founder) who make relatively small investments in very early–stage companies. An angel may be a classmate, friend, family member, or business associate of the founder. In some cases, there may be one or even two degrees of separation, where the founder is introduced to the angel. Angel investors will tend to behave more like traditional private equity investors, who are discussed in the "Private Equity" section. However, it is important to remember that angel investors have some unique characteristics. With a personal relationship to the founders, they may be swayed by some of the founders' interests and motivations. Even though they are making relatively small investments, as individuals, these investments may represent a significant portion of their net worth, and as a result they may use a different financial calculus than a large institutional investor would. For example, an angel investor who puts $300,000 into a start-up company may have a total net worth of $5 or $10 million. While $300,000 does not "break the bank," if the company does well and that investment is worth $10 or $15 million, the sale of the company or at least the angel's stake in it, will be a life-changing event for the angel investor. You need look no further than some of the angel investors in large technology companies in the late 1990s to see examples of dramatic increases in wealth.

Venture Capitalists

Venture capital has been around for decades but has reached new prominence in the last 15 years. Venture capital firms are usually made up of a small number of professionals who have built a fund of committed investments from institutional investors and in some cases very wealthy individuals. The business model of a venture capital firm is to find a number of promising, early-stage businesses, make a series of investments, help these businesses to develop and grow, and hope that a small number of these investments will yield significant upside. By definition, venture investing is the exercise of, to coin a baseball term, "swinging for the fences." Venture capital firms expect that a large percentage of the investments they make will be worthless, that a smaller number will yield modest results, and that a very small number will yield spectacular results. Some venture capital firms would argue with this assessment and say that they focus on more conservative business models, in effect trying to hit a lot of doubles and triples, but it is generally safe to say that venture capital is a relatively high-risk exercise, investing in early-stage companies without proven track records. The upside to this risk is that venture capital firms will get to invest in companies at relatively low valuations. Once invested, a venture capital firm will usually try to help the business succeed. Venture capitalists sit on board of directors, make industry connections, and often even install members of management into companies in which they have invested. Some venture capital firms operate like Japanese *keiretsu*.[9] These firms will create a network of investments and then work to ensure that each of their portfolio companies works with other relevant portfolio companies to help each other succeed (the same can be said for other private equity firms discussed later in this chapter).

Venture capital firms are, at the end of the day, beholden to their investors. They need to show performance in order to raise larger funds and, in some cases, even to keep the funds they have raised. The two measures of performance are (1) time and (2) quantity. The shorter the period between making an investment and reaping a reward, the better. The greater the return on that investment, the better as well. Often, these two measures will come into conflict. When a venture capital firm is faced with the option of selling its stake in a portfolio company, it must balance the benefit of an immediate win against the possibility of an even greater win in the future. A venture investor and a potential Seller will have to consider this balance not only in terms of this particular investment but also in terms of their broad portfolios. If a venture fund has not been able to sell many of its portfolio positions, it may be under pressure from its investors to reach a "liquidity event." This may drive the venture investor to consider the bird in the hand of an early sale versus the two in the bush of continuing to grow a portfolio company. By contrast, a venture capital firm that has recently sold off many portfolio companies or that has recently received a large inflow of investment funds may have an incentive not to sell a portfolio company but rather continue to grow it, hoping to yield even better returns in a few years.

A final point on venture capital firms, which also applies to other private equity firms, is discussed in the following section. In most cases, the employees and partners of a private equity firm or venture capital firm receive most of their financial compensation in the form of "carry." A venture capital partner may receive a base salary, but the vast majority of her compensation comes in the form of a share of the upside in the investments she makes. As a result, partners in venture capital and private equity firms have a very personal and immediate financial stake in Strategic Transactions by their portfolio companies. The sale of a portfolio company at a significant premium to the valuation at which the venture capital firm invested will translate immediately into a large financial windfall for the partner at the venture capital firm. As a result, the time and return forces that impact a venture capital firm have a similar derivative impact on the individual partners in that firm. On a personal, financial level, they must weigh the size of the financial windfall of a sale against the time required to receive it.

Private Equity

Much of what has been said for venture capital firms can be said for private equity firms. The model is very similar but generally at a later stage in a company's development. Private equity firms, as the term is commonly used, generally invest in well-established businesses with a proven business model. The most common model is for a private equity firm to make an equity investment in a midsized, privately held company. Often these are companies that have either been grown through venture capital investing or, often more slowly, through organic growth. In recent years, private equity firms have often not made investments in technology and software companies. This is because those companies have grown so rapidly that they have jumped directly from venture capital to going public. Like a venture capital firm, a private equity firm will make a large investment in the company with the hope of helping it to grow and develop, and eventually either be sold to an acquirer or taken public. While in some cases a venture capital firm may help fund acquisitions by its portfolio company, this is not that common. By contrast, private equity firms will often help fund an acquisition strategy. Thus, it is more common for private equity firms to be investors in companies that are Buyers as well as Sellers. Another difference between venture capital and private equity is that private equity firms are more likely to be acquirers themselves. Early-stage companies that venture capital firms invest in are usually still fairly dependent on their original founders and management team. By contrast, a private equity firm may often seek to acquire companies that are mature enough but their founders are long since gone or at least not essential. The following section discusses the management buyout and leveraged buyout variation on this.

The incentives of private equity firms are pretty much the same as venture capital firms. They take in large pools of investments, buy stakes in companies, and seek to drive to liquidity events, where those stakes yield substantial returns. Like venture capital firms, they are focused on the balance between time and return. The biggest difference is in terms of scale. Private equity firms tend to make larger investments in more established companies. The companies they invest in, by virtue of their size and maturity, are probably less likely on average to fail but also less likely to yield dramatic results. The private equity firm is swinging for doubles and triples, less likely to strike out but also less likely to hit a home run.

Leveraged Buyout and Management Buyout Firms

One variation on private equity is the LBO and/or the MBO. An LBO is simply the process of acquiring a company where the purchase price is heavily financed by debt. When a company is relatively mature and stable and generates strong, positive cash flows, it may be possible to borrow heavily to fund an acquisition since the cash flows make repayment of the debt highly likely. The advantage to a Buyer of an LBO structure is that it can purchase a relatively large company with a relatively small amount of its own money. The downside is that the company going forward will be heavily burdened with large interest payments to cover the debt and the debt holders must be paid in full before the equity holders can recognize a return on their investment. In some ways, an LBO has the same financial characteristics as buying an option on a publicly traded security or buying stock on margin. If the company does well, the return can be dramatic, but if the company does badly, your entire investment can be wiped out very quickly. Another variation on a private equity acquisition is the MBO. In a traditional LBO an institution like a private equity firm purchases a company with a large amount of debt. In an MBO, the management team themselves acquire the company with funding that is usually a combination of equity from their own pockets and from a private equity firm in debt as in a traditional LBO. The presumptive advantage of an MBO is that a management team with a deep knowledge of the business has a powerful incentive through a large financial stake in the success of the business. Of course, an MBO is only as successful as the capability of the management team to run and actually improve the business. It is important to recognize the separate incentives of the management team in an MBO. In many ways, managers in an MBO are in the same position as founders. In effect, they are taking a company and "restarting it" as a new entity under their control. Both financially and personally, they are in a similar position to a founder.

Public Investors

At some point in its life cycle, many companies will choose to go public. The initial public offering (IPO) has developed something of a mystical quality, particularly in the last two decades. While it is a seminal event in the life of the company and in the lives of the individual founders and early investors, it is really not so different from earlier investments made in the private company by the parties discussed so far. A public company is simply a private company that has chosen to sell its shares to a number and type of investor that triggers regulations concerning its conduct and communication with those investors. U.S. securities laws, in particular the 1933 and 1934 acts[10], are basically designed to protect investors, notably those smaller and less sophisticated investors who may not be able to protect themselves. In general terms, the acts provide that once a securities offering is being made to more than 35 unsophisticated investors, though it is allowed an unlimited number of sophisticated investors,[11] it is deemed a "public offering" and needs to begin complying with a large number of regulations, which are largely concerned with ensuring that those investors receive sufficient and accurate information about the performance of the company.[12]

Once a company is public, its shares, in effect its ownership, are held by a much wider variety and dramatically larger number of investors. In addition to the investors already described, there are two general categories of public investors: (1) individual investors and (2) institutional investors.[13]

Individual Investors

Individual or "retail" investors make up a large portion of the public markets. Both the size and activity of individual investors in the public markets have grown over the past few decades. On average, individual investors will own a significant portion, if not a majority, of most public companies. One recent study found that individual investors owned approximately 70% of outstanding shares in a survey of over 7,000 publicly traded companies.[14] Individual investors are the largest, if not sole motivation, for U.S. securities regulations and the operation of the Securities and Exchange Commission (SEC). Since these investors are rarely financial professionals, they have a very limited ability to understand the markets or the financial performance of individual companies. Since almost all have "day jobs," they certainly cannot follow the performance of a company in the kind of detail that institutional investors or the private investors can. Individual investors depend on a variety of surrogates to provide them with their views and investment strategies with regard to the market and with regard to individual companies. These sources include brokers, financial news sources, and even friends and family.

While it is hard to make generalizations about such a large population, it is fair to say that individual investors tend to hold shares of stock for fairly long periods of time. With the exception of "day traders," most individual investors take a buy-and-hold approach to shares of stock. However it is clear that this approach has eroded over the past decade as the Internet has brought real-time data and low-cost trading to individual investors. Today it is not safe to assume that an individual investor checks his portfolio once a quarter or even once a month. Many individual investors check their portfolios daily or even hourly. Since there is such a broad range of sophistication among individual investors, they can often be swayed by dramatic news reports, trends, and styles, and, most of all, by panic. This is not to say that panic does not affect institutional investors as well. But, perhaps because they monitor the markets less carefully, it is harder to correct misperceptions on the part of individual investors. This is clearly a very personal view on my part, and many would actually argue that individual investors are no less sophisticated and no less accurate than most institutional investors. One difference is clear, however. Individual investors get their information about public companies largely through news sources (both online and offline) and their brokers. This is a substantial difference from institutional investors.

Institutional Investors

Broadly defined, institutional investors are any large entities that make active and large investments in the public markets. These entities include insurance companies, pension funds, mutual funds, endowments and nonprofit institutions, and even massively wealthy individual and family investment vehicles.[15]

Different institutional investors can have substantially different motivations and investing methods. Some are judged on short-term performance like mutual funds, and others are judged on much longer–term performance like university endowments. Institutional investors also vary in terms of their interests in becoming actively involved in the management of companies in which they invest. Many large institutional investors specifically avoid becoming involved in all but the most important issues.[16] Some institutional investors may avoid involvement in these issues because it creates a conflict of interest with other parts of their business. For example, Prudential Insurance may have large investments in a company like General Motors (GM), while also being a provider of insurance services. Other institutional investors may choose to avoid involvement in management issues because they believe that they are a surrogate for individual investors. They choose to focus solely on maximizing the value of their portfolio through buying and selling securities rather than trying to influence the management of the companies in which they invest. However, other institutional investors have chosen to take an active role in the management of companies in which they hold a large stake. Given their size, these institutional investors may hold a significant amount of stock to represent a material voting block of shareholders. In these situations, they can have a significant impact on the management of the company. In the last decade, some large institutional investors, notably state pension funds, have become much more activist in wielding their voting rights to impact the management of companies in their portfolios.[17] One particularly good example is the California Public Employees' Retirement System (CalPERS), which in the early 1990s commissioned a study that suggested a strong correlation between stock price performance and active involvement by CalPERS.[18] CalPERS has been particularly activist, for example in withholding votes for five Hewlett-Packard Co. directors, citing the Palo Alto computer and printer maker's noncompliance with CalPERS corporate governance guidelines.[19]

Whether they are activists or passive shareholders institutional investors are always very active in managing their investments. Unlike individual investors, institutional investors have teams of analysts who work full-time to monitor their portfolios and make buy/sell decisions. Also, unlike public investors, institutional investors usually have a far richer set of data sources to make those decisions. While, in theory, public companies must share information with all investors equally, in practice, there are informal channels by which companies will communicate with large institutional investors. These can include one-on-one meetings between large institutional investors and the management of the company or an invitation to investor conferences hosted by investment banks where management will speak. In addition to these informal channels, institutional investors are also more likely to take advantage of sources of data that are made public but are usually too detailed or time-consuming to be absorbed by public investors. A good example of this will be the quarterly earnings call. While technically any member of the public can dial in to the quarterly earnings call of a company, in practice, few public investors participate. These meetings are largely sources of data for institutional investors and Wall Street research analysts. Speaking of which, access to one-on-one conversations with Wall Street research analysts is another unique source of data for institutional investors. While public investors may get to read the research put out by these analysts, institutional investors will usually have access to direct contact with the analysts.

While, in theory, institutional investors should be more sophisticated and stable investors in companies, in practice, they can be just as volatile and uncertain in their investing strategies and reactions to company news as individual investors. However, by their nature, they are each dramatically larger than individual investors, and in many cases, a single institutional investor may own a material chunk of one particular public company. It is not unusual to find public companies, particularly smaller public companies, with a single institutional investor holding 5 or even 10% of the company's stock.

CORPORATE STAFF

This chapter has discussed Buyers and Sellers as singular entities, but it is important to remember that behind the veil of a corporate legal entity there are dozens, hundreds, thousands, or even hundreds of thousands of individuals who manage and operate that company. The actions of a company are a coordinated amalgamation of the judgments, biases, motivations, and decisions of those individuals. Just as from a distance a flock of birds or a school of fish may look like a single entity, moving, turning, slowing, speeding up, one may anthropomorphize a company and view it as an individual, but, in fact, it is simply a "flock of management birds." Let us briefly discuss four key groups who are the most influential in shaping corporate decisions.

Board of Directors

The board of directors holds an odd position in the no-man's-land between shareholders and employees. In a private company, the board of directors has a relatively easy job. They usually represent the voices of the small number of large shareholders who own the business and can defer directly to those large shareholders for any major decisions. Things are different with a public company. The board of directors of a public company can rarely turn to shareholders and get their views. With the exception of a very rare population of issues that will go to a shareholder vote, the board of directors has to use its own judgment to reflect the best interests of the shareholders. Even in the case of a shareholder vote for companies with a large population of individual shareholders, the board of directors holds tremendous sway over the decision those shareholders will make, since relatively uninformed public shareholders, and even some relatively passive institutional shareholders, will look to the board for its recommendation. Technically speaking, board members are employees of the corporation, though with the exception of the executive officers (CEO or CFO), this is not their full-time job. Most public corporation board members are current or retired senior executives of other large corporations or notable and well-respected leaders of public institutions such as universities or not-for-profit institutions.

Board members have several conflicting incentives. Financially, while they are not as wedded to the company as senior executives and employees, they usually do have significant financial stake.[20] Board members also usually derive a significant amount of professional prestige from being on the board of a public company. Board members often have personal or professional ties to the company or to the members of senior management. Finally, by becoming board members, these individuals take on the potential for personal liability. While a successful suit against a board member is very rare, it is theoretically possible for board members to be held personally and financially responsible for their actions in that role. Financial and accounting scandals in the last decade have substantially heightened board members' concerns about this latter issue, and the new requirements of the Sarbanes-Oxley Act have begun to address them and focus board members and management.[21]

While the board of directors is involved in the overall management of a company, they generally operate at "a 10,000 foot level." The board of directors will usually defer to the management team and employees of the company for the day-to-day management of the company. However, when a company considers making a dramatic or "company-changing" decision, such as entering into a Strategic Transaction, board members must descend from the clouds and focus on the details. A board of directors will be actively involved in the consideration of any Strategic Transaction. It is important for a board of directors to be actively involved in these kinds of transactions, since they have such a dramatic effect on shareholder value and the value of the company. It is also important to involve the board of directors, since such transactions (as will be discussed in Chapter 7) are most likely to generate adverse incentives for employees and management that create a need for greater oversight by the board of directors. While for most business decisions, even very large ones, the board of directors will defer to management for analysis and usually decision making, in the case of Strategic Transactions, the board of directors will become actively involved not only in making the decision but also in analyzing the facts. The board of directors will usually call on outside advisors in addition to advice and analysis from management. Those outside advisors will be discussed in more detail below.

Executive Management

The executive management team of a company are the top echelon of the employee base. The management team is usually made up of a small number of key employees who have control over the day-to-day operation and functioning of the business. Depending on the size and complexity of the business, the management team can consist of 2, 5, 10, or even 20 employees. The nature of the business will also determine who is considered among the ranks of executive management. For example, in a technology company the CTO (chief technology officer) will clearly be among the executive management team. By contrast in a consumer products company, the CTO may be relegated to a more junior rank, while the CMO (chief marketing officer) would be one of the most important and senior roles.

Members of the executive management team are at the pinnacle of their careers. They are usually highly skilled and highly respected in their areas of expertise. They are generally very well compensated with both cash and equity in the business.[22] With this compensation comes great responsibility. First, the executive management team is responsible for the overall performance of the company. In all but the most strategic and far-reaching issues (where the board of directors may become involved), the executive management team has the final word on the strategy and actions of the company.

When it comes to Strategic Transactions, executive management teams have a complex set of incentives and motivations. It is important to recognize that while these executives are usually skilled, professional, and experienced managers, they are also individuals with personal incentives and goals. The executive management team of a potential Buyer will likely have a natural incentive to complete an acquisition. In most cases, the CEO of a $2 billion company would much rather be the CEO of a $3 billion company. This incentive is not only driven by ego (though this motivation should never be underestimated) but also by financial goals. Managing a larger business usually translates into better financial compensation and a better career track. By contrast, management of a Seller may also have an incentive to complete a transaction. In most cases, executive compensation includes a large amount of equity that vests over time. However, in the event of a Strategic Transaction in which the company is sold, that vesting usually accelerates. This, coupled with "golden parachutes"[23] and other arrangements, usually translates into a significant payday for executive management of companies that are sold. However, by contrast, the executive management of a potential Seller may have an incentive to avoid a transaction. Clearly, being the CEO or an executive of a public company is potentially more prestigious than being the general manager of a division of the acquirer. It is not uncommon to see public company CEOs fighting to keep their company independent, and in many such cases the Buyer will appeal to the board of directors going "over the head of the CEO."

While the board of directors will certainly get actively involved in any Strategic Transaction, executive management still has substantial control. Executive management can stimulate the conversation to begin with by either proposing an acquisition or beginning negotiations with an acquirer. It can get the ball rolling. Executive management can also have a substantial impact on the results of a negotiation. Though the board of directors may seek the advice of outside advisors, in most cases, they will remain highly dependent on the advice, analysis, and opinions of the senior management team on whom they have learned to depend.

It is extremely rare that a transaction will be completed with the Buyer without the management team of the Buyer being actively supportive of a deal and usually present for the deal. Since the board is dependent on the management team to integrate an acquired company and run the overall business going forward, the board will rarely undertake an acquisition without the support of, and in fact, leadership from the management team. When a company is being sold, there are some exceptions to this rule. In some rare cases, a potential acquirer may appeal to the board of directors or even directly to large shareholders of a potential Seller. This will particularly be more likely if a previous approach to the management team has been rebuffed. However, this tactic is fraught with challenges, since the management team will have a substantial impact on the views of the board of directors. Thus, the vast majority of acquisitions are primarily led by the management teams of the Buyer and the Seller. This is somewhat less true for privately held companies. In the case of privately held companies where ownership control is highly centralized, large shareholders may take an active role in Strategic Transactions, eclipsing the role of management. An excellent example of this is found in the case of portfolio companies of private equity firms. In these cases, a single shareholder may have control or effective control of the company coupled with an active strategy for driving to a liquidity event. In such situations, the private equity firm may well drive the decision making and be actively involved in the negotiation process of a Strategic Transaction.

Line Management

The term "line management" is used to describe managers of individual business units within a company. In some cases, line managers may also be members of the executive management team, but even if they are not, they have a substantial impact on the performance of the company. At the end of the day, line managers drive the core engines that generate revenue for a company. Setting aside their potential role as a member of the executive management team, a line manager may have very little involvement in a Strategic Transaction with one notable exception. If a Buyer is acquiring a business that is going to be integrated into and/or under an existing line of business, that line manager will be intimately involved in the transaction. For example, Unilever manufactures the Dove brand of soaps. If Unilever were to acquire a small soap manufacturer or competing brand of soap, one can reasonably assume that the general manager of the Dove business would be deeply involved in the transaction. Any time a company acquires a business that it plans to roll into an existing line of business, the line manager will end up holding the bag in the sense that after the transaction is complete, she will have the responsibility for running this new business, integrating it into her existing business, and ensuring that the acquisition is a success. Line managers also have an important role to play prior to a transaction's completion. Since the line manager and her team are the experts in their particular field, they will often be involved in setting a strategy that ends up driving an acquisition. They will also be likely most familiar with all the potential players in the space and, thus, with potential acquisition Targets. Similarly, their expertise in the industry means that they probably have the best assessment of these potential Targets in terms of a variety of factors, including brand, technology, customer base, and management team. Different companies have different views on who should lead an acquisition process. Certainly, if the acquisition does not fit into an existing line of business, executive management and the Corporate Development team will have to take the lead. But when the acquisition does fit into an existing line of business, line management is always involved and, in some cases, has to not only support but also sponsor a transaction. Unless line management has lost the confidence of executive management and is on their way out, it is unlikely to see a company acquire a company in an existing line of business without the enthusiastic support of the line manager. Thus, in these transactions, line management is not only involved in postdeal integration but also in strategy, Target selection, due diligence, and, in some cases, active negotiation.

In most cases, line management will tend to be supportive of acquisitions that fall into their business. An acquisition grows the line manager's business and provides him with new capabilities and new resources. In a sense, an acquisition allows the line manager to use the corporate coffers to build his business. Some line managers may view acquisition funding as free money from headquarters. Quite the contrary, there is usually a clear quid pro quo. In order to justify the expenditure of an acquisition, the deal will have to be projected to be financially attractive in the future. Once the acquisition is done, the projections used to justify it will become the responsibility of the line manager. In the simplest terms, a line manager's financial goals for the coming years will be increased by the amount of the financial performance expected from the acquired business. When this quid pro quo is properly managed, the incentives to the line manager are properly balanced. However, the line manager wants to drive an acquisition that helps her grow her business (as with the CEO, being the line manager of a larger business is always more interesting/attractive). But the line manager is signing up to deliver the financial projections that justify the acquisition, and failure to do so can be a setback for her career. In some ways, it can be argued that this creates one of the closest ties between employee and shareholder incentives. In theory, the line manager should only support acquisitions where she can deliver or outdeliver the financial performance that justified the purchase price.

It is important to note that this theory is not always effective in practice. Time is a factor. Gaining the full benefit of an acquisition often takes years. The process of integrating an acquired business and then reaping the benefits of the synergies between the two businesses is, by definition, a long process. In many companies a management career involves many moves and changes in role. To the extent a line manager expects to move on from her current role in the coming years, she may be willing to sign on for unrealistic financial projections for an acquisition, knowing that she will be in an entirely different role by the time the chickens come home to roost. In practice, line managers are often able to avoid blame for bad deals and missed financial projections. In part, because the future is inherently hard to predict, and outside factors as well as, if not more often than, managerial incompetence may be to blame for an acquisition failing to perform. In addition to leaving a role, a manager can cite market forces and unexpected changes for the failure of an acquisition to live up to its projections.

In most cases, when a company is being sold, line managers will have a relatively limited role. In part because being acquired is usually not a good thing for a line manager. While in some cases the acquiring company may provide the line manager with a better platform to perform on or better career opportunities, as a general rule, to the winner go the spoils. If the acquiring company has a similar business, the line manager of the Target is not likely to end up running the combined business. However, line managers do have to be involved to some extent in the sale. In most cases, a Buyer will want to meet with line management to assess their value individually. The line manager is also the most useful source of information for a Buyer on the details of that business's operations and future performance. Thus, in the case of the Seller, the line manager is likely to be at least somewhat involved in a strategic acquisition from the point of view of providing due diligence information to the potential Buyers.

Corporate Development

Effectively executing Strategic Transactions requires some special skills and expertise.[24] Companies that make regular use of Strategic Transactions as a tool for growth generally seek to develop an in-house expertise in the form of a Corporate Development team.[25] As a result, Corporate Development teams tend to be formed in companies that have embarked upon, or plan to embark upon, the fairly regular use of Strategic Transactions. Unless the Seller has a history of being an acquirer, it is much less likely to have a professional Corporate Development team to manage the sales process. This may be one of the reasons that Sellers are more likely to be highly dependent on investment banking services than Buyers.

The Corporate Development team is at the heart of any Strategic Transaction. Throughout this book, as the various parts of a Strategic Transaction are discussed, you can assume the Corporate Development team has a significant role in executing or at least managing the tasks and processes. Different companies give different levels of responsibility to their Corporate Development teams. Corporate Development may take responsibility for all or some of strategic planning, broad acquisition planning, Target selection, due diligence, negotiation, valuation, internal processes and presentations, and integration. There are different philosophies about how to split the work among the Corporate Development team, other staff functions such as legal and operations, and line management and staff. Much of how this work is split up will depend on the nature of the business, the CEO's management style, and, of course, the wealth of strengths of each area and its members. The most common areas for Corporate Development to take ownership of include: identifying specific Target companies once a strategy has been set, negotiation of a deal, valuation, internal presentations and approvals, and overall process management. This last item should not be underestimated or overlooked. A large part of executing a Strategic Transaction successfully is in managing the process efficiently and effectively and bringing to bear resources from a variety of places within the company. In a sense, the Corporate Development team works like a conductor with an orchestra, bringing together and coordinating staff from throughout the company and throughout a variety of functions. This emphasizes perhaps the most important expertise that the Corporate Development staff have, namely a familiarity with the deal process and the key steps required to get a deal done.

The corporate development staff has an interesting set of incentives and motivations. They tend to be high-performing and ambitious executives. In some companies, they are pulled from the ranks of other specialties, such as finance and legal. In other companies, they are recruited from the ranks of professional advisory services, such as investment banks, law firms, and consulting firms. While some companies have a static Corporate Development staff, in most companies Corporate Development is a temporary post leading to other areas of management or at least has the potential to be that. While, in theory, Corporate Development staff should be judged not only on the deals they do but on the deals they choose not to do, in point of fact, closed deals are usually a primary metric of their success. What I mean here is that shareholder value can be destroyed by a bad deal just as it can be enhanced by a good deal, and as the leaders of the deal process, it is incumbent on Corporate Development teams to stop bad deals from happening. However, just as with proving a negative, it is difficult to demonstrate value added by deals avoided. For most Corporate Development executives the clearest demonstration of value added to the company is the deals they have closed. Similarly, in companies where Corporate Development staff move on to other positions in the company fairly regularly, there is a danger that they will move on before the deals they have done can be determined to be successes or failures. This creates the potential for an adverse incentive from a Corporate Development staff to the advocates of the deal rather than advocates of shareholder value.

ADVISORS

Even for companies with a regular acquisition program and a sophisticated Corporate Development team, Strategic Transactions are significant and risky events. Strategic Transactions also tend to be some of the most complex and, at the same time, uncertain transactions that a company can do. Finally, the dollars at stake in a Strategic Transaction tend to be huge. All this creates a powerful incentive for companies to employ advisors. In the face of a risky and uncertain $500 million debt, who would not be willing to spend an extra million or two to provide some incremental comfort and certainty that all the i's are dotted and t's are crossed? Outside advisors also provide a certain amount of "cover" for executives and board members. When employing advisors, they can point to yet another step as well as an outside and theoretically independent party who supports the soundness of their judgment in doing the deal. It is important to keep in mind, however, that different advisors can have vastly different incentives, points of view, and expertise when providing advice on a Strategic Transaction.

Lawyers

When discussing lawyers, it is useful to start with a simple premise: Strategic Transactions, or, for that matter, any financial or business transaction is at its heart a contract or transfer of legal ownership. In a very real sense, law is the language of ownership. As will be discussed further when talking about due diligence in Chapter 7, in a Strategic Transaction, you only buy, sell, or own what the legal documentation says you do. Thus, lawyers are integral to any Strategic Transaction. While most corporations have their own internal lawyers, these are usually supplemented by outside counsel. Outside counsel usually comes in the form of lawyers from an established law firm. Outside counsel, as these lawyers are usually referred to, provide a variety of things that usually are not available when simply using internal lawyers. They provide expertise in niche and specialty areas, including Strategic Transactions themselves. Unless a company does a huge number of Strategic Transactions, inside lawyers usually will not have the same expertise that M&A and securities specialists at law firms will have. The same is true for such specialty areas as tax, intellectual property, and litigation, to name a few. Outside counsel also provides peak manpower. Strategic Transactions tend to create the need for a very large amount of legal work in a very short period of time. Corporations usually do not like to staff up their legal departments to handle such peaks and, thus, outside counsel provides the extra manpower to handle these rushes of activity.[26]

Outside counsel also provides a certain amount of independence. For some CEOs, corporate executives, and general counsels, outside counsel may act as a *consigliere*. Outside counsel can provide an independent, unbiased view on a wide variety of issues. In particular, outside counsel can help the board of directors and executive management navigate the challenges of determining their fiduciary duty and balancing their obligations to shareholders, employees, and the community. While in-house counsel, notably the general counsel, can also serve this role to a certain extent, outside counsel is far more separated from the internal politics and bureaucratic infighting of the corporate structure.

This brings up a particularly important point about outside lawyers. With rare exceptions, lawyers charge for their services purely on an hourly basis. As a result, they are generally entirely indifferent to the outcome of a transaction. Lawyers get paid whether the deal happens or not. This allows lawyers to be relatively unbiased and balanced advisors. The only obvious adverse incentive created by these economics is an incentive to be overzealous and excessively detailed, since the more work the lawyers do, the more they are paid.

Law firms vary in size dramatically from solo practitioners or groups of perhaps a dozen lawyers all the way up to the megafirms with hundreds or even thousands of lawyers on staff. Some firms focus on particular specialties, notably intellectual property, but most firms, particularly the larger ones, aim to provide a full range of legal services to their clients. Within a given law firm, there is a range of different lawyers, in terms of both seniority and specialty. In the broadest terms, lawyers are separated into litigators and transactional lawyers. However, there is a variety of subspecialties, including ones that cross the line in between these two areas. For Strategic Transactions, there will usually be a specialist who is a corporate lawyer, focusing on M&A or securities transactions. That lawyer will usually be supported by specialists in areas such as taxes, intellectual property, labor, and litigation. There is also a range of seniorities within a law firm. Again, there are two broad categories of associates and partners. Law firms are almost exclusively structured as partnerships, and, generally, lawyers at law firms rise through the ranks as associates for a decade or more before earning the right to be offered partnership. In a Strategic Transaction, the partner will tend to serve as the strategic advisor to the client and, potentially, the lead negotiator. Senior associates may take up some of these roles as well as broad management of the transaction process from a legal point of view. More junior associates will have specific tasks such as the reviewing of due diligence documentation and the drafting of contract documents.

While outside counsel clearly adds value with specialty expertise and manpower, they can also provide great value from the general wisdom that is acquired by doing a large number of transactions. Thus, they will often move beyond the very specific tasks of executing a deal and become very general advisors to their client companies.

Investment Bankers

In a Strategic Transaction, I would argue that, among advisors, investment bankers play the "ying" to the lawyers' "yang." That is, in many ways, the two groups of advisors complement each other, not only in terms of their particular skills but also in their approach and general demeanor with regard to a transaction. Whereas lawyers look at the downside and will often argue caution, investment bankers tend to be advocates for the deal. Whereas lawyers focus on legal rights and remedies, investment bankers focus on financial terms and dollar values.

While I will not go into extensive detail on the structure and role of investment banks, it is useful to lay a broad outline as the context for this discussion.[27] The structure of investment banks has been changing substantially over the past few years and will likely continue to change. While there is no standard form for what an investment bank must be, let me set out an example of the standard large investment bank structure. Most of large investment banks are now part of really large, even massive, financial institutions. These institutions usually include a commercial bank that lends to corporations, a retail brokerage operation that provides brokerage services to individual investors, a research operation that provides research on stocks to both individual and institutional investors, a sales and trading operation that executes stock trades for large institutions, and an investment bank.

As seen in recent years, there are many inherent potential conflicts of interest among these various pieces of an investment bank. For purposes of this discussion, I will focus on the specific investment banking operations within these larger financial institutions. Investment bankers are financial and transactional experts who advise corporate clients on transactions. Generally speaking, these transactions include equity offerings, debt offerings, initial public offerings, acquisitions, divestitures, mergers, and a variety of other large financial transactions. When advising clients on offerings of securities, investment bankers are generally compensated through their role as underwriters, where in simplest terms they are paid a percentage of the total volume of securities sold by their sales and trading and brokerage units. This percentage could range from less than 1% for investment grade debt offerings to well over 5% for initial public offerings of stock. Similarly, when advising clients on Strategic Transactions, such as M&A, investment bankers are generally paid a percentage of the dollar value of the transaction. It is exceedingly important to note that in both cases investment bankers are only paid if the transaction is successfully executed. While investment bankers are, on rare occasions, paid retainers or fees purely for advice, the vast majority of investment banking profits come from payments that are contingent upon the success of the deal. As a result, investment bankers have a massive incentive to press for the successful conclusion of a Strategic Transaction. A modest, but countervailing, force on this incentive is the fact that investment bankers seek to maintain a long-term relationship with their clients. Thus, an investment banker will be hesitant to press for a highly unattractive transaction, since that advice could doom any future business from the client. However, there is a powerful force to the notion that a bird in the hand is worth two in the bush. It is commonly accepted that investment bankers will usually seek to be advocates for the deal and that their advice must be viewed in this light.

As with outside counsel, investment bankers have specific areas where their expertise is most obviously used in Strategic Transactions, but the potential for a much broader advisory role. The obvious areas where an investment banker has a role include: identifying potential Targets, brokering initial conversations between parties, valuation, financial structuring and structuring of financing options for a transaction, and, in some cases, managing the sale process. But, as with outside counsel, investment bankers conserve a broader consigliere role, particularly where they have developed long-term relationships with their clients. As with outside counsel, investment bankers tend to have extensive experience with a large number of transactions. They are often also industry experts who usually have insight into the trends among competitors. Finally, investment bankers have a deep expertise in market forces and generally a good understanding of the likely market impact on a company's stock of a Strategic Transaction.[28]

When advising a client on a Strategic Transaction, investment bankers are usually paid a success fee, which is tied to the size of the transaction. While it is not unheard of for investment bankers to be paid a retainer of some sort, and they are often reimbursed for out-of-pocket expenses, the vast majority of their advisory revenue is based on a success fee structure. The range for such fees will vary with the size of the deal and the relationship with the client, as well as market forces. Exhibit 2.2 provides an example of a fee schedule that an investment bank might offer, with a sliding percentage scale based on the size of the deal.

One last point is useful to consider with regard to investment bankers. While most other advisors are hired in reaction to the decision to engage in a Strategic Transaction, investment bankers try to actually stimulate that decision. A significant part of an investment banker's time is spent "pitching" client companies on potential transactions. While the pitches certainly make an argument for the capabilities and "résumé" of the investment bank, the majority of this material is concerned with providing the client company with intelligence, industry insight, transaction ideas, and information on specific Targets. While part of the purpose of the pitches is to stimulate a specific transaction in the hope that the investment bank that brought the idea will naturally be hired to help execute it, pitching companies is part of a broader effort to provide general value to the companies. In fact, active acquirers usually identify Targets on their own but

EXHIBIT 2.2   Investment Banking Advisory Fees Example

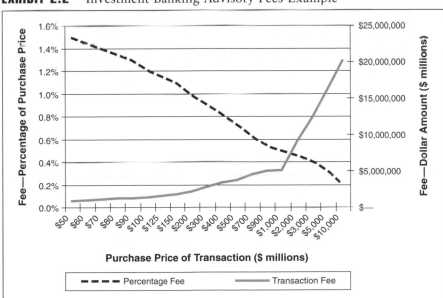

when choosing investment bank advisors, will often give the business to banks that have provided valuable intelligence and general information over the prior months or years. Ironically, in many cases, a bank can spend years billing a client and end up being paid an enormous sum for a very small amount of work. In some ways, high investment banking fees are really a method of rewarding investment banks for years of unpaid advice and information.

Auditors

In general terms, auditors provide two related assurances in a Strategic Transaction. They tell the Buyer that the Target's financial performance is as advertised and that the way it is described in the Seller's books is the way it will impact the Buyer's books once the Seller is consolidated with the Buyer. On the Seller's side, the auditor's services are a prerequisite to making a company saleable, in most cases. Like law firms, auditor's firms can range in size from a few accountants to tens of thousands, in the case of the few largest firms in the world. The largest auditing firms today do far more than simply produce financial reports. They provide advice on how to structure a company financially as well as tax and accounting strategies. More broadly, the largest auditing firms also have related consulting and advisory services. Some even provide investment banking services. Like the investment banks, the auditing firms have to manage potential conflicts of interest between the units providing auditing services and those providing other advisory services and consulting.

In a Strategic Transaction, the Seller's auditors will prepare financial statements in preparation for a sale. In many cases, the Seller has had its financials audited for years, and the financials prepared for a sale are simply an update or perhaps even the financials prepared in due course. In other cases, particularly for smaller Sellers, there may not have been previous audits, and a full audit is completed specifically in anticipation of a sale. However, in most cases, for a Seller of any reasonable size, and particularly with nonfounder shareholders, it is likely that auditors have been used well prior to the decision to sell. Auditors for the Sellers will sometimes be called on to discuss their audits and results with potential Buyers. For the most part, though, auditors for the Sellers are simply performing the standard financial practices of any standard financial audit.

There are two types of potential auditors who may work for a Buyer. First there is the auditor who provides the Buyer with an audit of its own financial statements. This firm will, of course, be in the best position to advise the Buyer on how the acquired company's financials will be reflected on the Buyer's own financial statements. In many cases, a Buyer will hire its own auditor to review the books of a potential acquisition Target as well. In other cases, particularly when the Buyer's auditor does not have sufficient expertise based on industry or geographic region, the Buyer may hire a second accounting firm to review the financials of a potential Target. An excellent example of this occurs when the Target is located in a country where the Buyer's auditor does not have local staff familiar with local accounting procedures and policies. Cross-border transactions like these present a particular challenge because the Buyer must be sure to determine how the Target company's financials will appear when converted to its home country's auditing and accounting standards.

Auditors are generally compensated on a project and/or hourly basis. In the case of auditing financials for a regular client, the auditor can usually make a relatively accurate prediction of the amount of effort involved and will usually provide the client with a project price or even a commitment to a particular price. Variable hourly rates are more likely to be used when an auditor is called on to do due diligence on a Target, since there is much more uncertainty about the amount of work required.

Auditors have a powerful incentive to come up with the best possible treatment for financial data to benefit their clients but there is a countervailing pressure to comply with auditing standards or risk huge legal liability. As seen with the accounting scandals of recent years, auditors hold huge potential liability for violating, for helping their clients to violate, those standards.[29]

One cannot overestimate the importance of the role auditors play in Strategic Transactions. Relatively obscure differences in accounting treatment can have a dramatic impact on financial statements. Without properly reviewed audited financials, the Buyer takes a huge risk that the numbers will look much different on its books than they did in the offering memorandum it was given by the Seller. For the Seller, a lack of audited financials can either make their company entirely unsaleable or at the very least result in a substantially reduced price as the Buyer values the Seller with a worse-case scenario in mind.

As a general rule, and in particular after the events of the past few years, auditors, like lawyers, tend to take a very conservative approach to Strategic Transactions. Like lawyers, auditors are paid for their time rather than for the success of a transaction. This, coupled with the very real possibility of legal liability, will press auditors to take a very conservative posture.

Consultants

Consultants are an often overlooked participant in the Strategic Transaction process. In part, this is so because they focus their energies on the earlier stages of the deal and are rarely involved in the final closing of a transaction. However, their impact on early strategic decision making is amplified during the course of the deal process. Early work by consultants can change the Target, general sector focus, or even the choice to do a deal at all.

As with other advisors, consulting firms can vary in size dramatically, from global behemoths to solo practitioners. Consultants can have a range of different focuses. Some firms focus on broad- and high-level strategy work; McKinsey & Company is notable in this area. Smaller firms may focus on a particular sector or subsector seeking to differentiate themselves from the large firms with deep industry knowledge. Still other firms, which are often subgroups of the very large firms, may focus on particular processes, such as technology systems integration or human resources. While consultants may find themselves involved in various parts of a Strategic Transaction, the most common places to find a powerful impact from consultants are in early-stage strategy development and in late-stage due diligence and integration planning.

Strategy is the bread and butter of many large consulting firms. As a result, they are often involved in the broad decisions that will drive a choice to do Strategic Transactions and the choice of where to focus those Strategic Transactions. For example, the consulting firm working with a large company can help it develop the strategy that includes global expansion and then help it reach the decision to the best way to expand in certain markets is to acquire local platforms. In some cases, consulting firms will go as far as to help the company identify specific Targets, though this usually is where they step aside in favor of the company's Corporate Development team, line management, or investment bankers.

Once a company is far down the road of doing an acquisition, consultants will often reemerge to assist in due diligence and integration planning. Consultants are helpful in due diligence because they usually have deep industry or area expertise. For example, human resources consultants may be brought in to review and compare the benefit plans of the Target and acquirer. Environmental consulting firms are almost always used when there is any amount of environmental due diligence, such as the review of the environmental condition of a factory or other industrial facility. Consultants can also be very valuable in helping an acquirer plan the integration process. Here, consultants bring both expertise in and experience in a large number of prior integration exercises, as well as an independent and outside view. The independent and outside view is particularly important, since part of the integration process involves making a "best-in-class judgment" on a variety of areas between the Target company and the acquirer. This is an area where, despite best intentions, the acquirer or line management may have in-hand biases. For example, while the acquirer or line management may be loyal to the brand and product name it has spent years developing, consultants may determine that the acquired company's brand and product names are more valuable and should be adopted by the combined business.

Like auditors, consultants are usually paid on a project or hourly basis. While they do not have a powerful bias to be deal advocates, they do have a strong bias toward change in general. In contrast to auditors, who derive a steady stream of income from regular annual and quarterly audits, consultants make their money when a company chooses to change. Developing strategies and action plans for strategic change is the bread and butter of consulting firms. Therefore, if consulting firms have an inherent bias, it stems from their focus on making big and sudden changes in companies.

With the exception of deep industry and sector specialists, consultants tend to be generalists. Their expertise is in process, analysis, and decision making rather than in a particular industry or area. This, however, is a broad generalization, and certainly many consultants develop industry focuses, and some consultants choose to specialize. However, generally speaking, strategy consulting firms bring value through their understanding of how to attack, analyze, and solve problems.

One last note on consultants and their personal backgrounds. Consultants tend to be highly educated and very sophisticated business people. While the career path of a consultant can certainly involve progressing through the ranks of the consulting firm to a senior partner role, many, if not most consultants, actually end up in the ranks of corporate management. This is a particularly powerful synergy for consulting firms, who, in effect, seed their clients with members of their own staff. While this is certainly true for other advisors, such as law firms and investment banks, consulting firms seem particularly adept at it. Most large strategic consulting firms actually maintain alumni networks and online job postings to help place current consultants who may be passed over for partnership and former consultants, who continue their association and relationship with the firm years after departing.

Advisor Staff

When dealing with the various kinds of outside advisors, you need to have at least a basic understanding of the different levels of staff members and their roles in an advisor's organization. This is important to a company in terms of both managing costs and understanding the roles and expertise of the specific people with which you are working. The general categorization of staff and then a few specific comments about the different types of advisors will be provided next.

Broadly speaking, advisor staff can be categorized in three groups: (1) junior, (2) midlevel, and (3) senior staff. Certainly there is a smooth gradation as these professionals become more senior, but, in terms of the work they do, these three segments are a useful separator. Junior staff are concerned with detail work (for example, financial modeling, reviewing material, or drafting of basic documents). Midlevel staff are primarily concerned with process and deal management, as well as with the oversight of the junior staff. Senior advisors spend most of their time in sales mode as rainmakers, selling services to clients. The rest of senior staff time is spent giving general oversight to the team and guidance on the most challenging issues, and providing clients with strategic advice and serving in the consigliere role.

In a law firm, the team is divided into paralegals, junior associates, senior associates, and partners. Paralegals have only a college education and are not attorneys. They are largely concerned with the basic tasks of document management and processing. Junior associates are newly minted attorneys, who will do much of the drafting of basic legal documents, legal research, due diligence document review, and basic process management. Senior associates are more seasoned attorneys, who will draft the more complex documents, serve as primary negotiators, and manage the entire deal process. Partners are literally that—equity holders in the firm. They are very senior lawyers, who are responsible for bringing business into the firm and managing clients. They will also provide guidance to the senior associates on the most complex issues and may take the lead in particularly high-profile negotiations.

Investment banks have a similar structure but with a larger range of titles. Additionally, there is not the inherent regulatory difference between lawyers and nonlawyers. Analysts[30] are the most junior staff, usually just out of college. They are largely concerned with the mechanics of building financial models and doing basic financial research. Associates are newly minted MBAs, who are concerned with more complex financial modeling, the drafting of pitch material, and some basic process management. Vice presidents have usually left behind modeling and most pitch drafting and are more focused on developing pitch ideas, managing live deals, and sometimes pitching clients. Directors are usually focused on very high–level deal management and pitching clients. By this point in their careers, bankers are usually largely rainmakers and are the primary contact point for small and midsized clients. At the director level, they are judged on their ability to bring in business. Managing directors are almost entirely focused on pitching clients and maintaining client relationships, with only a modest amount of time being devoted to very high–level deal management.

Similar structures apply to auditors and consultants, with partners focused on bringing in business, midlevel staff focused on managing projects, and junior staff doing the guts of the work on those projects. While titles may vary from firm to firm, it is important to recognize the range of roles and understand the level of advisor that is servicing you. The classic story of one big consulting firm in the late 1980s is that all the staff would wear very similar blue suits and white shirts. While part of this may have been corporate culture, likely another goal was to make all levels of staff look very similar so that it would not be as obvious to the client that while a very senior and seasoned consultant pitched the project, far more junior staff then showed up on-site to execute it. This is not to say that you want to demand the most senior staff for all your work. This is where the business model of the advisor becomes important. Since investment bankers are paid on a success basis, the cost does not vary based on the staff they use, and the client has an incentive to push for as much senior involvement as possible. By contrast, for firms that charge hourly rates, managing the staff provided by the advisor can help manage costs. You do not want a law firm partner or even a senior associate managing your due diligence room or drafting basic documents. For an hourly-based advisor, it is often productive to press for more junior staff involvement, since they are charged out at dramatically lower rates.

REGULATORS

Almost every business and financial transaction is regulated in some way by the government and/or the courts. Strategic Transactions are no exception. One needs to differentiate here between the regulation of Strategic Transactions themselves and the regulation of the companies taking part in a Strategic Transaction. In some cases, there will be an overlap between the two because regulators of a business or a particular entity have special rules or regulations regarding Strategic Transactions by that entity or in that business.

Setting aside industry- and company-specific regulation, there is one main driver to the regulation of Strategic Transactions and that is investor protection. Strategic Transactions between privately held companies are relatively lightly regulated, with the companies generally required to comply with state laws concerning how corporate decisions must be made and authorized. Beyond receiving proper authorization from the board and shareholders of each company, a merger of two private companies usually requires the filing of a very short and simple form. The vast majority of regulation of Strategic Transactions focuses on public companies and seeks to ensure protection of investors, particularly individual or retail investors. Generally speaking, these regulations are no different in theme and intent than the broader regulations governing public companies. The only difference is that, with the stakes being higher in a Strategic Transaction than in most corporate decisions, the focus of regulators on ensuring fair treatment of investors is sharpened and heightened.

Securities and Exchange Commission

The SEC was founded to protect investors. It is armed with the regulations inherent and derived from the 1933 and 1934 securities acts. It is important to remember the context of the SEC's birth, the aftermath of the crash of 1929. At the risk of making too much of a generalization, I think it is safe to say that the SEC is primarily concerned with protecting the rights of individual and less sophisticated investors. Exemptions to many of the SEC regulations are available to companies whose only investors are large and sophisticated. The assumption here is that large sophisticated investors can protect themselves with much less help from the SEC but that individuals and the cliché "widows and orphans" need significant protections when investing in companies. Since Strategic Transactions, and particularly the sale of a company, have such a singular and dramatic effect on the financial interests of individual investors, it is not surprising that these transactions receive a great deal of focus from the SEC. Two particular areas that receive focus are: disclosure and fiduciary duties. The SEC and the regulations that empower it have a tremendous focus on ensuring that individual investors receive fair, full, and accurate disclosure of a potential transaction, allowing them to make an informed decision in the event of a shareholder vote. The SEC also focuses on the fiduciary duties of the board of directors and executive management of a company, seeking to ensure that they act in the best interests of the shareholders and in good faith. It is important to note that in addition to empowering the SEC to enforce these and other policy goals, the securities acts create some broad rights for individual investors to sue companies and, in some cases, directors and officers directly. In a sense, one might argue that the private law firms who represent investors and assemble class actions function as another pseudo-regulator.[31]

State and Local Regulations

While the SEC is by far the most visible regulator of companies, and the federal securities laws, the most visible regulations, most small private companies are actually primarily regulated by state law. Companies must incorporate in a particular state and are then deemed, like individuals, to be residents of that state and subject to that state's laws. One of the reasons that so many companies choose to be domiciled in Delaware is that their regulations are fairly friendly toward businesses, and their state courts are fairly sophisticated in adjudicating corporate law issues. Wherever a company is domiciled, it will be governed by state laws and state regulators. In most cases, the regulations governing Strategic Transactions for private companies are fairly straightforward, and many are even modeled on Delaware's regulations.

Industry Regulators

Most industries or lines of business in the United States (and for that matter most countries) are governed by some industry-specific regulations and industry-specific regulators. These may be both federal and state regulators. For example, the Federal Communications Commission (FCC) regulates owners of radio stations, television stations, and other broadcast media. While most of an industry regulator's focus will be on the operation of the business in ordinary course, many will also have regulations concerning or limiting Strategic Transactions. It is essential to understand these industry-specific regulations when considering a Strategic Transaction. An excellent example is again found with the FCC where there are strict guidelines concerning foreign ownership of radio stations. In most cases, industry regulators will have little to say about Strategic Transactions, but in those rare cases where they do, the impact can be dramatic and, in some cases, entirely block the transaction from happening.

International Regulators

A final category to consider is international regulators. Any time a U.S. company does business outside the United States it is likely subject to some regulation by the host country. Similarly, a non-U.S. company's actions, even within the United States, are likely to be regulated by its home country. In an increasingly globalized market, more and more Strategic Transactions involve companies with homes in different countries or, at the very least, companies doing business in multiple countries. When doing a deal that touches another country, it is important to consider that country's regulations and regulators.

One broad theme that crosses all regulators is: better safe than sorry. Failure to consider or address regulatory requirements in a Strategic Transaction can be a painful misstep. Failing to file even the simplest forms or comply with the simplest regulations can create a huge headache or even damage a transaction. As is true for many other areas of specialty, using advisors with the right background is usually a good investment in a smooth deal. When doing a transaction, it is important to remember not only the regulatory schemes and bodies that govern your business but also those that govern the counterparty's business. For a Buyer, acquiring another company means acquiring its regulator and regulations. Like marrying into a family with a difficult or trying cousin, buying a heavily regulated business may still make all the sense in the world, but you need to prepare for the accompanying discomfort.

OTHERS

Most of the direct and indirect stakeholders in a Strategic Transaction have been discussed, but there are other parties who will often take an interest. Their impact on the transaction also needs to be taken into account. Even if they cannot directly affect the transaction, they can impose costs or create benefits to the companies involved.

The Public

Strategic Transactions are watched not only by members of the public who have an equity investment in one of the companies but also often by the public as a whole. The reputation and image of a company with the general public can be affected by a Strategic Transaction. For example, if a large software manufacturer acquires a large outsourcing operation in India, this can create or emphasize a public perception that the company is sending American jobs abroad. This may or may not be a fair assessment and, of course, there are many other ways to offshore jobs without making an acquisition. Nonetheless, the high-profile nature of the Strategic Transaction may attract more attention and create a public perception that negatively impacts the company's sales. You need to consider the impact that a transaction will have not only on your investor base but also on the public in general. This is particularly true for companies with products or services aimed at the retail market.

Customers, Partners, and Competitors

Even for companies that do not sell to the public, a Strategic Transaction can have an impact on customer perception. Customers may view a transaction as positive if they see it as enhancing the capabilities of their provider or perhaps as negative if they see it as shifting focus away from the service or product that they are concerned with. Customer perception is often a primary Target of the public relations' effort of a strategic acquirer, who may seek to spin the deal as bringing benefits to its customers from things like a broader product range or a greater geographic reach.

A deal can also impact the perceptions of partners in powerful ways. The best example is a situation in which the acquisition brings a company into direct or indirect competition with a partner. While you may not want to tell a partner about a transaction before it is complete, it is important to manage these perceptions.

A Buyer also needs to be concerned with customer and partner perceptions from the Seller side. When acquiring a company, it is important to consider how the acquired company's customers and partners will view the transaction. Reactions can vary dramatically. Some customers may view the transaction positively as giving them a much larger and more stable supplier. Others may have a negative reaction either because they are worried about getting lost in the shuffle of a large company or because they have chosen in the past specifically not to do business with the Buyer. Customer perception is an often ignored land mine that can do substantial damage to a Strategic Transaction.

Competitors will also have a reaction to many Strategic Transactions. They may be intimidated by the increased strength of the Buyer, or they may even be pacified by an appearance that the Buyer is heading in a different direction (away from them). The deal may spur them to become more aggressive or to shift away from a line of business. In some cases, a

Strategic Transaction can even spur a competitor to either make acquisitions of their own or to approach the Buyer about a sale. In an industry that is consolidating, competitors often have the choice to "get big or get out."

The Press

In some ways, the press is a surrogate or an amplifier for the parties just discussed: the public, customers, partners, and competitors. In general, these parties are most likely to learn about the transaction from, and certainly to have their perceptions of the transaction delivered by, the press. Here, the press is defined broadly to include everyone from *The Wall Street Journal* and CNN to the Motley Fool and even online bloggers. One advisor whom I have not mentioned previously is the public relations (PR) firm. PR firms and in-house PR specialists may have an important role in Strategic Transactions in terms of crafting the story and/or amplifying the story to the press. When there is danger of damage to one of the above-discussed relationships, PR can help nullify the damage. For example, a company buying an outsourcing operation abroad can try to emphasize the number of jobs it continues to create at home. When the transaction can have some positive benefits, the PR firm can help spin that story with the press. One good example here is the merger of COSI and Xando. By combining a popular regional sandwich shop with a popular regional coffee-house, the merger aimed to create a more attractive destination for customers and to differentiate itself from the competitors on both sides. Certainly good public relations work was likely used to help create a clear story for the press of a new kind of coffee shop with great food or sandwich shop with great coffee.

NOTES

1. For a much more detailed and extensive discussion of this topic, see Michael E. S. Frankel, *Deal Teams: Roles and Motivations of Key Players in Mergers, Acquisitions and Equity Investments* (Boston: Aspatore, 2004).
2. Ranked by number of deals over period from December 1, 2000 to June 13, 2002. TheDeal.com, June 24, 2002, citing Mergerstat, Los Angeles.
3. The time horizon during which a financial Buyer will hold an acquired company varies based on the type of acquisition and the model the financial Buyer is following. As a general rule, you can expect financial Buyers to maintain control of the company for several years. Some financial Buyers seek to sell an acquired company as quickly as two years after a transaction, while others hold companies in their portfolios for five years or longer.

4. Good examples are Meredith Brown, Ralph Ferrara, Paul Bird, and Gary Kubek, *Takeovers: A Strategic Guide to Mergers and Acquisitions* (New York: Aspen, 2001); Lou Kling and Eileen Simon, *Negotiated Acquisitions of Companies, Subsidiaries and Divisions* (New York: Law Journal Seminars, 1992); and Philippe Very, *Management of Mergers and Acquisitions* (Hoboken, NJ: John Wiley & Sons, 2004).

5. The roles and motivations of these various players are covered in greater detail in Michael Frankel, *Deal Teams: Roles and Motivations of Key Players in Mergers, Acquisitions and Equity Investments* (Boston: Aspatore, 2004).

6. As Jim Collins discusses in his book *Good to Great* (New York: HarperBusiness, 2001), many of the greatest companies have been founded on a general theme rather than a specific product.

7. As you will see in the "Corporate Staff" section of this chapter, many of these same things can be said of senior management and even the board of directors.

8. These categories are by necessity somewhat arbitrary. The goal here is not to define the width and breadth of private investing, but simply to try to generally categorize private investors.

9. *Keiretsu* is defined as a group of companies affiliated and associated by agreements and various levels of cross-ownership that work together and cooperate to enhance their businesses and profitability.

10. The Securities Act of 1933 and the Securities Exchange Act of 1934.

11. Again in general terms, a sophisticated investor, termed an "accredited investor" is an individual who passes one of several different tests of sophistication, discussed in detail in sections of the Securities Act of 1933. The simplest tests of an accredited investor are any individual with an income in excess of $200,000 or net worth in excess of $1 million. Rule 501, Regulation D, Securities Act of 1933.

12. The discussion of the U.S. securities laws has been overly simplified here. There is a rich literature, which provides much more detailed information about the regulations imposed on public companies. Excellent examples include *Securities Regulation* by James Cox, Robert Hillman, and Donald Langevoorts (New York: Little Brown, 1991) and for the definitive treatise on the subject see Louis Loss and Joel Seligman, *Fundamentals of Securities Regulation* (Boston: Aspen, 1999).

13. Note that institutional investors may also be investors in private companies. Increasingly over the last two decades, large institutional investors such as pension funds, mutual funds, and insurance companies have begun to invest in nonpublic companies. However, both by virtue of the inherent stability and size of public companies and the protections provided by public company regulations enforced by the SEC, large institutions still tend to hold the vast majority of their assets in investments in public companies rather than private companies.

14. Norbert Michel, "Most Stocks Are Held by Private Investors," *WebMemo* #265 (Heritage Foundation, April 18, 2003).

15. Most people associate institutional investors with entities like mutual funds, such as Fidelity, and insurance companies, such as Prudential. However, it is important to remember that large pools of wealth, and thus investment, are held in other entities such as nonprofit institutions, for example the Harvard Endowment, and state pension funds, for example the California Public Employees' Pension Fund, known as CalPERS.

16. Good examples of issues that will likely attract the attention of even the most passive institutional investor include a sale of the company, a massive merger, or accounting scandals.

17. Robin Sidel, "Money Managers Raise Activism Among Investors," *The Wall Street Journal* April 13, 2001.

18. The 1993 study examined the performance of 42 companies targeted by CalPERS between 1987 and 1992. It showed that the stock price of these companies trailed the Standard & Poor's 500 Index by 66%, in the five-year period before CalPERS acted, but outperformed that index by 41%, in the following five years. "Why Corporate Governance Today? A Policy Statement," (California Public Employees' Retirement System, August 14, 1995).

19. "CalPERS withholds votes for H-P board members," *Sacramento Business Journal* (March 10, 2004).

20. Board members are usually paid an annual cash compensation as well as given stock options. While director compensation varies widely, it is not unusual to see board members well paid, $20,000 to $50,000 per year, and given significant equity stakes.

21. A large industry has emerged to address the new requirements of Sarbanes-Oxley, and all the major accounting firms have developed extensive services and materials to assist their clients in compliance. A huge literature has also emerged. For example, see Scott Green, *Manager's Guide to the Sarbanes-Oxley Act* (Hoboken, NJ: John Wiley & Sons, 2004).

22. It is not unusual to see members of the executive management team of Fortune 500 companies being paid millions of dollars in cash and tens of millions of dollars in equity annually.

23. This term is used to refer to terms in executive employment agreements providing for large, or even massive, bonus payouts in the event of a sale of the company (and sometimes the firing of those executives).

24. As a Corporate Development executive, I must admit to a certain inherent bias. Some people may certainly argue that Strategic Transactions can be accomplished by any sophisticated and experienced business executive. However, my counter to that argument would be to point to the proliferation of Corporate Development specialists and in-house Corporate Development staff in most large corporations. I will leave it to the reader to decide whether this is an essential tool or simply an extra luxury.

25. A quick comment on nomenclature is useful here. The terms "Corporate Development" and "business development" are often used interchangeably. In general, Corporate Development denotes Strategic Transactions, including mergers, acquisitions, divestitures, joint ventures, and equity investments. The term business development is used for both those kinds of transactions as well as what I will call strategic sales, generally meaning very large strategic sales to large strategic customers. For ease of understanding, I will use the term Corporate Development to describe the staff focused on Strategic Transactions.

26. An excellent example here would be the due diligence exercise, where dozens or even hundreds of boxes of contracts and other legal documents may need to be reviewed in a matter of weeks or even days.

27. For a more detailed description of investment bankers and their role in Strategic Transactions see Michael E. S. Frankel, *Deal Teams* (Boston: Aspatore, 2004).

28. Again, this is an area where pundits may be skeptical. Some people will argue that investment bankers and Wall Street, in general, have little ability to predict movements of the market. I will leave that debate to others and simply say that there is certainly consensus among investment bankers and many of their clients that they provide expertise. Certainly recent changes in, and the increased separation of investment bankers from research analysts, has had a negative impact on their ability to give insight into likely market reaction and reaction by institutional investors to the announcement of a transaction.

29. Even before the recent spate of litigation, auditors were paying huge settlements. In 1999, Ernst & Young paid $335 million to Cendant shareholders, and before it was dissolved, Arthur Andersen paid $110 million to Sunbeam shareholders in 2001. Stephen Taub, "Andersen Pays $110 Million in Sunbeam Settlement," CFO.com, May 2, 2001.

30. I'm referring here to investment banking analyst as opposed to research analysts. On the research side, the term "analyst" is a broader term, denoting everyone from the most junior to the most senior staff.

31. There is a long and rich debate over the value of class actions. Some argue that class actions are a powerful tool for protecting individual investors and creating negative consequences for directors, officers, and companies who may violate their trust. Others argue that class actions have gone too far and are now primarily a tool for class action law firms to enrich themselves. I leave it to readers to come to their own view, but I suspect the truth lies somewhere in the middle.

CHAPTER 3

Decision to Buy or Sell

The decision to make an acquisition, and certainly the decision to sell a company, is one of the most important and impactful decisions that a company can make. Certainly, the decision to sell has a powerful finality to it. Selling a company is the ultimate endgame. However, the decision to buy can also have a dramatic impact. While, unlike a sale, it is not the last and final decision of a company, it will usually have dramatic impact on the business and is hard, if not impossible, to reverse.

As we will discuss in detail below, the decision to buy or sell is not a single and simple decision but rather the sum and result of a great deal of strategic analysis and thinking. It is essential for a company to put a great deal of thought, effort, and resources into the analysis, strategy, and planning behind that decision making. This is important because of the gravity of the decision but more important because this analysis can affect the quality of the decision. A thorough analysis of why and when to sell can help direct the Seller to the best sales transaction and maximize the value for shareholders. Whether this means crafting the business to make it more saleable or simply identifying the Buyers likely to pay the most, the analysis done in deciding to sell will be a valuable tool in maximizing shareholder value once the decision is made. Similarly, the analysis and strategy that goes into a decision to buy can help focus the Buyer on the type and size of target that most fits its needs and strategy.

Many books on M&As discuss the various reasons to acquire, but few go into as much detail about the reasons to sell. This chapter will discuss both. It will begin from the Buyer's point of view, considering the reasons that the company might choose to make an acquisition. It will then turn to a company's decision to sell. Keep in mind that each side's thought process informs the other's strategy. For example, understanding that a Buyer's reason for acquisition is a need to expand geographically can help the Seller to craft its business and its sales pitch to appeal to the Buyer. Similarly, understanding that a Seller's motivation for sale is a belief that larger players are about to enter its market can help a Buyer motivate a sale by, for instance, emphasizing its own plans to enter the Seller's space.

REASONS TO BUY

While every company may want to get larger, pure growth is rarely a good reason to make acquisitions. In theory, any acquisition must pass the test of being the best strategy for enhancing shareholder value. Of course, in theory this test should apply to every decision that a company makes. However, one needs to remember that this is a very theoretical and subjective test. In the real world, the goals and motivations of the individuals running a company play a large part in the decision to make acquisitions. When you consider the decision to buy, it is useful to keep in mind how an acquisition will affect the careers and financial stakes of the key decision makers. For the rest of this chapter the Buyer is presumed to be a single decision maker, and the company as a whole is assumed to be making rational decisions in its best interests. Keep in mind, however, that, beneath the veneer of these decision-making processes, there are often personal biases and goals at play. For example, a CEO who wants to be in charge of a larger company may justify acquisitions with perfectly valid or even flawed strategic rationales.

The foundation of almost any decision to acquire is a "build versus buy" analysis. While a company may not formally assess these two alternatives and compare them in every case, there is a build alternative to almost every acquisition. That is, the assets, capabilities, technology, or other benefits from acquisition can almost always be built from scratch for some cost and over some period of time. There are some rare exceptions to this rule, where it is theoretically impossible to duplicate whatever the value associated with the acquisition. For example, if a company has a strong patent on a technology, or a singularly powerful brand, one could argue that it is impossible to build. However, even in these cases, it can be argued that a competing brand or a competing technology could theoretically be built. The question is always one of cost, time, and practicality. Later in this section, all the different variables that can drive an acquisition will be discussed. In each case, it is possible for a company to build rather than to acquire. Before making the decision to acquire, a company should always look at the build option. Building and buying each have some distinct advantages and disadvantages no matter what the asset or resource being built or bought is. Building will usually allow a company to develop an asset to exactly match its strategy and its existing business. This is the difference between buying off the rack and having something tailor-made. Building will often be less expensive or at least will allow the cost to be spread out over the period of the build. Building also gives the company the flexibility to make changes on the fly during the build process in response to changes in its needs. Finally, building is completely within the company's control, depending only on its ability to marshal its own resources. Building also has some distinct disadvantages. It may require expertise that the company does not have. For example, building an operation in a new geographic region may require local cultural expertise that the company does not have (by definition, since they are not currently operating in that region). Building also takes time. Building a capability or an operation or an asset can take a significant amount of time. In business, time can be a very precious commodity, and opportunities lost during the delay caused by a "build from scratch" strategy can be very expensive. Building can also be distracting. Since it requires the focus of management and resources from many parts of the company, it can distract those resources from other focuses.

Buying appears to be a much simpler alternative. This may be why it is so seductively attractive as a strategy for expanding a company. Buying has the advantage of speed, since it usually takes far less time to acquire a company than it does to build a similar capability from scratch. Buying also allows the acquirer to obtain instant expertise. Again, in the example of a geographic expansion, the Buyer gets not only operations in the new region but also likely a local staff familiar with the local culture. There are some significant and often overlooked pitfalls to buying. The obvious one is cost. Buying a company can be very expensive, and the purchase price usually comes in the form of a single large upfront payment. Buying is also an off-the-rack exercise. As such, buying is likely to produce some challenges in terms of integration, mismatches in culture, and other differences between the ideal asset that the Buyer is looking for and what it actually gets. Buying also has an inherent uncertainty. While the Buyer can do due diligence and try to gain a complete understanding of the company it is acquiring, there are inherent limits to how deep that understanding can go. Almost every Buyer encounters at least one, and often many, nasty surprises after it completes an acquisition.

At the end of the day, there are some situations where a build strategy is best and some where a buy strategy is best. The challenge for a potential acquirer is to analyze the alternatives well, taking into account the pitfalls and risks of each. It is important not to overlook the downside and dangers of buying. Building will tend to look daunting, since all the work that has to be done is laid out in front of you in a clear and intimidating way. Buying may look deceptively simple, but it is not. When you couple the challenges of integration with the potential risks of acquiring a business with unknown flaws, liabilities, and other nasty surprises, buying can be as daunting a task as building. As with deciding between buying an off-the-rack suit and having one tailor-made, the right decision will vary in each situation. If the suit in the store requires little alteration, it can be a fast and easy way to dress yourself, but at some point, if too much alteration needs to be made to get a proper fit, it may actually be easier to get a suit made to order.

The build versus buy analysis provides value even after a company has decided to buy. Going through this decision-making process will help a Buyer sharpen its views on what it needs and how much it is willing to pay for it. Having thought through and quantified the build alternative will help put an acquisition in context. For example, even if a company has decided that acquiring is a better way to enter a market, if the price of a potential target is too great, it may actually decide that the build option is cheaper. Analyzing the build versus buy options also brings to bear many of the resources that a company will require during the acquisition and integration process. From engineers to sales and marketing executives, the people who would develop a build strategy will often be those who will help assess potential targets and plan integration.

While buying certainly has its challenges, the time value of money cannot be overestimated. This may be the single greatest pitfall of a build strategy. In fast-moving markets and high-growth sectors, a matter of years or even months can mean the difference between capturing early dominance and struggling to be relevant. When assessing a build strategy, one must consider not only the costs of the actual build but also, and more important, the cost of time. It may often be worthwhile to pay a substantial premium to acquire an existing business in order to enter the market quickly.

Now, let us discuss the specific reasons that a company can decide to acquire. In many, if not most, cases more than one of these reasons will apply. It is useful to identify the individual reasons, however, since this helps the Buyer to prioritize its goals during the process of negotiation and integration and also ensures that the Buyer will not lose track of the underlying business purpose during the excitement of the deal. Certainly, many parts of an acquisition target can be attractive, but it is important to keep the focus on the core issues and assets that are driving your acquisition strategy. Keeping these priorities in mind can also help during negotiation when you have to consider where to concede and where to stay firm.

Customers and Market Share

Perhaps the single most powerful and obvious reason to acquire another company is for its customers. In essence, customers are the driver of revenue, and revenue is the first goal of business. Customer acquisition can come in many flavors. Buyers may simply seek to acquire more customer relationships. Buyers may also seek to acquire different kinds of customers. Different kinds of customers can mean new geographic regions, new demographic segments, or even new legal entities (such as business customers versus consumers).

Customer segmentation is a complex science, and I will not attempt to duplicate it. However, it is helpful to consider at least some of the ways that customer populations can be sliced and diced. Customer "types" can include:

- Different age groups (young adults, baby boomers, retirees, etc.).
- Credit and wealth levels (FICO [Fair Isaac Credit Organization]) scores and credit ratings — wealthy, middle class, low income, etc.).
- Geographic region (rural, urban, suburban, Northern, Midwestern, European, Asian, etc.).
- Business versus individual (individuals, sole proprietorships, small business, large enterprise, etc.).
- Level of use (heavy users, occasional users, one-time customers, etc.).
- Gender (male, female).
- Niche focus (hobbyists, entrepreneurs, housewives, yuppies, etc.).

In the case of customer acquisition, the build versus buy analysis is fairly obvious. Acquiring a company allows one to acquire a large pool of customers in one fell swoop. The alternative is to spend money and time on the more traditional methods of customer acquisition, including marketing, advertising, and sales. In most industries, the cost of customer acquisition is a fairly well-analyzed and well-documented dataset. This is particularly true for industries with large volumes of small customers, notably retail. In this case, the build versus buy comparison can often be fairly exact.

When a Buyer's primary reason for acquisition is the customer base of the target, the Buyer needs to consider the issue of degradation. In some cases, the transaction itself can damage the customer base. To the extent the customer base is damaged or reduced by virtue of the transaction, the Buyer should consider the acquisition of the customer base net of that degradation. In simple terms, the Buyer needs to consider the customer base it will be left with after the deal, rather than the customer base that the target has on a stand-alone basis. There is a variety of ways that a customer base can be degraded. The most obvious is simple size. If a percentage of the customers defect as a result of the transaction, the total customer base is reduced. The customer base can also be degraded in quality to the extent that the transaction leads the customers to be less loyal, to be less committed, or simply to spend less money.

There are several reasons that a customer base can be degraded as a result of an acquisition. The simple pain of change can cause damage to a customer base. It is difficult to entirely mask the process of integration from a customer base. When a company acquires another company, the target's customer base is likely to experience at least some changes. The most obvious examples might include new billing formats, new service levels, a new sales force or sales representatives, and even changes to the product itself. As part of integration planning, the Buyer will clearly try to minimize the impact on its customers, but some pain is almost unavoidable. This discomfort can cause customers to abandon the provider or, at the very least, to lower their threshold to consider switching to a competitor. For example, if my local bank were to be acquired by Citibank, it might try to integrate their online bill payment platforms. Even if the resulting platform had more features and functionality, I would still be faced with the annoyance of learning a new website and new commands. This would certainly lower at least one of the barriers keeping me from considering moving to another bank, since whether I stay or go I will have the same annoyance of learning a new online bill payment system.

In addition to the inherent pain of change, sometimes an acquired company's customers have to deal with the pain of inferior service from the Buyer. Again, the Buyer may try to minimize this by retaining best-in-class levels of service and product. However, often weaknesses in a Buyer's business will bleed into an acquired business. Again using the example of a local bank acquired by a large national bank, you can imagine that as the more stable and familiar an employee base at the local bank gets integrated into and mixed with the larger more volatile employee base of the national bank, the result might be that instead of the same familiar friendly faces at my local branch, I am now faced with new bank staff, who are not familiar with me or my business and are thus far less appealing to work with.

Stickiness is also a factor in degradation. Some products or services have an inherent stickiness once the first sale is made. In effect, the initial purchase creates some barrier to change—a level of "pain" the customer will feel if it switches providers. Understanding how sticky a product or service is, will help the Buyer predict likely degradation. For example, if GM purchases a particular part from an outside vendor, and has specifically designed a vehicle around this part, it will find it difficult and costly to change providers. The Buyer of this vendor will likely find it fairly easy to retain GM as a customer unless the Buyer does something to make it so unappealing for GM to stay that it overcomes the inherent "pain" of making a switch.

A somewhat related source of degradation is found in the case of a partial Seller. When the target is not a complete company but rather a division of or piece of a company, the Buyer risks damage to customer relationships as it severs the division it is buying from its parent. In these situations, customers are used to receiving multiple services and products from a single company and must now deal with two different providers. In a sense, this is the reverse effect of the natural synergy of bringing the target's products together with the Buyer's products to create a single suite. Sometimes, this can be alleviated through ongoing relationships with the Seller of the division. The effort to minimize damage to the customer base will be discussed as part of the broad discussion of integration planning in Chapter 9. The important point to remember here is that, when acquiring a customer base, you need to consider what you are acquiring net of the inherent damage to that customer base of doing the transaction. It is not what the Seller has, but what you will be left with that is important.

Related to the issue of degradation is the issue of legal contracts with customers. There is a huge difference between a customer that makes each individual buying decision anew, and one that makes a long-term commitment as a customer. In most cases, customers are not bound to use a particular supplier and are free to take their business elsewhere. For these customers, the question of degradation is paramount. The Buyer needs to assess how much of this customer base it is likely to lose as a result of the deal. However, sometimes customers sign long-term contracts and are committed to make purchases from a company. Such customers are particularly attractive to a Buyer, since they eliminate the issue of degradation. Or do they? When a company has long-term contracts with its customers, one of the key issues in due diligence is whether these contractual relationships can be transferred. Many such contracts will have explicit clauses releasing the customer from obligation if the company is acquired or goes through a "change in control." A Buyer needs to identify not only whether customers are under contract but also whether that contract will survive the deal.

Geographic Reach

Geographic expansion is another very common reason to do an acquisition. Expanding into a new geographic region is challenging on a variety of counts. In addition to the logistical challenges of setting up a local operation and facilities and developing relationships with local suppliers and customers, there is a broader challenge of understanding and operating within a new local culture. For some companies and in some situations, acquiring a local presence is easier and faster than building one. The build versus buy analysis will weigh heavily on how different the new region is from the current region in which the company operates. For example, a company expanding from New York to New Jersey may encounter few challenges and few differences. By contrast, a company expanding from the United States to Asia may face a global list of challenges in adapting its business to local customs. Acquiring a business in a new geographic region provides several specific advantages and benefits. We can separate these benefits into two broad categories: (1) local market expertise and (2) local market operations.

Local market expertise will encompass a broad range of issues. A company operating in the local geographic region will have an understanding of business practices and broad cultural issues. It will understand the standards used in business and, in particular, the standards used with regard to the product and services that it is providing. It will also have a deep understanding of local customer needs and practices. For example, a company providing credit services in Brazil would understand that while most of the population do not own their own homes, many own vehicles, and it is standard practice to borrow money with the security of a vehicle, much like a home equity loan in the United States. Local expertise can also include an understanding of the local economy and the local competitors. Local expertise is something that is often undervalued and underappreciated. While it can certainly be built, the time and effort involved can be substantial. This is particularly true because this expertise must permeate every part of an organization from the sales force, who must interact with local customers, to the product development team and engineering team developing features and functionality. Even local financial and legal practices require specialized expertise.

Local relationships are an even more valuable asset than local knowledge and often are absolutely critical to successful business operations. In many markets, local relationships are the difference between success and failure of a business. Local relationships encompass not only knowing people in the local market but also having developed a reputation in that local market. Someone with local relationships will know who the right people are, what their strengths and weaknesses and goals and limitations are, and how to make connections with them. In many less developed, and even some more developed, markets, reputation is a valuable currency. In these markets, reputation and credibility are more important than financial capacity in gaining the confidence of partners, suppliers, and customers. This brings us to an important point. Local relationships are important across a variety of axes. To operate effectively, one needs local relationships not only with customers but also with suppliers, partners, regulators, and a variety of other parties. Perhaps even more so than local knowledge, local relationships can take a great deal of time to develop, and there are no shortcuts.

Certainly, a company can try to acquire local relationships and knowledge through selective hiring, but as any human resources expert will tell you, hiring a business from the ground up is a long and exhaustive process in and of itself. And certainly, while individuals may bring a reputation, that reputation will only partially translate to the newly created business.

There are also very concrete values to an existing local business. Even with expertise and local knowledge, the infrastructure of the business can be expensive and time-consuming to construct. Facilities, operations, information systems, supplier relationships, and a variety of other physical assets and systems need to be built. Certainly, building from the ground up allows for seamless and perfect integration with the parent company's operations, but this comes with the cost of substantial delays in time to market.

The benefits of acquiring to create a local presence and the cost of the billable alternative vary substantially based on how different the new geographic region is from the home operations of the company. As a general matter, crossing national borders substantially increases the value of acquisition and the cost of build. However, not all borders are created equal. Certainly the difference between the United States and Canada is dramatically lower than the difference between the United States and China, or even the United States and Mexico.

One last point to consider on geographic reach. Shortly, the goal of acquiring people will be discussed. While acquiring a business in a new geographic region is not entirely about people, the more one focuses on local market expertise and relationships, the more important it becomes to retain the people who are acquired as part of the business.

Technology/Product

Acquisitions often allow a company to take a fast path to new technologies or products. As with customers, the acquisition of technologies and products can usually be compared to a fairly quantifiable build alternative. However, like brand (which will be discussed in the next section), technology and product are sometimes impossible to duplicate to build a strategy. If the target company has patents or copyrights on its technology or products, it may be effectively impossible to build something exactly the same. One excellent example are drug companies, where a successful patent means that another company cannot simply duplicate the drug exactly but must go through a longer and more difficult process of trying to develop a different drug with the same effect.

One of the attractive features of acquiring a company for its technology or product is that you are less dependent on things out of your control like employer tension. In fact, when a company is acquired for its technology or product, the Buyer will often only retain a small portion of the employee base, notably those with specific expertise in the development of that technology or product.

The acquisition of a new technology or product can fit into a Buyer's business strategy in a variety of ways. The new product can be added to the Buyer's existing products to create a broader suite and add to its existing customer base. The advantage here is that the Buyer is able to leverage all of the expense and resources devoted to its sales effort and, hopefully, increase the amount of revenue it gets from each of the customers by adding another product to its list. When this is the strategy, that Buyer needs to consider how the product will fit with its other offerings. It needs to consider such matters as the quality of the product and the standards and protocols used. For example, a large videogame maker might be interested in acquiring a smaller competitor to broaden its product line quickly, rather than trying to take the time to write more games. In this case, it would certainly need to consider the platform on which the games operate. A game manufacturer that made most of its games for PlayStation® would not want to acquire a smaller company that made most of its games for Xbox.

New products are sometimes acquired as a means of expanding into new businesses and new customer bases. In this situation, the Buyer may be less concerned about fit with its existing product line, but it needs to consider the ramifications and all the other resources that would be needed to allow the business to flourish. Usually, a Buyer will want to expand in a way that allows it to leverage at least some of its existing resources such as its manufacturing operations, its sales force, or its brand. So, even when a product is not being acquired to fit neatly into an existing suite of other products, the Buyer needs to consider how the product will integrate with the parts of its business that would be relevant.

A Buyer will sometimes look to acquire technology rather than a complete product. This technology may be "front end" or "back end." Front-end technology will include technology that can become a component of a product that the Buyer offers. For example, a cell phone manufacturer might acquire a company with technology for very small cameras so that it can create a picture phone. Back-end technology includes the acquisition of technology that will be used in the Buyer's operations, perhaps to make those operations more efficient or more effective. Unlike front-end technology, where the Buyer is more likely to need exclusive control and an exclusive license for the technology, often back-end technology can be licensed, purchased, or leased. For example, General Motors uses robotics systems in its manufacturing operations but likely does not own any of the robot manufacturers but simply buys the robots. However, in some situations, the technology may be so crucial that the Buyer needs to actually own it. Perhaps, the Buyer is seeking to create a competitive advantage by preventing competitors from having similar technology in their back-end systems.

While the build strategy is often an option with technology and products, a potential Buyer needs to consider not only the cost and time of building from scratch but also the benefits of trial and error. Products and technologies rarely work perfectly the first time, and through the process of development you gain valuable insight into everything from functionality to customer needs. One of the advantages of acquiring technology and product is that you often get something that has evolved through many relations and may have features that would not have emerged in the first generation of your own build process.

When acquiring a product and customer-facing technology, it is important to differentiate between the value of the product and technology itself and the value of the brand. This is not always an obvious distinction. For example, while the Sony Walkman cassette decks were certainly well-designed products, it is not clear how much of their success and market dominance came from the quality of the actual product as opposed to the accumulated reputation of and loyalty to the Walkman brand.

Brand

Brand is a particularly hard to quantify, yet clearly valuable, asset that many companies have. Certainly, no one would deny that names like Coke, Apple, Nike, and McDonald's have huge value, in and of themselves, for the reputation for quality and the level of customer loyalty that are associated with them. The build versus buy analysis for brand is particularly difficult to quantify. One can certainly quantify the marketing dollars spent to reach a certain number of customers, a certain number of times; however, this does not translate necessarily into brand quality. In some cases, it may be impossible to duplicate the brand quality no matter how many marketing dollars are spent. Perhaps more important, the amount of time necessary to develop a brand can be enormous. To some extent, it seems as if technology, customers, and local market presence can be built more quickly, the more money that is spent on them. By contrast, certain brands and certain levels of brand loyalty just take time. Many of the most powerful brands have taken decades or, in some cases, centuries to develop.

The challenge for a potential acquirer is that while it may not have an effective build option, it may also be very difficult to attach a particular value to a brand. In most cases, Buyers will fall back on trying to quantify the customers and revenue that are derived from the brand. When you go down this path, it is important to remember not only the revenue that the target derives from its brand but also the revenue that the Buyer may be able to derive from the brand. For example, if your target is a single product, but the Buyer has multiple products, the Buyer may be able to use the brand to enhance sales across its entire product line. By contrast, the Buyer also needs to give significant thought to the risk of brand degradation. Transferring a brand effectively through an acquisition is particularly challenging and risky. A brand itself, like fine glassware, is easy to crack or even shatter. During the course of a traumatic event, such as an acquisition, it is easy for a company to take a misstep and do substantial damage to the brand. In some cases, even the most well-meaning and careful Buyer can damage the brand by its very nature. Some brands have value specifically because they are associated with small "rebellious" companies. And the very act of an acquisition by a larger conglomerate can damage that brand. Again, as with customers, the Buyer needs to consider the value of brand, not as it is currently held by the target but as it will be held and operated by the Buyer, taking into account both potential enhancement and greater use and potential degradation.

People

People have already been discussed in the context of geographic expansion and technology and product. There is a variety of reasons why people can be the driving force behind an acquisition. In a tight employment market, it may be attractive to acquire a large number of employees quickly and without growing through a recruiting process for each one individually. Some areas of specialty may be particularly valuable and rare, and it may be easier to acquire them through the acquisition of a company. In some cases, the focus may be on the rank-and-file employees. For example, a company with a large, well-trained, and particularly effective sales force may be the target for an acquisition. In this case, the attraction is acquiring a large prebuilt sales force that is particularly attuned to customers and effective. By contrast, in other situations, a company's senior management team may be the focus. In other cases, it is often the technology team. This latter example is most often true for companies with unique or patented technology. In most cases, the goal of acquiring people will be coupled with a related goal. For example, companies with unique technology usually have fairly unique technological staff, and companies with strong and deep customer relationships often have a particularly talented and skilled sales and marketing group.

Acquisitions focused on people can be among the riskiest and most challenging. This is because—not to overstate the case too much—we live in a country where indentured servitude is illegal. That is, when you acquire a technology, or a facility, or a brand name, it is yours to keep, but when you acquire employees, they are only yours until they decide to leave. This is one of the classic challenges of acquiring companies like consulting firms, where it is said, "the value of your business walks out the door every day at quitting time." Any business that is highly dependent on its people always operates under the risk that those people will quit and leave. However, when you acquire a company, where people are a significant asset, the risk is even greater. An acquisition introduces new factors and elements that can affect your ability to retain those employees. As discussed further in Chapter 9, the target company's employees may find themselves subject to different compensation structures, new benefit plans, and a new corporate culture. They may also find themselves the beneficiaries of large cash payouts if they had significant equity in the target company. For these reasons and many others, employees of the target company often choose to leave after an acquisition is completed. While this particular degradation of assets can be somewhat addressed through a proactive effort to woo these employees and, in some cases, special retention bonuses and contracts, losing employees once a deal is done is a real and common risk.

The build option is also fairly obvious and often fairly appealing in this situation. For the same reason that employees can walk away after a company is acquired, they can walk away, or more accurately be hired away, from their employer. Through aggressive recruiting practices, the use of headhunters, and rich compensation packages, the company has a clear build option to acquire talent directly. Certainly, this may not give the company access to any particular employee, but in most cases, it allows the company to hire the requisite talent. The most notable exception is likely to be very senior executives of a target company, who are motivated financially much more by the value of their equity stake than by their salary. However, these are also the employees most likely to be lost after a transaction is completed, since they are likely to have gotten a huge financial windfall.

The combination of an obvious build strategy and the inherent risks of the buy strategy (through "the degradation of the asset"), means that doing an acquisition to acquire people is a relatively rare strategy. In many cases, people are a strong consideration and a significant asset, but it is relatively rare that a company will make an acquisition solely to acquire people. In cases where it does, tremendous focus needs to be placed on how to retain that talent, when you risk having your entire purchase price "walk out the door at the end of the day."

Economies of Scale

Economies of scale is often a business school professor's favorite reason to do an acquisition. In a nutshell, the assumption is that bigger is better, or at least more efficient. When driven by economies of scale, the Buyer immediately looks to gather more customers or more product volume to run through its manufacturing or other product provision operations. This is a common strategy in industries where a significant amount of costs are fixed costs. In these situations, every incremental sale or unit of product produced is usually highly profitable as measured against only the variable costs. For example, if the company builds a manufacturing facility, it would have invested in significant fixed costs. The company has a powerful incentive to try to generate enough sales to run that manufacturing facility at full capacity, thus spreading the fixed costs of the facility over as many individual sales as possible. An acquisition is a fast and easy way to increase volume and, thus, achieve greater economies of scale.

In a sense, the build versus buy analysis here is really similar to that done under a customer acquisition. The difference is that the benefits are more substantial when you can assume that the customers of the acquired business will be serviced on the existing manufacturing platform of the Buyer. Thus, in this situation, the value of time and speed to market increases, as does the potential premium that the Buyer can pay, since it w ill be able to rely on substantial synergies when it shuts down the target's manufacturing operations and moves all of the target's volume onto the Buyer's own platform.

When an acquisition is driven by economies of scale, it is particularly important to consider the challenges and costs of integration. Economies of scale come at a substantial upfront price. One should never underestimate the cost of integrating products, operations, manufacturing, and other factors under a single platform. As a general matter, achieving economies of scale through acquisition is an exercise in upfront costs (purchase price and integration costs) that yields substantial long-term benefits. The Buyer needs to recognize the full extent of the upfront costs and the time it will take to achieve them.

Differences/Market Position

Like economies of scale, differences/market position-driven acquisitions are really an adjunct to other reasons already discussed. When a Buyer acquires a target to strengthen or bolster its market position, it is likely doing so through the acquisition of the target's customer base or, in some cases, their geographic placement, product, or brand. However, there is a distinct difference in this particular category. Acquisition of additional customers or product is an end in and of itself. By contrast, defense or growth of market share is a goal achieved vis-à-vis other players in the market. In this situation, the Buyer is focused not merely on growing its business but also on maintaining or expanding its position relative to its competitors. In some markets and segments, there may only be room in the long term for a limited number of players. This is particularly true of markets where margins are low and economies of scale are significant, and customers gravitate to really large players and brands. There are many other reasons why market share may be, in and of itself, an important strategic goal. For example, in some industries, if a company achieves sufficient market share, it can become the de facto standard and actually yield market power over its partners and suppliers. Without opining on the validity of the claim, certainly the Department of Justice has made the claim that this is what Microsoft did with its massive and dominant market share in the PC operating systems segment. Market share also provides credibility. For example, potential partner companies may look to market share as an indicator of the strength and longevity of a company's business or product line.

The build versus buy analyses that were discussed above apply to a market share goal. In a competitive sector, however, big jumps in market share will be hard to achieve quickly to a build strategy, since presumably a company's competitors are all making similar efforts.

One final, and somewhat tangential, thought on market share. There is nothing inherently wrong with the goal of gaining market share. In fact, this is, by definition, one of the primary drivers of business in the capitalist model. Gaining market share can lead to economies of scale, which in turn can lead to greater efficiency and, in many cases, lower prices. The law has, however, put some notable limitations on efforts to acquire market share. Suffice it to say that antitrust law it is primarily concerned with maintaining and fostering a competitive business environment.[1] When considering an acquisition driven by the goal of gathering market share, a Buyer needs to be sensitive to issues of antitrust regulation. In some cases, antitrust regulations may actually bar a transaction. Even when they do not, Buyers need to be careful about how they describe and discuss market share goals. As any lawyer will tell you, discussing the goal of acquiring market share through an acquisition can be a risky proposition to the extent that it creates the impression of anticompetitive behavior or anticompetitive goals. When market share is a significant driver of an acquisition, the Buyer would do well to consult its attorneys early in the process and heed their advice not only in how and whether to do the deal but also in how to describe and discuss it.

Several of the key reasons that a Buyer will choose to acquire have been discussed. There are some universal themes. The build option is nearly always available and should always be considered carefully. The potential for the degradation of assets is a real risk that needs to be taken into account. Integration efforts, costs, and time need to be factored in as well. All this said, many Buyers quite rightly consider acquisitions to be the optimal strategy for achieving some of their goals.

One final thought on the reasons to buy. While this section has been very analytical in discussing rational economic reasons for a company to acquire, it must circle back on the individuals who make those decisions. It is rare to find a CEO, senior executive, or business unit manager who does not want to run something larger and more permanent. Organic growth is hard and slow work and acquisitions are an attractive, and often seductive, shortcut. It is common to find senior executives who drive an acquisition strategy aggressively even when it is not entirely clear that this is the optimal route to growth. In other cases, you may occasionally find companies that, for whatever reason, are talented at doing deals and perhaps less talented at organic growth. In some cases, you even find companies that are effectively acquisition machines, whose real expertise is effectively acquiring companies and then creating synergies between different acquisitions they have done. Regardless of the drivers of an acquisition, however, it is still important to anchor to the business reasons for doing a deal. By identifying these reasons upfront and understanding them deeply, you can ensure that focus is put in the right places during due diligence, the negotiation of terms, and integration planning.

CHOOSING TO SELL

If choosing to acquire is like a battle, choosing to sell is the entire war. It is the final decision that will close the books on the venture and the final scorecard that will tally the success of the business. As such, the decision is usually long fought and subject to a great deal of debate. This is as it should be. It is rare that there is a specific point in time when it is clearly optimal to sell a company, and so usually a judgment call must be made about likely future events, including the performance of the company, its competitors, and the industry as a whole. In many cases, this discussion will take place over a matter of months or even years. Particularly in the last decade, many companies have been built with a sale as the explicit goal. For everyone involved in the company, a sale is a dramatic personal and professional event. As will be discussed shortly, these personal incentives can often drive a sale decision very directly. However, let us begin the discussion at the business level with a consideration of the reasons that a business might choose to sell.

Business Reasons to Sell

In this section, the Seller is considered as a unified corporate entity and it is assumed that the management and owners act with one voice, focused solely on maximizing shareholder value. As will be seen in the next section, this is an assumption that is often tested by conflicting personal goals. That said, there are several reasons why a company might choose to sell. All these reasons are based on the notion that the company has likely reached a peak in terms of its inherent value and that shareholder stakes can be maximized by selling rather than by continuing to operate the business. In theory, the calculation that should be done here is to compare the growth in shareholder value that can be achieved by the company to the alternative uses of capital available to the shareholders. As discussed in detail in Chapter 8, every entity or individual has a cost of capital and alternative uses of capital. If an investment cannot return the cost of capital, it is a bad investment in any case, and if it cannot achieve the same level of returns as an alternative use of capital, it is an inferior investment. In concrete terms, if one expects the stock of the company to appreciate by 10% a year, but investors could get a 15% return at similar risk levels by putting their money elsewhere, the company is an inferior investment. The challenge is to assess when a company reaches that inflection point where it is no longer the best investment. As a general matter, people focus on the question of how the company will grow rather than the alternative uses of capital for the investors. Each investor may have different uses of capital, and unless a person is a large sophisticated professional investor, he or she may have no idea what those alternative uses of capital are. The good news is that, in most cases, this is not a close call. Rather, a Seller usually faces a situation in which it will not just slow down slightly but either slow down dramatically or actually decline. If you believe that long-term decline in value is in the cards for a company, it is a no-brainer to decide to sell and reposition your capital—even a savings account or Treasury bills will yield better returns. The big question is whether the company is approaching this kind of turning point and when it will hit. This is particularly important for high-growth companies, since selling too early means leaving a lot of value on the table. This was the conundrum faced by investors during the tech boom, when even if they recognized that the bubble would eventually burst, they did not want to get out too early and miss the rest of the upward ride. Certainly, those who sold tech stocks in 1999 regretted their decision, though not as much as those that held on to those same stocks past 2001.

Market Timing

The nature of market cycles naturally leads to the first reason that a company will choose to sell. Regardless of the performance of a particular business, all companies are subject to the movements of the overall market. In a recession, even the most robust stocks will suffer. One could argue that in a down market, alternative uses of capital also suffer similar losses, but one needs to remember the always-present "do-nothing" alternative whereby an investor can hold his or her money in cash. As a result, even if a company is performing well, if a down market is coming, it can maximize shareholder value by selling and leaving shareholders with cash.[2] As any stockbroker will tell you, trying to time the overall market is a risky proposition. It is even harder to complete a sale process, which usually takes months, in timing with the movements of the market. If a company knows that it will likely have to sell in the short to medium term, market timing may help to maximize the value of the sale, but trying to sell specifically in time with the market is fairly risky. For example, if a company believes that it will start to encounter very heavy competition from new entrants to its space in the next three to four years, it might use market timing to determine when, during that period, was the best time to sell. However, if a company has no other reason to sell, it is rarely a good idea to sell simply because it believes the market is near a peak.

Industry Cycle Timing

One step down from market timing is industry timing. Most industries move in cycles. Sometimes those cycles are related to the market and sometimes to other economic factors. An example is the demand for new housing. When interest rates rise and/or the economy is weak, demand for new houses may decline, and when interest rates are low and/or the economy is strong, demand may rise. This is a trend that will repeat itself in the long term as demand ebbs and flows. Trying to time a sale to match these types of industry trends is challenging for the same reason that more general market timing is. However, since trends in your particular industry will have a more powerful and direct impact on the value of a company, and since they may be easier to predict for an industry player, it is often easier for a company to time a sale based on market trends. For example, interest rates bottomed out in 2004 and began to rise. Many mortgage providers and other companies that generated business based on refinancings of home loans likely were able to predict that their industry had reached a cyclical high and might have tried to sell at that peak. An industry trend differs from an overall market trend in a couple of important ways. First, it may have a more dramatic impact on companies in that particular industry.

By definition, the market overall has a hedging mechanism, since it is the aggregate of a variety of industries that rarely all move in the same direction. Individual industry cycles can be far more dramatic. Second, since an industry trend may not correlate to the overall market, the alternative investment opportunities may not decline with the value of the business. For example, in a strong economy with rising interest rates, home builders may suffer, while electronics makers flourish as people use their new wealth to buy televisions rather than to make down payments for new houses (which are more expensive due to higher interest rates). Additionally, to the extent that potential Buyers come from other industry sectors that are not faring as well, a Seller may still be able to command a strong price even if its own industry sector is declining. For example, when book sales are declining dramatically, but sales of books-on-tape are rising, a book-on-tape company might be willing to pay top dollar for a publisher despite declining revenues because it needs content for its books-on-tape.

The challenge is, of course, that most Buyers will also be aware of these trends and will discount the value of the business accordingly. As discussed in Chapter 8, there is a big difference between the value of an acquisition to the Buyer and the price it will be willing to pay. The latter is driven by the perceived market value, and if the rest of a sector is in decline, a Buyer may not be willing to pay a high price, since it presumes that it could buy other similar companies at a low price. Since these industry cycles repeat themselves, like market cycles, unless there is an urgent need to sell or this cycle is perceived as particularly high or strong, it is not necessarily urgent to sell at the peak, since there will always be the inevitable next peak. Like market timing, industry cycle timing is a useful tool once a company has decided to sell, in order to maximize value. If one believes that the cycle is truly just part of a repeating pattern, there is no particular reason to sell because of industry cycles. However, since these cycles often take the better part of a decade to repeat, and often it is hard to tell if they indeed will repeat, if a company wants to drive to a sale in the medium term, it may want to be opportunistic and sell during a market peak rather than risk having to ride out a down-market longer than they intended.

Hitting the Plateau

Even a well-run business, in a market segment that is growing, can hit a plateau or even begin to decline. In some industries, there is a natural market space for small niche players and another for the "big boys." In some cases, there is a large chasm separating the two, and it is very difficult for a company to make the leap. For example, the difference between a local chain of restaurants and a national chain is dramatic. While Starbucks made the leap, many other local chains that have had success in their home city market may not be able to. The plateau can also be hit by a company that outgrows its clothes—meaning its own capabilities. We will discuss the ways this can happen shortly. Some companies hit a plateau when they dominate a product market but do not have the capability to expand beyond that niche. This is common in the technology space where many companies develop a "better mouse trap" technology but cannot expand beyond that single offering. These companies are often bought by larger technology companies, and their products are added to the Buyer's full suite. Cisco is a particularly good example of a large technology company that often acquires smaller single-product technology companies. Another kind of niche is a particular customer base. You can imagine a company that sells clothes very successfully to teenage skateboarders but does not know if it has the capability to address a wider range of customers effectively. The challenge, of course, is for the Buyer to maintain the strength of the acquired company's position in that niche, while expanding it.

Whether the niche is a geographic space, a product line, or a customer base, a company that has hit a plateau within its niche must either choose to press on and try to grow into a new space or consider a sale. When a company hits this kind of plateau, a sale may become a more attractive strategy. In a sense, the idea is that the company does not have the resources to reach the next level, but the right Buyer might, and, thus, the sale makes the company more valuable—a value that the Buyer and Seller will likely split. Hitting the plateau can be a frustrating experience for a company, since it is not a sign of failure but a natural limitation of the business and/or the team. It is like a high school athlete who is told that no matter how hard she trains, she does not have the innate skill, or simply the right physical attributes, to continue in her career. A great example is that of ballet students who grow too large, or football players that do not. It is also challenging to hit a plateau, since it is rarely clear-cut and obvious. In most cases, the company will be developing plans for growth and expansion into new markets, customer bases, and products. In some cases, small companies have effectively broken through these barriers and become huge successes. Starbucks is an example of a company that broke the geographic barrier spectacularly. Dell is a great example of success expanding beyond a core product line. Cadillac has had recent success expanding into a totally new customer demographic with its Escalade SUV. So, the temptation will always be there for a company that has hit a plateau to try and make the leap. The challenge for management and owners is to make the key judgment call of whether the company is capable of making that leap or whether it is best to sell. It needs to balance the risk of failure to leave the plateau against the greater returns for doing so.

Fundamental Adverse Change

Beyond hitting the plateau, sometimes a business faces the risk of serious decline. This can be the result of something company-specific or general to the industry or sector in which it operates. In both cases, the company may try to maximize shareholder value by selling before this decline begins or at least before it substantially damages the company.

Some industry trends are not cyclical but are one-time events or permanent trends. If an industry is going through such a change, a company may find itself looking forward to a sustained, or even permanent, period of decline. This is a more obvious and powerful driver to a sale than cyclical industry trends, since the opportunity to sell at this level may not come again. One example of this kind of change is a shift in regulations that changes the playing field for the business permanently. Businesses usually fight such regulatory change for obvious reasons. As a result, major new regulation of an industry will often be driven by either new factual/scientific discoveries or changes in broad public policy goals. For example, the discovery that asbestos may/can cause cancer suddenly triggered new regulations of the use and disposal of the material and dramatically reduced the value of asbestos-manufacturing businesses. Similarly, the new regulations in many cities, notably New York, barring smoking in public establishments has arguably damaged the value of bars and other venues where smoking was previously allowed.[3] A related topic is the class action lawsuit. New discoveries about the adverse affect of products on consumers usually trigger massive lawsuits. However, to the extent a company has been sued, it is likely too late for it to sell the business without having that damage factored into its price.

An industry can also suffer decline as a result of natural changes in the market. The classic example is that of the buggy-whip sector, where the advent of motorized vehicles led to a huge and inevitable decline in the demand for buggy whips. An industry or a particular company can decline as a result of outside influences, such as the development of a technology or changes in customer demand. The recent popularity of the low-carbohydrate diet has had this kind of impact on manufacturers and retailers of bread and other carbohydrate-rich foods.

There are also many drivers to company-specific decline. In some cases, the fault may lie with the core business model or product, while in others it may lie with the management team. Whatever the reason, when a company's business begins to decline, and there is no confidence that the trend can be reversed, a sale may be an attractive option. The key question the company needs to ask is whether the factor that is driving the decline will be relevant to a potential Buyer. If it is, the Buyer will likely not pay a price above what the company is worth as a declining stand-alone business. However, if the Buyer is able to rectify the problem or simply avoid it, the Buyer may be willing to offer greater shareholder value than continued independence. For example, if a technology company has a great product but an ineffective sales force, a larger company with a strong sales force might find the company very attractive.

Outgrowing Your Clothes

Many small and start-up companies eventually outgrow their clothes. While a few can overcome their limitations organically, many can be significantly hobbled by these inherent limitations. In this situation, a sale to a company with more advanced capabilities can be the best way to maximize shareholder value. There are a variety of ways that a company can outgrow its clothes, and some will depend on the nature of the industry. This section will discuss some particularly common examples.

Management

Small and start-up companies are usually run by entrepreneurs. While some of these managers will have experience running large organizations and operating in large companies, many will be serial entrepreneurs who have spent most of their careers in start-ups. This is actually a distinct advantage early in the development of a business. New and struggling businesses require a wholly different set of management skills than do large and established ones. A serial entrepreneur is likely to understand and be prepared to deal with the pitfalls and challenges of starting a business. However, as a business grows, the skill set required in a management team changes. In most cases, the original management team will largely be retained as a company grows. You can argue that this makes sense. Why would you replace the very managers who helped launch and grow the business so successfully? As a result, many companies are faced with the challenge of a management team that really does not have the right skills to manage the company at its present size, nor to deal with the challenges of trying to make the leap off a plateau. The inherent loyalty felt by shareholders toward the team that helped build the business can exacerbate this problem.

Sometimes, a company's shareholders and founders will be wise enough to see the need for a new kind of management talent and will recruit new managers as the business grows. Yahoo! is a good example of this as the founders and shareholders chose to hire a seasoned "big company" executive to be the CEO.

The challenge of outgrowing your management talent drives deep into an organization. Not only the CEO and top executives but also the entire management team may lack the right skill sets as a business grows. While the company certainly has the option of trying to upgrade its management team, often this is a daunting task, and during the transition, the company risks damaging its business. In this situation, a company may consider a sale. The advantage of a sale is that the Buyer presumably has a deep bench of the right management talent and may be more effective at inserting those skills quickly than the company could be on its own. As you can imagine, selling a company because you have outgrown your management is a particularly sensitive exercise. The management team is often offended by the implication that they do not have the skills to continue to grow the business, and selling a company without the support of the management is difficult. However, the financial windfall that will usually attend such a sale may help to motivate management.

Capital and Resources

Even if the company's management team is up to the challenge, sometimes a company simply does not have the right resources to continue to grow. As they say, "the spirit may be willing, but the body may be weak." To rise above a plateau, or simply to continue growth, sometimes requires capital and resources that a company does not have. In some cases, the company may be able to draw on its investors, or new investors, but in other cases, it may be difficult to bring enough capital to bear. There are several good examples of such resource constraints.

The growth rate required of some company resources is fairly linear or even declining. Economies of scale will mean that certain costs rise at a slower rate than the growth of the company. For example, once an employee benefit plan is developed, the incremental cost of adding new employees to it is very low. Similarly, if you have set up a full call center, the cost of each additional call is extremely low. However, during certain periods in a company's evolution, some costs will take a dramatic and sudden leap upward. A company entering a new business with a high level of regulation will suddenly incur much greater costs in complying with those rules. A company that offers a technology solution and reaches a certain size may be required by regulation, or by its customers, to implement much higher standards of security and reliability. Perhaps the best example is found with technology platforms, where costs of growth are often not linear but take giant single leaps. For example, once you hit the maximum capability of one kind of processor, it may be an order of magnitude more expensive to move up to the next level. When a company hits this kind of wall of cost, its growth can be stunted if it cannot bring the right resources to bear.

Whatever the nature of the resource constraint, the issue often boils down to money. While a company can always try to raise additional capital, sometimes the amount needed is too much for a small company to demand. Even if the business model is sound, investors may be hesitant to make a very large bet on a very small company. This is often the case for a company with a great product but one that relies on a massive infrastructure before it can be effectively sold. Such a company cannot afford to move in baby steps but needs to spend an enormous amount up front. For example, building out a cable network in even a single city is so expensive that a small company could never think of trying to accomplish it. A low-tech example would be a fantastic consumer product that is only cost-effective in huge volumes.

Even though the product is a clear winner, investors may be hesitant to seed a small company with enough money to manufacturer the product in the massive numbers needed to make it profitable. In such a case, selling to a larger Buyer with the capital and resources to execute on the vision may be the best way to maximize the value of the company and the interests of the shareholders.

Size/Critical Mass

The broader, but related, issue is that of overall size and critical mass. Beyond capital, there is a variety of other natural constraints to growth. Many companies are unable to break out of their niche position (to avoid the plateau as discussed above) because they lack the critical mass in some element of their business. While lack of critical mass is sometimes purely a function of capital constraints, it is often more complex. In some industries, there is a range of small players who are able to be successful in small scale. However, in many cases, these small players are unable to expand and compete directly with the large main players in their industry and are relegated forever to their niche.

One good example is the coffeehouse. In most towns and cities, there are single coffee shops that are highly successful. They may even be able to expand and maintain a small chain in close proximity to their original location. However, making the leap from a small chain in a single market, to a national or global brand like Starbucks is a huge challenge. To be a successful national chain, a company needs to achieve a high level of national brand recognition. The same story can be told for manufacturing businesses. Small niche businesses may be able to operate at low volumes, but to compete with large players, a manufacturer will usually need to achieve some level of critical mass to drive incremental costs down. You can imagine that it would be impossible to run a profitable auto company that only made 5,000 cars a year and sought to compete directly with GM or Ford on price. Niche players like Ferrari can survive at low volumes because they are not competing directly with the big players but filling a specialized demand that does not require critical mass and scale. Perhaps the most stark example of critical mass to support infrastructure is Federal Express (FedEx). To offer its service, FedEx needs to have a global transport network in place. In effect, the first package it ships costs billions of dollars. To be a sustainable business, the FedEx and UPS models both have a huge critical mass barrier.

This latter case is the most common example of a critical mass barrier where a minimum volume must be generated through a manufacturing infrastructure to make it cost-effective. This infrastructure can be a manufacturing plant, such as a pipe factory; a technology platform, such as a phone network; or a financial platform, such as a lending institution. In each case, there is a fixed cost to maintain the infrastructure, and if it is not spread over a minimum number of transactions, it is not going to be cost-effective.

Beyond manufacturing, there are other infrastructures and fixed-cost platforms that require a level of critical mass. A regulatory compliance infrastructure is another good example. Some regulatory structures require substantial fixed-cost investments, and those costs have to be spread across a large number of transactions to avoid making the enterprise a money-losing proposition. For example, to operate a mutual fund you need to comply with a variety of regulations under the Investment Company Act of 1940. If a fund does not have some minimum amount of investment on which it gets paid an advisory fee, the costs of simply being a mutual fund will exceed revenues.

Whether the critical mass barrier is in brand recognition, manufacturing volume, regulatory requirements, or any other required infrastructure, in some cases, a small company cannot achieve the critical mass to support the infrastructure. This creates a natural barrier to growth that may make a sale an attractive option. To the extent the Buyer has the capacity to build, or more likely already owns, the required infrastructure, it may be able to make the business more profitable and higher growth than it could be on a stand-alone basis.

Cashing Out: Investor/Owner Reasons to Sell

Even when a business is not fundamentally constrained from further growth and success, the key players often have an interest in selling. Particularly for privately held companies, the sale decision is often made for reasons that have nothing to do with the success or operation of the business. While the performance of the business may open windows of opportunity for a sale, the key driver to the sale, if not the timing, can be totally unrelated to the business. Founders, professional investors, public investors, and management may all have reasons to seek a sale.

Founders

Several things can motivate a founder to seek a sale. For founders, a sale is usually a life-changing financial event that dramatically increases their personal wealth. Founders also often get burned out, as the stress and energy demands required to grow a business finally gets to them. Founders with an entrepreneurial bent may also find themselves less enamored with their role as a start-up matures into a larger, more bureaucratic and "corporate" business. Founders may also come to the realization that they no longer have the right skill set to run the business, and in the absence of easily acquired management talent, may see a sale as the best way to ensure the continued success of the business.

In most cases, the sale of a company will create a sudden and huge financial windfall for the founders. While in some cases these founders may already be incredibly wealthy, in most cases, the sale will have a dramatic impact on their lifestyle. For some founders, this will not be a great motivator. If the company is doing well, founders are usually able to pay themselves handsomely and have often taken chunks of money out of the business during various rounds of financing. For a person with modest tastes, the money she makes running a private company may be more than enough to meet all her needs. For other founders, who may have dreams of living an opulent life, the lure of a huge payoff may be highly motivational.

Even if founders are not motivated by the financial payoff of a sale, it may represent a painless way to exit the business. Founding and building a company is hard work and long hours. By the time a company is successful and large, the founders have often been working nearly non-stop for years. At this point, the founders may view a sale as an attractive exit option that allows them to leave the company—their baby—in good hands, while allowing them to finally reap the fruits of their labors by taking time off to relax and spend with their families.

Ironically, the success of a business may actually leave a founder feeling out of place. Most entrepreneurs work best in a small, rapidly changing, and unstructured environment. As a business grows and becomes more successful, a certain amount of structure and bureaucracy becomes necessary. For the founder, this is a mixed blessing. The inevitable result of major success is that the culture of the company she founded shifts away from the founder and becomes more corporate. It is not uncommon to find founders of large and successful companies remembering fondly the time when they were scrapping and struggling in a small shop. Serial entrepreneurs often return to their roots and start new small companies, which they again try to grow. For a founder who loves the small company start-up culture, a sale may be an easy way to exit the business that she now finds stifling and allow her to return to her favorite environment, a new start-up.

While a founder may sometimes not mind the more bureaucratic corporate culture that develops, the culture often cannot stomach the entrepreneur. The skills needed to start a small business and scramble to make it successful are not the same ones needed to run a large mature company. As a company matures, the skills of the founders may no longer be sufficient. The wiser founder recognizes this and brings in management talent with the right skills to run a larger company. The founders of Yahoo! are a good example. Early on in that company's growth they recognized the need for a more mature "big company" executive and brought in Terry Semel to run the company. While the need to bring in professional management does not always lead to a sale, once the founders have decided that they need to hand over the reins to a new executive team, the incentive to keep control of the company and not sell decreases substantially.

Of all the parties involved in a decision to sell, the founders usually bring the most emotional and personal preference to the issue. With the exception of management, most of the other parties to a sale decision are driven entirely or largely by financial incentives. Only the founders and managers take the issue personally and expect the decision to have an impact on their day-to-day lives and not just their wallets.

Professional Investors

Unlike founders, professional investors usually take a purely logical and financial approach to the issue of sale. That said, they have their own set of particular biases and preferences, which influence their view on the decision. Professional investors are focused on the performance of their investment in a company as it compares to alternative investment options they have for their money. They are also concerned about the investment in the context of their overall portfolio. For professional investors who are managing other people's money, there is also concern with perceptions on the part of their investors.

When a private investor puts money into a company, she has an expectation of both risk and return on the investment. Given a particular level of risk, the investment needs to be expected to have a particular level of return. For example, investment in a start-up needs to have the potential for a very high return, given the higher risk of failure, while investment in a large established business can be coupled with a lower expected return, given the lower risk of failure. The professional investor is always considering any investment against all the other alternative uses of her money. If a professional investor believes that the future continued return on an investment has dipped below its threshold level, it may seek a sale. For example, if the growth of a company is expected to slow down substantially, a professional investor may decide the time is ripe to sell the company and reinvest its money in a higher growth earlier-stage business.

Private investors also tend to focus on particular types and stages of investment. When a company evolves out of this "sweet spot," the investor may be tempted to sell. For example, an investor in early-stage technology start-ups may want to liquidate its position in a company once that company has become a large, slower-growing technology company. This is not only because the investment has different financial characteristics than the investor is used to but also because the investor's particular expertise and advice is no longer relevant, and it, therefore, will have less control or impact on the development of the business. In some cases, professional investors will sell to other professional investors as the company evolves from one's "sweet spot" to the others. It is not uncommon to see early-stage venture capital investors selling their stake to private equity firms focused on larger and more established businesses.

Private investors also have to consider the impact of a particular investment on their overall portfolio. Any private investor that is managing funds for others—such as private equity and venture capital firms—likely gives those fund investors regular reports on the overall fund performance. If the portfolio as a whole is underperforming there may be an incentive to trigger a liquidity event by selling a company that has performed particularly well to offset less successful parts of the portfolio. By contrast, if the fund has had a good year but is anticipating weaker times in the future, there may be an incentive to let their investment ride and realize the gain in the future. In some cases, a private investor may want to trigger a sale simply to demonstrate success to investors in its fund.

Public Investors

Unlike private investors, public investors in a company tend to hold very small stakes and take little if any role in the governance of a company. Whether they are individual investors or institutional investors, they tend to view their ownership of a company as a pure financial investment. Given this, they are likely to view a sale in the purest terms. In most cases, any offer to purchase the company at a price materially higher than its current market valuation will be embraced. The exception will be where the management or board of directors can convince shareholders that the company is undervalued by the market and that the offer, even if it is above the current market valuation, is lower than the value their stakes will achieve if the company continues to operate independently. This will be the situation in a hostile deal, where the board opposes an offer and the Buyer appeals directly to shareholders and launches a proxy battle to gain control of the board paving the way for an approval of the deal.

In rare cases, public investors can take a more active role in the management of a company. In situations where a public investor gains a material stake in the company, he or she may start to behave more like a private investor, taking an active role in management. In those situations, the private investor may be more likely to think beyond the immediate gain from a sale to the long-term potential of the company.

Management

Executive management has a combination of interests when it comes to a sale. In most cases, senior executives are both employees and significant shareholders. A sale can impact both their professional and financial futures. These personal incentives have to be balanced against their role as fiduciaries for the shareholders.

When a company is sold, three things can happen to members of the executive team. In some cases, the Buyer will actively seek to retain members of the team and view them as valuable, and in some cases essential, assets of the company. In this situation, a sale can actually be a boon for an executive's career. In other cases, the Buyer will view them with some measure of indifference, being willing to retain them but not viewing them as essential to the success of the integrated business. In this case, the executives may find the new role acceptable but often will find it underwhelming. In the last case, the Buyer will have no use for the executives and will either not seek to hire them or only seek to retain them for a short transition period. Which outcome is expected will determine how an executive views a potential sale.

While executives can develop the same emotional attachments to a business that founders develop, that level of esprit de corps and connection is less likely for executives. Senior professionals are more used to experiencing moves in and out of organizations, and since they did not create the company, but only grew it, they may be less likely to build an emotional tie to the institution.

A sale can also be a huge financial event for an executive. Senior management in most smaller companies has a significant equity stake. In the event of a sale, executives will experience a miniversion of the financial windfall that founders will get (and in some cases, a similar windfall). As with founders, this can cause management to lose interest and motivation as it dramatically changes their lifestyle. A financial windfall can be a huge incentive for executive management to support a deal.

As a general rule, while management may be subject to some of the same incentives as founders, they will tend to be more professional and rational in their reaction. They will also likely be more aware of, and subject to, the pressure to act in the interest of the shareholders. Given this, they will be more likely to take a rational approach to an offer to purchase, comparing the value received by shareholders to that which they can achieve as an independent company. However, there is an inherent bias against sale, since management will tend to be optimistic about their own plans and strategies for success.

NOTES

1. For a detailed discussion of this issue see Robert Pitofsky, Harvey Goldschmid, and Diane Wood, *Trade Regulation Cases and Materials,* 5th ed. (Brooklyn, NY: Foundation Press, 2003).
2. This assumes payment in cash. As discussed in Chapter 8, a Seller is often paid, in part or in whole, in the stock of the Buyer. In that situation, obviously the

Seller's shareholders are not eliminating overall market risk to the extent that it is going to damage the stock of the Buyer. However, to the extent they will be allowed to quickly sell the Buyer stock they get in the deal, they may be able to convert to cash and eliminate that market risk in fairly short order.

3. Note that sometimes such regulations can actually have the opposite impact, increasing the value of a business. For example, those few establishments granted "grandfather" exemptions to the smoking ban in New York are now hugely financially successful. If a company is in an industry that is newly regulated and it somehow avoids the impact of the regulation, it is likely to gain market share and be more successful. For example, if apple farmers use a certain pesticide to increase production, which is suddenly found to cause cancer and is outlawed, those few farmers that didn't use the pesticide will benefit from positive customer perceptions and the fact that their competitors suddenly have an increased cost that they do not have.

CHAPTER 4

Buyer's Preparation for the Deal

Given the combination of complexity and importance inherent in Strategic Transactions, it is well worth the investment to develop the right capabilities and team to execute the deal well and efficiently. If preparing properly has even a small incremental impact on the value derived from a deal, it easily pays for itself. To put this in perspective, gaining even 50 basis point (0.5%) of value on a $1 billion deal translates into $5 million in value. This effect is even more dramatic when considered in terms of avoiding a bad deal or in the context of doing multiple deals over time. Whether you are a Buyer or a Seller, developing the right capability to execute a deal can not only ensure that the deal goes smoothly but also actually add value to the transaction.

DEVELOPING A STRATEGY

Deals often appear opportunistically for Buyers—whether investment bankers pitch them, industry relationships bring the parties together directly, or the Target cold calls a senior executive. There is no rule that says a purely opportunistic deal cannot be a good one. Beyond pure financial synergy, a "found" deal may actually make sense long term for a Buyer and turn out to be an excellent investment of capital and resources. However, for the most part, doing an acquisition without an underlying strategy is fraught with risks. The most effective acquisitions are usually those that flow from a broad corporate strategy and then from a derivative acquisition strategy. They are also those deals that have obtained broad support and buy-in from both the board of directors and executive management.

Broad Corporate Strategy

I will not bother to make the argument for developing a broad corporate strategy, since there is a raft of literature and MBA coursework that takes that burden. It is fairly common wisdom that a company is well served by maintaining and constantly adapting a strategy that provides an overarching theme and direction for the business. The strategy helps to direct a variety of groups and efforts efficiently and in sync, and coordinates companies with multiple business lines.

If one posits that a corporate strategy is an important element of running a company effectively, it follows that any Strategic Transaction needs to flow from, and help drive, that strategy. Deals are some of the most impactful single decisions or actions a company can take, and so it is particularly important that they connect well with the corporate strategy. More importantly, Strategic Transactions are one of the most powerful tools for implementing corporate strategy and in particular for creating a sea change when such is required from a new strategic direction. Take the example of product development. If a new strategic direction calls for the development and launching of a new product line, a company can choose to drive that development organically over a period of months or years, or it can choose to acquire that capability in one fell swoop through an acquisition. When Strategic Transactions fit into a corporate strategy, they are powerful tools. When they do not, they can be a distraction at the very least and, at the extreme, can entirely derail the direction of the company.

Just as you would not choose the design of a house based on your preference for using a hammer as your tool of choice, as opposed to a screwdriver, strategy should not be driven by the goal of doing deals. However, the potential to do deals, or lack thereof, can help inform strategic decisions about what is possible. For example, if a company wants to spur growth and has the choice of growing geographically in Europe or Asia, the fact that there are a large number of attractive acquisition Targets in Asia and fewer in Europe can nudge the strategy in that direction. Planning for acquisitions can interact with the broad corporate strategy by showing where that particular tool can be used most effectively and where it is limited.

Strategic Transaction Strategy

Once a corporate strategy is established, a company needs to decide where it will use Strategic Transactions as the execution tool for that strategy. A variety of factors needs to be considered. Each particular area merits a build versus buy comparison, whereby the company compares its options to acquire as compared to relying on organic growth. In each area of potential acquisition, the company needs to consider several factors. The availability of Targets can vary widely and needs to be reviewed. Often connected to this is the market pricing for Targets. In a space with few attractive independent players, the premium to acquire one may be very high, driving the company to find the build option more attractive. The ease of integration is another factor to consider. Some capabilities or assets are so hard to integrate that it is more efficient to just build them from scratch. Similarly, one needs to consider the ability to transfer the core value of the asset or capability effectively. For example, it is often hard to transfer brand loyalty and market image to a larger acquirer. The image of a small "rebel" independent may be substantially damaged solely by virtue of such an acquisition. When considering where to use acquisition as a tool, a company needs to consider all these factors and determine where Strategic Transactions will be most effective. In addition to considering the build versus buy options in each individual case, the company needs to consider them in the aggregate. Capital, as well as capability, will constrain the volume of Strategic Transactions that a company can do. Even active acquirers, such as Cisco, have a limit to the number of deals they can do in a given period of time. In particular, given the focus of senior management on such deals, it is important not to overload the pipeline of transactions too heavily and risk not getting all the necessary components of a strategy in place.

Once you have determined the general areas of focus for an acquisitions effort, you need to develop a specific strategy for each such area. The strategy will include an analysis of the key requirements of a successful transaction. These key requirements will be driven by the underlying corporate strategy and can vary dramatically from company to company and deal to deal. In some cases, speed to market will be paramount, and in others, it may be maximizing financial metrics, such as return on equity. In most cases, there will be a number of different requirements that must be balanced and ordered. What, hopefully, emerges is a clear picture of the most attractive Target and the key goals of the deal. For example, imagine a clothing manufacturer with a corporate strategy of moving into the hipper younger segments of the market. One acquisition strategy might involve acquiring small boutique clothing design firms with cutting-edge designs. The primary goal would be to find a firm with the right design and style. A secondary goal would be to choose a firm where manufacturing could easily be taken over by the Buyer's existing and larger manufacturing operations. In this case, the Buyer might be relatively unconcerned with profitability or customer relationships, since it plans to sell the designs through its existing network of retailers. Finally, there would be a strong time-to-market element if the Buyer wanted to integrate this new line in time for the next year's fall fashion season. Setting out these goals not only ensures that the potential deal dovetails with the corporate strategy but also gives direction to the deal team, in terms of sourcing Targets as well as in terms of prioritizing issues during negotiations. In this case, there is a preference for very hip and cutting-edge, even if highly unprofitable, design shops, with a focus on retention of designers and staff rather than of existing customers.

Armed with this blueprint for the ideal transaction, the Buyer's Corporate Development team can now build a Target list and sort through the Targets based on the requirements. Of course, they also need to consider availability since, in most cases, not all potential players are for sale, and certainly not all are for sale at a reasonable price. The Buyer's team can then go about engaging with various potential Targets and trying to close a deal. In some cases, they may be more active, reaching out through surrogates (discussed below) and directly to the potential Targets. In other cases, they may be more passive, setting up criteria and then waiting for properties to become available.

This is by no means the only way to get a deal done but, hopefully, points out some of the pitfalls in acting without considering the broad corporate strategy and developing a particular acquisition strategy. The approach may vary from company to company and sector to sector, but the need to develop a conscious plan and approach is always there. Finally, it is important to remember that this is not a static environment. More so than in other parts of the company, in Corporate Development the world and fact patterns can change rapidly. An acquisition strategy must be able to absorb changes in the environment and adapt to them, while staying true to the underlying goals of the company and its strategy. For example, a cake company might seek to acquire a retail food chain to sell its pastry product as a dessert. However, if it finds few Targets, or if another larger player starts to compete for every deal, it may change its acquisition strategy to acquiring a coffeehouse chain, which also provides a channel for selling its product.

Board and Management Buy-In

As with the broad corporate strategy, an acquisition strategy needs the approval and support of the board and management. In some ways, it is even more crucial when planning a deal. Acquisitions are such singularly risky events that the decision makers need to have a high level of comfort. While it is certainly possible that without any advance notice the board or the CEO may approve a large deal, based on a single presentation, it is far more likely that they will balk at taking such a risk. It is usually very important to develop support for an acquisition strategy well in advance of bringing a particular deal up for approval. Even very sophisticated business leaders usually take time to gain comfort with a dramatic move like a large acquisition. An iterative discussion that provides them with the opportunity to ask questions and give feedback often can help shift them from wary to actively supportive. At the end of the day, it is hard to get a large deal done without fairly vigorous support from these decision makers. And of course to the extent that they are firmly set against the acquisition strategy, an early read will save the team weeks or months of wasted effort and allow them to focus on retooling the strategy to meet the approval of the board and executive management.

While at this early stage, you may not be able to spell out the details of a future deal, you will at least be able to set out some of the parameters developed in the acquisition strategy and get the decision makers comfortable with those key issues. Of primary importance will be variables such as the size of the deal, the type of business to be acquired, how it fits into the broad corporate strategy, and likely public and market reaction. The more detail that can be provided in these early stages, the less likely the decision makers will be to balk at the deal decision. Of course, the countering risk is that the natural uncertainty of an acquisition strategy may cause some of these variables to change midstream and leave the deal team looking unreliable. Thus, the key is to balance the level of detail provided with the need to try to develop early confidence in the acquisition strategy.

BUILDING A CAPABILITY

Whether a Buyer is planning to launch a sustained acquisition program or just do one deal, building the right capability is a necessary prerequisite to doing a deal and ensuring that it gets good value for its purchase price. A Buyer that is not planning a sustained program of acquisition may hesitate to put a large internal capability in place. Clearly, it does not make sense to build a large in-house Corporate Development team for a single deal. The balance between in-house resources and outside advisors allows a Buyer to create a balanced approach to doing a deal, depending on whether, and how often, it plans to do further acquisitions in the future. However, it is important to note that there is a limit to how far one can leverage outside advisors. A certain amount of company-specific knowledge is always required to do an effective deal. Thus, even when a Buyer is certain that there will be no follow-on Strategic Transactions, it will need to dedicate a certain amount of in-house resources to getting a deal done.

Corporate Development Team

As discussed above, members of the Corporate Development team are not only experts in specific skills, such as valuation and negotiation but also serve a broader role as the "traffic cops" of a Strategic Transaction. It is their job to manage all the resources, both inside and outside the company, that need to be brought to bear. Even for a Buyer planning to do a single deal, it is important that someone within the company fill this role and have the capability to manage the process and the network and credibility to make things happen in different parts of the company. For companies that are planning a sustained acquisition program, the Corporate Development team will usually form the foundation of that effort and becomes even more critical. When building a Corporate Development team, it is important to remember not only the specific skills the team members need to have but also the more ephemeral, but nonetheless essential, characteristics and credibility they need to have within the corporate structure to get the job done. Corporate Development teams are like fulcrums, allowing the company to leverage a variety of resources and skills throughout the organization, and unless they are strong enough and capable enough to fulfill this broader role, they will have trouble getting a deal done effectively.

Key Skills/Capabilities

This discussion can be separated into two areas: (1) specific skills sets and (2) general capabilities. In terms of specific skills sets, Corporate Development needs to have the financial acumen to do complex valuation exercises, as well as to review, understand, and assess financial statements. They also need to understand the overall transaction process and the key steps that need to take place in a deal, as well as the high points of integration planning and the challenges inherent in that exercise. While they certainly do not need to be lawyers, Corporate Development needs to have a high-level understanding of the legal structures and issues of a Strategic Transactions, since many of these issues will devolve to business judgments, where the lawyers will look to them to make the call. They also need to have a good general understanding of the Buyer's business and operations, as well as the business sector in which they are looking to acquire. As can be seen from this list, Corporate Development needs to be somewhat of a "renaissance organization." Every member of the Corporate Development team does not have to have all these skills, but to be effective, the organization must, in the aggregate, have all of them. And to be effective as a senior Corporate Development executive, an individual must have acquired the basic skills in all these areas.

Beyond these specific areas of skill, the Corporate Development staff needs to be generally skilled at adapting to new situations and problems, since every Strategic Transaction brings a unique twist or challenge. They need to be comfortable in stressful and fast-paced situations, since Strategic Transactions usually happen in quick crescendos, rather than slowly over long periods of time. The Corporate Development staff needs to be comfortable with, and capable of, speaking in front of senior executives and negotiating with them, since they will likely be presenting deals to their own executives and negotiating with those of the counterparty. Perhaps most difficult to plan and accomplish, Corporate Development staff needs to have credibility and authority within the company. Corporate Development is often an exercise of overseeing and managing the work of people who do not report to you but are seconded from other parts of the company. These people usually continue to have a "day job," and generally they will be compensated and promoted based on this primary job. It is common for employees to resent being staffed on Strategic Transactions and to view this work as a distraction from their real job— where they get paid.

To be effective, the Corporate Development staff needs to be able to command enough authority among senior executives to get the resources they need and to then motivate them to act. In most cases, Corporate Development staff actually have to spur employees to work faster, harder, and under more stressful conditions than they have in their current role. While part of this will come from choosing people with the right temperament and character for the Corporate Development role, that only goes so far. To have an effective Corporate Development team, a company needs to imbue that role and its deals with the right sense of importance throughout the organization. In some cases, this may be fairly easy. To the extent line managers are incentivized to get an acquisition done, they will help drive that sense of urgency and importance among their staff. In some cases, the executive management team must step in to press the issue. This will be particularly true for acquisitions that do not have an existing home within the current organization and, thus, do not have a sponsoring line manager.

As a result of this diverse set of skills required, Corporate Development staff can be recruited from a variety of places. In each case, they will probably arrive with some weak spots and some strong spots in their skill set and will need to "backfill" the weak spots. As a result, it is sometimes less important that the potential Corporate Development executive have a particular background and more important that he or she be smart and adept at picking up new skills and learning on the fly. As discussed above, common sources for Corporate Development staff include, but are not limited to, investment bankers, lawyers, consultants, finance executives, and even general line managers.

Role in the Organization and the Deal

As discussed in Chapter 2, the Corporate Development team functions as the conductor of an orchestra, bringing together a variety of internal and external resources and leading them down a single sheet of music in harmony and in time. In practical terms, this means lots of checklists, forms, meeting, call planners, and imposition of deadlines. This form definitely overlies significant substance. Strategic Transactions require a very large number of things to happen in unison and in sequence over very short periods of time. The conductor role is crucial and is probably more akin to a conductor faced with an orchestra that has rarely, if ever, played together and, in many cases, are entirely unfamiliar with the music to be played. The project management role of Corporate Development is crucial.

Corporate Development has work of their own to do as well. Generally, they are responsible for pitching deals within the company and getting approvals. While in smaller companies this may be a fairly easy task, in large corporations—the most likely active acquirers—this is usually a time-consuming and complicated task. In a large corporation, approval may be needed from several levels of management up to, and often including, the board of directors. Different companies will require different analyses to be done as part of that approval process, and usually these presentations for approval must lay out not only basic financials but also the full story and case for the acquisition, including the underlying strategy, financial projections, and integration plans. While some of these elements will obviously come from different sources, notably line management, Corporate Development is generally responsible for consolidating the material and crafting the story. They are also usually the primary live presenters.

Corporate Development sometimes has primary responsibility for doing the financial models—though in some companies this role is given to the finance group[1]—and is almost always responsible for doing the valuation work. They almost always lead the due diligence effort, and while they can usually pull resources, particularly experts in areas like technology, operations, and marketing, they are ultimately responsible for ensuring that timely and thorough due diligence is completed. Corporate Development will rarely have ongoing responsibility for integrating an acquired business postclosing, but they are often responsible for fleshing out the initial integration plan or at least working with line management to make sure that it is done. In most organizations, this work will be a prerequisite to obtaining final approval to consummate a deal, and since Corporate Development usually seeks that approval, it naturally falls to them to ensure that all the component "ducks" are in a row before pitching a deal for approval. Given this, Corporate Development naturally ends up as the dumping ground for the odds and ends that fall through the cracks in the process. Since they are the leaders and advocates of the deal, they will step in to take on work and projects that somehow get left undone, and boxes that get left unchecked.

As a result of all this, when building a Corporate Development team, it is as important to consider breadth of skills set as it is to consider specific skills. Corporate Development leaders are true jacks-of-all-trades, who need to be flexible and adaptable. They need to be assertive and aggressive enough to negotiate, yet politic enough to marshal resources from throughout the company. M&As are usually hit or miss exercises, and so when building a Corporate Development team, you need to consider not only the workload of a live deal but also the work involved in chasing down the hundreds of potential deals and the dozens of failed deals that usually precede and follow every successful deal. This is not to say that a Corporate Development team needs to be huge. For most companies, even fairly acquisitive ones, the team is made up of fewer than 10 professionals with a small support structure.

Corporate Development teams are, by their nature, top heavy. Since much of the heavy lifting can be resourced from other parts of the company, the Corporate Development team will tend to be staffed by seasoned professionals with minimal analyst-level and administrative support. Most Corporate Development teams look like an inverted pyramid with a large number of senior professionals and a small number of junior ones. Thus, while the teams are usually small, the compensation levels are usually high. This is particularly true because of the background of the team members.

Many Corporate Development team members are either hired from consulting or investment banking firms, or recruited from the population of highly successful and well-compensated internal "stars." Travel and entertainment expenses can also be high, because Corporate Development teams spend a lot of time on the road meeting with potential Targets. Like a SWAT team, a Corporate Development team will tend to be a small but elite group of well-funded professionals called on to act quickly and aggressively—melodramatic but true.

Advisors

In most cases, you would not hire advisors until you are well into the process of a Strategic Transaction, but in some cases, you will want their help earlier in the process, and even when they are hired in the heat of a deal, you need to know in advance whom you will call. It is important to establish a network of relationships with potential advisors well before a deal gets hot. Consultants are often hired to help develop the broad strategy for a Corporate Development effort. In other cases, they are brought on to support a particular deal. Similarly, while investment bankers are almost always paid on a success fee basis for deals, they are usually hired after an extended series of meetings and discussions with the company over a period of months or even years. In the case of investment bankers, and to a lesser extent consultants, part of the reason for lots of predeal interaction is that the "pro bono" work they do when in sales mode prior to a deal or engagement represents a significant amount of the value they bring. Investment bankers, in particular, are often hired as much to compensate them for work done prior to the engagement as for work they will do on the deal itself.

However, there is a more important reason to work with advisors in advance of a live deal. Once a transaction goes live, everyone will need to move quickly and effectively. Being familiar with your advisors' capabilities and staff before starting work is important. By working with advisors prior to a deal, you will be able to ensure that they understand your company, its business and operations, its goals, and even its culture. Similarly, you will be able to assess the quality and capabilities of the team that is servicing you. This will help you to choose an advisor and to build confidence in that advisor's views and analysis.

Beyond consultants and investment bankers, a variety of specialist advisors may be used on deals. In some cases, these are specialists you cannot possibly get to know before the deal. In this situation, it is usually best to defer to someone with the expertise to choose the right firm or person.

Often, a company will turn to its established outside advisory relationships to choose other "secondary advisors." For example, a company might depend on its legal counsel to hire environmental consulting firms, or on its consulting firm to hire a technology integration specialist, or on its investment banker to hire an asset valuation specialist.

Other Corporate Resources

Building a Corporate Development team is a good start, but it is just the tip of the iceberg in terms of the resources necessary to execute a Strategic Transaction. Resources from throughout the company will need to be harnessed to prepare for and execute a Corporate Development effort. The initial strategy that drives the effort will need to involve the strategic planning team as well as business leaders and executive management. Once a strategy is built, sourcing potential deals will require help from members of the business unit management teams particularly familiar with the sectors, products, and companies on which the strategy is focused. Once a deal becomes live, resources will be needed from relevant business units as well as staff functions for a variety of roles, including integration planning and more critically due diligence. While the specific requirements will vary from deal to deal, they could include staff with expertise in technology, product development, marketing and sales, finance, risk, real estate, and a variety of other areas. In particular, legal and corporate-level finance and accounting staff will play a critical role in any Strategic Transaction. One option is to staff a Corporate Development team with a deep bench of experts in topics ranging from marketing to technology. In most cases, this is a highly inefficient solution and one that still does not provide the Corporate Development team with specific understanding of what the relevant business unit is doing. At the same time, to be effective a Corporate Development team needs access to such resources on a fairly regular basis as it reviews opportunities, engages in due diligence, and tries to close deals. One trend is to create virtual teams, where staff from relevant business units are assigned as the "go-to" people when Corporate Development needs support.[2]

DEVISING A PROCESS

Running an effective and efficient Corporate Development effort is a lot like conducting an orchestra. You need not only the right set of players but also a single piece of music from which you all play. Sourcing opportunities that are actually a good fit, and then executing on those opportunities requires a lot of different resources, processes, and analyses to all come together in a coordinated manner. In the absence of a well-thought-out process that is tailored to the needs and culture of a Buyer, a Corporate Development effort can fail to effectively drive deals and even do damage to the company.

Leveraging Expertise

When developing a Corporate Development effort, one needs to make a judgment about the importance, likelihood, and impact of deal flow from that effort. In a large and active Corporate Development effort, resources from throughout the company will need to be harnessed to execute the deals. The more those resources are arranged and leveraged in advance, the more effective the effort will be. However, calling on resources outside the Corporate Development team in advance of a live deal is a drain on other parts of the business. For example, during due diligence one may need technology specialists from the IT department; however, those resources all have "day jobs" that are important to the core operations of the business. The more and the earlier those resources are pulled toward deals, the greater the impact on the business.

For a company with a sufficiently active and developed Corporate Development effort, other parts of the company can actually budget and plan for this resource drain, since it becomes relatively predictable. In the most extreme cases, departments will actually staff in anticipation of a regular flow of deals and expect that, at any given time, a certain number of their team members will be working on deals. For most companies with less active, mature, and predictable Corporate Development efforts, it is hard to commit the budget necessary to create this kind of buffer in staffing and resourcing throughout the organization. However, failing to make any effort to plan for the use of corporate resources will make it nearly impossible to execute a deal quickly and efficiently. For most companies, there is a happy medium. Corporate Development can develop a plan for the resources it is likely to need in upcoming deals and share these plans with the parts of the company that are likely to have to contribute the resources. Corporate Development can also keep leaders in those other parts of the business informed about the progress of potential deals. Finally, Corporate Development can educate business leaders about not only what resources will be needed but also specifically what those resources will do. This will help business leaders throughout the organization to better plan for the sudden jarring effect of a deal going live.

Take, for example, a business where brand is an important asset—the apparel industry for instance. When considering the acquisition of an apparel company, the quality and strength of the brand can be a significant variable in the value of, and even the very reason for acquiring, a Target company. When the acquisition goes live, the Corporate Development team will need to call on resources from the marketing and/or product development groups to determine and evaluate the brand of a Target company. This evaluation must take into account not only the value of the brand as a stand-alone company but also the value of the brand when consolidated into the brand portfolio of the acquirer. Establishing this need in advance will allow the leader of the marketing group to consider the people on her staff best able to assess this value and what information they will need to have at their disposal. The leader might need to combine experts in brand value with members of her team with an understanding of the future branding strategy of the company. For example, if the Gap had a strategy of going "up market," you might imagine the value of the Ralph Lauren brand being particularly significant to them as an acquisition Target. Bringing business leaders into the thought and planning processes for a deal will make them better able to support the deal when it goes live.

In practical terms, Corporate Development can begin by meeting with key business leaders and giving them a sense of the overall Corporate Development strategy. It is also important to review the deal process, since many business managers, even very senior ones, may never have been involved in a Strategic Transaction. Corporate Development can provide a framework and overview of the kind of resources that will be needed, as well as the specific deliverables and timetables. It may be helpful to create a standard form due diligence report and timeline of a transaction. Of course, the need to get buy-in and marshal resources from business leaders must be balanced against the need for secrecy. By their nature Strategic Transactions are highly confidential, even within a corporation, and there may be limits to what even senior business leaders can be told about Corporate Development plans, but the more that can be shared, the better prepared these leaders can be.

Special mention should be made of some resources that are particularly critical to any Strategic Transactions. Legal and finance/accounting staff needs to be put in a separate category from other corporate resources. In some ways, they are really de facto members of the Corporate Development team and need to be far more closely aligned with any Corporate Development effort. This is particularly true of legal staff, who will, effectively, sit beside Corporate Development in the negotiation of any deal.

While other corporate business leaders need to be kept abreast of Corporate Development efforts, the legal staff needs to be more intimately involved at a much earlier stage. From the point of initial contact with a potential counterparty (and sometimes even before), the legal staff needs to be inserted into the process.

Approval Process

A Strategic Transaction is among the most significant and dramatic single decisions a company can make. As a result, one cannot overestimate the importance of the approval process. More importantly, it is essential to map out and design the approval process to ensure that it does not bog down, or even block, a successful deal. This is not an idle concern. It is not uncommon to find potential bidders on an acquisition dropping out of the process because the necessary internal approvals cannot be received in time. To be sure, this will almost never be the reason given to the other side, but it is a common occurrence. This is not a problem limited to large multinational corporations. Even smaller companies can find approval a challenge. In fact, since they are less likely to have formalized structures and chains of command, sometimes smaller companies will find the approval process more cumbersome rather than less.

The legal approval requirements for a Strategic Transaction are not discussed in great detail in this book but it is important to remember that any deal that can have a material impact on a company, and certainly all sales of companies, are governed by the legal requirements that regulate the operation of companies.[3] Some deals will require shareholder approval, others may be approved by the board of directors, and others may require only approval from executive management. The level of approval will usually correlate to the size of a deal, although other factors can enter into the equation. For example, if a $100 billion public company is acquiring a $20 million private company it will need neither shareholder approval nor board approval. In fact, for a deal like this, which represents such a small portion of the value of the acquiring company, authority will likely be delegated to the general manager of the subsidiary or unit doing the deal. Surely, someone like Bill Gates will often not be approving, nor perhaps even be aware of, a deal of this size. However, other factors, such as public relations and legal exposure, can certainly affect the level of approval. If an acquisition Target operates in a particularly controversial or risky business, where the acquisition can be expected to generate negative press reports or some other significant risks to the company, more senior approval may be required. For example, when acquiring a company in a controversial business like pornography or perhaps tobacco, or when acquiring a company that operates in a risky market like, perhaps, some countries in Africa with political instability, higher levels of corporate approval may be required.

Where legal and regulatory levels of approval end, internal business standards take over. While the CEO may end up giving the final approval to a deal, she certainly does not want to see every single potential deal that is proposed anywhere in the organization. Deals usually require a series of approvals, which act not only to ensure proper authority and compliance with corporate bylaws but also as a filter for deals so that the higher in the organization a deal rises for approval, the more senior the staff that has previously vetted it and approved it. Every company will have different levels and processes for approval, but they all tend to follow some tiering system in which different deals require different levels of approval, and the higher in the company the approval goes, the more people have to approve it along the way. It is crucial to establish in advance what the standards are for approval and who the right people are at each level. If this is not clearly established in advance, there is a huge danger that a deal either will get bogged down as the deal team searches the organization for the right person or, even worse, will be done without the right approval being given. For example:

- Deals need approval from the head of Corporate Development and the line manager who will own the business.

- Deals require approval from legal.

- Deals involving large asset pools require approval from risk.

- Deals above $10 million and those that have no line manager (i.e., new businesses that will stand on their own) require additional approval from the divisional CEO.

- Deals above $100 million require additional approval from the corporate CEO.

This is only one example and an approval process needs to be tailored to each company and, particularly, to the nature of its business. For example, in most companies, intellectual property is a relatively minor issue, but for a movie studio or large publisher, intellectual property rights and, thus, intellectual property counsel are at the core of any deal. The key is to establish well in advance what the approval standards are and who the authorized approvers are. Appendix D provides an example of a standard approval process that a company might use for Strategic Transactions.

The next step is to consider how to obtain approval. Anyone approving a deal is going to want to be given a fairly detailed presentation about the deal. While each such presentation could be developed on a one-off basis, this will slow down the process and often lead to a situation in which the approver is not getting the information he needs. Ideally, a company should establish fairly standard presentation forms to be used when presenting a deal and specify the kind of analysis that needs to be done. As discussed in Chapter 8, different companies have different ways of viewing the financial impact of a transaction. When presenting a deal, it is important to identify the key metrics that are most relevant to the company and include them in any deal presentation. The same can be said for due diligence, integration, and broad strategic justifications for the deal. In a perfect world, the company would establish a standard presentation and analysis form, which could be used at every level of approval with minor adjustment—ensuring the most streamlined process for approval. In practice, approval is rarely that well orchestrated in a company, and one might argue that, given the variations from deal to deal, there will always be the need for adjustment. However, some standardization of forms and analyses will go a long way toward preventing the Corporate Development team from having to reinvent the wheel and ensure that approvers' expectations are met in terms of the material given to them when asked to approve a deal. Appendix E provides an example of the key topics covered in an approval presentation for an acquisition.

Organizational Buy-In

Effective execution of Strategic Transactions requires both formal and informal approvals. Formal corporate approvals are a necessary, but by no means sufficient, condition to a successful Strategic Transaction. As discussed above, while the Corporate Development team may lead a deal, the vast majority of the manpower and effort required to get a deal done is contributed from within the line businesses and other areas of corporate staffing. Perhaps more important, effective integration—which, as discussed, is the single most important determining factor in the success or failure of a deal—is almost entirely handled by staff in the line business and with little direction from the Corporate Development team. Failure to get broad organizational buy-in to a deal can either block the deal from successfully closing or ensure its eventual failure during the integration process.

A surprisingly wide swath of employees is relevant to completing a Strategic Transaction. Most corporate staff functions, such as legal, finance, real estate, and human resources, will be critical. The management and many of the senior staff of the relevant line business will also be important. The larger number of line employees necessary to do due diligence and integration planning will also be essential. As discussed in Chapter 7, almost every area of specialty in a line business will be involved in either due diligence or integration of an acquired business. Other related entities, such as labor unions, are also needed to support, or at least not to oppose, a deal. Of the dozens or hundreds of people involved in a Strategic Transaction, only a handful are actually members of the Corporate Development team. Without support from the myriad of other participants, Corporate Development staff will be like the police trying to manage an unruly mob.

Certainly, it is rare to see open rebellion within a company. If the CEO approves a deal, it is unlikely that anyone will openly refuse to participate, but as we all know, there is a huge difference between grudging participation and active support. Tactics like work slowdowns and sickouts have long been used by labor unions to stymie corporate efforts, while avoiding a formal strike. Whether it is a pilot quadruple checking his systems and delaying a flight, or a five-year-old dragging his feet as you walk down the street, there are a myriad of ways that someone can impede progress without formally standing up as a roadblock. Therefore, it is essential to not only get formal approval through channels but also to get a broader organizational buy-in that will make employees not only willing but also enthusiastic participants in a deal.

This is not always possible. Strategic Transactions, by their very nature, bring chaos and change to an organization, and there are almost always winners and losers. Not everyone will be happy about a deal, and many may oppose it either for personal reasons or philosophical ones. Some employees may be concerned that the deal will damage their careers or even risk their jobs. For example, if a company with a small unit providing consulting services seeks to acquire a larger consulting company, the employees in the consulting division may worry that they will be overshadowed, or even entirely replaced by, the larger unit being integrated. Employees may have more theoretical opposition to a deal, simply believing that it is the wrong approach for a company. Certainly, it is possible that when Ben & Jerry's was sold to Unilever, many employees opposed the deal for fear that it would dilute or even eliminate some of the strong cultural foundations of the company, such as a focus on charitable and environmental causes.

While you cannot please all of the people all of the time, getting buy-in from most employees, and at the very least from their managers, before doing a deal will be critical to its successful execution. In my view, the key to this exercise is communication and proper incentives. Communicating the high-level logic and strategy behind a Strategic Transaction not only helps employees understand their role and do it better but also gives them a feeling of ownership in the transaction. Strategic Transactions are, by their nature, secretive, so there will be significant limits on one's ability to communicate. However, even creating a broad understanding of the general goals behind Strategic Transactions and the intent to do them will go a long way to getting employees comfortable. For a Buyer, the emphasis of this message should be on the value it brings to the whole company and to the employees' specific business unit. While a company will not be able to communicate the details of its M&As strategy, it may be able to communicate the intent to consider Strategic Transactions and tell employees how and why this will enhance the business. Once a deal starts and employees are brought under the tent of confidential information, it is important to communicate the goals of the deal clearly.

Beyond making the employee feel involved, you need to consider the incentives of the employee. To the extent possible, linking the success of the deal to employees' incentives will ensure that they are enthusiastic participants. On a broad level, to the extent that you can allay fears about layoffs and redundancies, you will do much to garner the support of employees. Knowing that the deal will not result in damage to their career will be incredibly important to them. Showing how the deal will help their organization grow will also be important. It is as, or more, important to link the deal to very personal incentives. Remember that, for most employees, a Strategic Transaction is not a full-time long-term role. It is a sideline to their "day job" and is often viewed as a distraction. Companies doing Strategic Transactions, particularly those that want to maintain a sustained and ongoing Corporate Development effort, would be wise to ensure that employees are rewarded for their involvement in successful deals. In some cases, this may be a formal bonus structure and in others simply a strong message to managers that performance on a deal should be considered and echoed in annual performance reviews. Often, the reward can come through a new role. In many companies, an acquisition creates opportunities for promotion as employees are inserted into the acquired division, often in roles with far greater responsibility. Whatever the method of incentivization, it needs to be communicated to the employee in advance of the deal. It is no use to reward employees *ex post* for good work on a deal; they need to know in advance that the reward is coming. The need for proper incentives rises up through the organization. Even senior executives need to be properly incentivized. Usually, the general manager of a business has a built-in incentive to do an acquisition, since it will result in her managing a larger business. Other managers need to be considered. Even seasoned executives have personal incentives, which need to be managed, and since their view of a deal impacts the incentives of all below them, it is especially crucial that they be supportive. If a unit manager is not actively supportive of a deal, it is unlikely that any of her staff, whose bonuses and careers are driven by her reviews, will be particularly supportive. Like Reagan-era economics (at least in theory), management support of a deal follows the trickle-down theory.

PLANNING THE MESSAGE

As one of the more dramatic actions a company can take, Strategic Transactions will tend to evoke a strong reaction from most related parties, both internal and external. In some cases, the impression that people have of a deal can be as important as the actual impact it will eventually have. Whether it is market reaction and its immediate impact on the stock price, or employee reaction and the resulting impact on morale, the impression and reaction that people have to a Strategic Transaction can have immediate and material impact on a company long before the real financial impact of a deal is determined. Once a deal happens, a company needs to manage the message both internally and externally (and we will discuss this further below); however, there is a lot that can be done in advance of announcing a deal to plan and even start to telescope the message. While a company may not be able to disclose the details of ongoing negotiations or even the acquisition strategy it is developing, it may be able to lay the groundwork by both planning the eventual message and sending initial more general messages.

The goals of these messages to the various constituencies are discussed in greater detail in Chapters 9 and 11, but, in the broadest terms, one can think of these messages as alleviating concerns and building optimism about the deal. In advance of actually being prepared to send out a message on a deal, you can still set up the mechanisms that will do so at the right time. It is useful to identify the person responsible for drafting both internal and external messaging. This will usually be someone in the public relations and/or investor relations group. It is also helpful to identify the various groups that will have input or need to approve such messages and try to identify a point of contact. This will often be the same person from the group involved in the deal itself. It may also be useful to start to talk in broad terms about the kind of message that you want to send. Doing all of this well in advance will help to ensure that, during the heat of a live deal, effective messaging is executed well and in a timely manner. For example, if a deal is announced at 7 AM on Monday morning, a press release outlining the deal and explaining its value to the company had better hit the press wires before the market opens. Otherwise, the market may take a negative view of the deal and punish the stock of the company before it has a chance to tell the story of the deal.

Beyond preparing for the message on particular deals, there is some messaging that can be done in advance. A company that is planning a sustained Corporate Development effort, or even one that is just planning a single deal, but one where news is likely to leak, may consider sending a broader message about its general goals in advance of a specific deal. If a company is planning to embark on a series of acquisitions, it might be well served by explaining the rationale for the broad strategy to the market well in advance of announcing its first deal. Providing the same explanation to key customers or to employees may also help avert surprise and concern when a deal is announced. For example, a company planning to expand geographically by acquiring similar businesses in new markets should consider some advanced messaging. Explaining this broad strategy to the market may actually bolster its image and will certainly give the market time to absorb the idea of an acquisitive strategy in new markets. Reviewing the strategy with employees will help alleviate fears, in some cases, that the strategy will lead to an offshoring of their jobs. Presenting the strategy to customers as a way to broaden the company's reach to better serve their international needs will be a plus and will avoid concern that the company is shifting focus away from their home market.

NOTES

1. It can be argued that ceding financial modeling to the finance group is a good way to counteract the "deal advocate" bias inherent in Corporate Development. The finance group has no vested interest in the success or failure of a deal and is free to turn a skeptical eye to the financial projections and synergy assumptions of the projections. For companies with complex accounting policies, this will also ensure that the financial pro forma presented accurate represents how the acquired company will impact the Buyer's financials.
2. One article cited a recent study by Ernst & Young, noting that "many companies are moving toward using what E&Y calls 'virtual teams.'" Ken Klee, "So Who's On Your Team?," *Corporate Dealmaker* (December 9, 2004).

3. For a discussion of the legal requirements for approval of a Strategic Transaction, take a look at J. Fred Weston, Kwang S. Chung, and Susan Hoag, *Mergers, Restructuring and Corporate Control* (Englewood Cliffs, NJ: Prentice Hall, 1990), and for a more detailed technical discussion see Ronald J. Gilson and Bernard S. Black, *The Law and Finance of Corporate Acquisitions,* 2nd ed. (Westbury, NY: Foundation Press, 1995).

CHAPTER 5

Seller's Preparation for the Deal

O nce the decision is made to sell, a Seller's strategy is largely done, and the focus narrows. Deciding to sell a company, or a piece of a company, is only the first step, and a great deal of effort needs to be expended to ensure that shareholders and/or the parent company get maximum value in the deal. A Seller will go through many of the same exercises described in the previous chapters for a Buyer's preparation for a deal. However, there are some notable differences and some additional steps that Sellers need to take.

BUILDING A CAPABILITY

While a Seller, by definition, does not plan to repeat the process, as a Buyer may, it is nonetheless essential that a Seller develop a capability to conduct a sale. The modest investment in a team, a process, and the requisite knowledge can pay huge dividends when measured in even an incremental difference in price received. Selling a business requires a lot of preparation and the right team of internal, and usually external, specialists. Sellers should have this capability well in place before launching a sale process, to ensure not only that they maximize price but that they are able to get a deal done at all.

Corporate Development Team

Sellers may not need a long-term Corporate Development team, but they will need a team dedicated to managing a sale process. In some cases, where a company plans to divest many pieces over a sustained period of time, it will actually make sense to build a Corporate Development team focused on repeated sales. In either case, an in-house team needs to be assembled to manage the process. A lot of work goes into a sale, and, just as with a Buyer, a Seller will need a central team to control the process. The same kind of people can be used in a Seller's Corporate Development team, but there are some notable differences. Most fundamental is the fact that a Seller's Corporate Development team are working themselves out of a job, if their goal is a complete sale of the company. These staff members can be expected to focus on the career impact of this odd situation, and it is important to properly incentivize them to perform well. It may even make sense to give them the same kind of change in control bonus structure that senior executives will often get, to ensure that they do not have an adverse incentive against closing a deal. Even where only parts of a company are being sold, there are concerns for the morale and incentives of the Corporate Development team. Where the divestiture is an exception, and most of their work is doing acquisitions, a sale can actually be an exciting challenge for the team. However, where a company is embarked on a long and sustained string of divestitures, the Corporate Development staff may be hard to motivate. Since, by their nature, sales cause a company to shrink rather than grow, there is not the same prestige and enthusiasm for running sale processes. Staff may worry that their careers will not be enhanced by doing these deals—quite reasonably so. It is certainly less impressive to say that one sold one-third of the company at a good price, than it is to say that one made the company 50% larger with astute deals. Growth is always sexier than even the most managed, careful, and prudent decline.

Advisors

Sellers will also need to retain the same kind of advisors that a Buyer will need. If a company is being sold in its entirety, the stakes are obviously higher. As a result, the use of advisors becomes less optional and more mandatory, as the board of directors will be heavily focused on ensuring, and providing evidence, that they have acted prudently. Even when only a portion of the business is being sold, the more labor-intensive nature of a sale process makes advisors more likely to be needed. Since the Seller is usually in the role of fielding multiple offers, and sometimes negotiating simultaneously with multiple partners, it is more likely that it will need advisors to provide both expertise and pure manpower. It is important to remember that, as with the Corporate Development staff, advisors to a Seller have some adverse incentives. Unlike a Buyer, which represents a potential repeat customer, a Seller (unless a partial Seller) is by definition a one-time client. Advisors may have an adverse incentive to "go easy" on potential Buyers, since the moment the deal closes, that counterparty become a potential client. Most advisors are far too professional to allow this incentive to affect their behavior, but it is an important difference to keep in mind. At a less dramatic level, advisors to a Seller will certainly be less inclined to cut costs or discount services, since there will be no opportunity in the future to recoup these losses on future business. Partial Sellers are perhaps less attractive to advisors than Buyers, since they are generally "shrinking" entities. However, they still offer the opportunity for ongoing relationships and repeat business, and thus create far fewer of these adverse incentives.

Since a sale process is generally fairly complex and requires more preparation (as this chapter will discuss) than a purchase process, Sellers usually are well served by retaining advisors earlier. This is even more so for Sellers that do not have a well-developed Corporate Development team with the expertise to start the process of preparing a company for sale.

While a sale process will generally be more work for advisors, it also has the advantage of greater or more certain fees. For advisors who are compensated on the quantity of work, such as lawyers and accountants, a sale process will usually take more time and generate higher fees. For advisors paid on a success basis, such as investment bankers, a sale process has a far higher likelihood of yielding a successful result, and thus a fee. For example, if a company puts itself on the block and attracts five potential bidders, and if each of the parties retains an investment bank, the Seller's investment banker is highly likely to be paid, unless the deal entirely falls through. By contrast, each Buyer's investment banker has only a one in five chance of representing the winning bidder and thus receiving compensation.

Other Corporate Resources

Just as with a Buyer, a Seller will have to marshal a variety of corporate resources to effectively complete a sale process. The team managing the deal will have to call on staff from the same set of corporate and line functions. In fact, the sale process usually requires far more dedication of resources, particularly in the preparation stages. The challenge here is that, unlike an acquisition, a sale or divestiture is usually not good news for employees. In most cases, the sale of a company puts many people's jobs at risk. A sale is also a hit to morale, since it often implies a failure of the company. It is rare that a sale represents much potential upside, financially, personally, or for the careers of most of the Seller's employees. Motivating staff to contribute to the process and work hard is far more challenging for the Seller. Again, as with Corporate Development staff, incentives — either concrete financial incentives or the promise of greater career protection—are often a useful motivational tool. The use of corporate staff is also hampered by the need for greater secrecy. The potential damage to a company, if the fact that it is considering a sale gets out, is far greater than for a Buyer. This information can affect the value of the company in the public markets, in its relationships with customers, and certainly in the morale and retention rates of its employees.

Since the Seller must actually build a case for the value of the business, rather than just complete due diligence on someone else's business, a Seller is likely to need to involve more members of senior management. Members of senior management will also be important because the skills and expertise of the management team may actually be an important factor in the value of the business. Showing the Buyer the quality and experience of the Seller management team can materially increase the value of the business, in some cases. Finally, senior management will need to be actively involved since, as will be discussed later in this chapter, a Seller often has to make substantial changes in the business in order to maximize its value in a sale. In a sense, the work distribution of a Seller is the reverse of a Buyer's. Buyers put modest effort into the initial stages of a deal, with the workload increasing after the deal is complete, and integration needs to be done. By contrast, the majority of a Seller's work occurs before the deal starts, in preparing the business for sale, and peters off quickly as the deal closes. As a result, early involvement of senior management and early dedication of resources are even more crucial to a successful sale than they are to an acquisition.

MAKING THE BUSINESS MOST SELLABLE: CLEANING IT UP

Selling a company is like going "all in" in a game of poker. It is a single final decision that will irrevocably determine the value of the investment for shareholders. The stakes could not be higher to maximize the value of a deal. As discussed in Chapter 6, this leads Sellers to consider a variety of structures, when running the selling process. However, well before launching the sale of a company, a Seller can do much to influence the eventual outcome and final valuation. Preparing a business for sale can take months, or even years, but, given the financial impact of even a slight incremental change in valuation, it is well worth it.

The amount of work necessary, and possible, to make a company more sellable will vary dramatically. Large public companies usually have the least work to do, while small privately held companies have the most potential for change. However, it is important to note that even the largest public company can take significant steps to increase its value to a potential Buyer. Private companies not only have to focus on business fundamentals but also on a variety of standards that will make a review of their operations "apples to apples" with a Buyer. These changes include conforming to financial and legal standards and procedures. Public companies are already required to comply with financial reporting standards and provide a fair amount of visibility into their operations through public disclosures. Their efforts will largely be focused on shifting their fundamental business operations to suit a potential Buyer.

Making a business more saleable takes a fair amount of effort and burns valuable resources. In some cases, it can also force decisions that may not be optimal for the business itself. For example, designing a technology platform to be highly scalable and compatible with platforms used by larger companies in the space may make the company more saleable, but if those changes are not immediately necessary for the business as a stand-alone entity, they will impose costs on the operation that would otherwise not have been needed. Therefore, the decision to make a company more saleable usually requires significant strategic thought and commitment. Certainly, at the fringes, there are small things that can be done with little incremental effort, but for the most part, the decision to make a company saleable entails costs and significant distraction for the management team and is made consciously at the board or even shareholder level. Note that the decision to make a company more saleable does not have to be made at the same time as the decision to actually sell. In a sense, this decision is a hedge or option. A Seller that is contemplating sale may decide to invest the effort well before making the final decision about sale.

As discussed, the decision to sell is sometimes made for strategic reasons, when a company reaches a point in its development or growth where it can maximize shareholder value only by selling and/or being part of a larger company. In other cases, companies are developed with the plan, from the start, of selling. This latter situation is more common with private equity backing. Since private equity investors have a fairly short time horizon on their investments—often three to five years—unless the company grows dramatically and can be positioned for an initial public offering (IPO) quickly, sale is the most likely liquidity event for the investors. While they may always hope for an IPO, they need to plan for a sale.

The best context in which to discuss making a company more saleable is to consider the needs of the Buyer. While it sounds fairly obvious, it is surprising how many companies do not take these issues into account as they develop. Perhaps part of the reason is that few entrepreneurs or CEOs like to consider their role as that of developing a business for sale. While shareholders may view the sale of a company as a success, most CEOs set their sights on creating a long-lived, significant, and independent business. A CEO's goal is to be Bill Gates, not a division head for a small part of a conglomerate. The kind of personality it takes to start and run a company does not easily lend itself to actively planning for a sale. Nonetheless, such planning must be demanded, to maximize the value in a sale.

Needs of Buyers

Predicting the needs of likely Buyers is more an art than a science. The first step is to try to predict likely Buyers. The Seller then needs to consider both the nature of the Buyer's business and its own. There will be a high variance between industries and even between specific Buyers, over how much value they place on different factors. However, there are some factors that are likely to be important to almost any Buyer. Nonetheless, investing time in seriously considering the likely nature of the Buyer is an important prerequisite to investing resources in any of these efforts. In this section, several broad categories and ways in which a Seller might improve its business or operations to make the business more saleable will be discussed. Note that these are generalizations that may not all be true for any single business but will serve as a guide to thinking about how to make a business more saleable.

There are, however, a few key themes that run through all of these areas and are worth noting. Visibility is always important, as was discussed above. The more visibility a Buyer has into a Target's operations, financials, and business, the less risk they will contribute to the acquisition. Ease of integration is another key theme. A significant percentage of all deals end up failing in terms of value creation for the acquirer.[1] Integration is the single biggest source of failed acquisitions, and eliminating even a few integration challenges can substantially enhance the value of a business.[2] Familiarity may breed contempt between individuals, but it provides comfort to an acquirer. Organic damage from a deal is another key theme. Some areas of a business, like fine china, can be damaged in a move. Creating effective "cushioning" to minimize damage alleviates another key concern for Buyers.

Human Resources/Compliance

For many businesses, people are the core asset. Making sure that a company's compensation and benefit structure is industry-standard and similar to that of potential Buyers provides several benefits. In terms of visibility, it gives the Buyer comfort that it will not be acquiring hard to price and potentially expensive benefits obligations. Even more critical is the impact that benefits have on integration. The closer a benefits package is to the one the Buyer offers its own employees, the better. There is a danger, particularly if the Target is large and/or integrating directly into an existing business where staff will be commingled, that the Buyer will end up with pressure to adopt the "highest common denominator," since it is particularly hard to lower the benefits of one group of employees, and sustaining two varying sets of benefits risks significant employee discontent. For example, if the Buyer provides three weeks of vacation and the Target provides four, it will be very hard to shorten vacation for the acquired employees, and expensive to lengthen it for all the existing employees. Either way, the difference between the two benefits structures will be painful for the Buyer during integration. An even more disastrous result occurs where each of the two packages has stronger and weaker components, and there is pressure on each side to trade up to the stronger components of the other employee group, yielding a benefits plan with the best, and most expensive, of both worlds. A related integration problem is the question of morale that results from adjustments to benefits and compensation. If the acquired business's staff will have compensation materially reduced to match the Buyer's business, there is a significant danger of losing many of those employees. For a business where employees are a valuable asset, this can be disastrous. As a company considers a potential sale, it needs to start aligning its compensation and benefits structure with the industry. The biggest areas of concern will probably be compensation, equity or options, vacation, and medical benefits. This will vary based on the nature of the workforce. In small high-technology companies, huge options grants may be the biggest issue, while in manufacturing and labor-intensive businesses, medical benefits and vacation may be more sensitive.

Other issues to consider in this area include unionization, regulatory compliance, and legal liabilities. Trying to integrate union and nonunion shops is very challenging. However, it is clearly far easier to allow a union to expand than to force it to contract. The biggest challenge will be attracting a Buyer with a nonunion workforce to a Target that is unionized. The

Buyer has to not only contend with the union for acquired employees but also consider the impact of giving the union a "beachhead" to its larger workforce of nonunionized employees. In some industries, particularly labor-intensive ones with large pools of nonexempt hourly employees, compliance with federal and state labor laws is a significant issue. Ensuring that a business complies with these regulations should be important, regardless of sale, but a Seller also needs to consider regulations to which it is currently exempt but which may affect a Buyer. For example, a particularly small company may be exempt from some requirements to provide handicapped-enabled facilities, but an acquisition by a larger company may trigger those obligations. The breadth and depth of potential regulations should not be underestimated.

The moment a company is acquired, the new parent steps into its shoes with regard to all legal issues. A compliance failure that might have been overlooked in a small company may trigger immediate fines or legal action when the small company becomes part of a large company. A lawyer would say that a company must always comply with all relevant regulations, but it is recognized that, with smaller companies, there may be a temptation to cut corners. However, when making a company saleable, one must consider the impact of this corner cutting on the larger acquirer. Tightening up compliance and installing more complete procedures for monitoring and ensuring compliance will give substantial comfort to a potential Buyer.

A related issue is the matter of demonstrating regulatory compliance. Keeping complete and accurate records of compliance will give the Buyer and its lawyers substantial comfort, and also smooth the sale process. Some particularly common examples are getting environmental reviews of real estate, audits of financial statements (which will be discussed further under "Financials," below), and compliance audits for consumer protection regulations. For a large public Buyer, these kinds of records are not merely a matter of comfort but a mandatory prerequisite to any deal. Companies with deep pockets are highly concerned about inheriting liabilities and violations from an acquisition, since such companies are juicy litigation targets.

Finally there are human resource–related legal liabilities. While no one likes to be sued over these issues, the impact differs from company to company. A sexual harassment suit may be unpleasant for a small private business but may have a much larger impact on a large public company. One needs to consider not only the pure financial liability but also the nonfinancial impact, such as the public relations effect. A large public company, subject to press scrutiny, will be loath to acquire a business with a high-profile litigation that might garner national attention once it is associated with the bigger company. It might be well worth it to settle such suits in advance of a sale, since the cost of settlement is unlikely to go down once the larger Buyer is the inherited counterparty.

Technology

This area is particularly industry-specific. In some industries, technology is tangential at best and merits no serious thought in an acquisition. In other industries, technology is the absolute core of the business. In businesses where technology matters, it is important to consider maximizing value, creating defensible value, and integrating systems.

Maximizing the value of technology means ensuring that the technology remains valuable and that this value can be transferred and leveraged by the Buyer. Where technology is homegrown, it is important to ensure that all the intellectual property is protected. This is, of course, important, regardless of whether the company will be sold or not; however, clearly demonstrating that these protections have been put in place will be important to a Buyer. For example, a company should be able to demonstrate that it has filed patents and copyrights for its work and has put the right legal paperwork in place to ensure that anything developed by employees is the property of the company. The ability to demonstrate that the technology has been maintained and upgraded, to keep pace with changes in the state of the art, is, again, something that a company should be doing regardless, but having the documentation to evidence it will be important to a Buyer.

The value of technology, perhaps more than other parts of a business, can be determined by considering build versus buy costs. Unless there is a unique and defensible difference in the technology of a company, the Buyer can always choose to simply build a similar technology. This is not to say that this will make the technology valueless. The cost of a greenfield build (i.e., building a technology from scratch), coupled with the lost revenue and market position from the extra time to market, can make a technology acquisition very valuable. However, a defensibly unique position, usually through a patented or difficult-to-duplicate development, will add substantial value and take the Buyer away from build versus buy. This can be an important difference in valuation, since the pie that is split between Buyer and Seller goes from the cost of the build alternative to the total value of the business to the Buyer.

The third, and perhaps most important, aspect of technology is the issue of integration, broadly defined. In some cases an acquired company's technology is maintained as a stand-alone infrastructure, but, in almost all cases, there is some level of integration into the Buyer's systems. There is a variety of axes along which integration may occur. Since I am by no means an expert on technology integration, and other authors have devoted much work to the subject, I will limit my comments here but give you a rough idea of the myriad of issues.[3] The Buyer may want to consolidate systems on the same hardware platform and operating system, to minimize costs of maintenance, by having a single staff with the right expertise and by consolidating licenses. For example, if a Buyer runs on Oracle databases, by acquiring a company that also runs on Oracle databases, the Buyer may be able to consolidate the two licenses and save money. The Buyer will also be able to use a single database team with expertise in Oracle. A second axis of integration is between the Seller's technology and that of the Buyer's customers. One large potential synergy of an acquisition is the ability to sell the acquired company's products and services to the Buyer's customer base. However, if the acquired company's technology does not integrate well with that of the Buyer's customers, this effort will be hampered. Another axis is reliability, redundancy, and security. If the Seller's infrastructure is not "up to code" with the Buyer's standards, it may need to do substantial, costly, and time-consuming upgrades. Similarly, scalability is often an issue when a small Seller has built a platform to support its small number of customers, but the system must either be expanded or entirely redesigned to accommodate the dramatically larger volume of the Buyer's customers. In some cases, this may be as simple as buying a small amount of incremental hardware, but, in other cases, it may require a quantum leap in technology that can make the acquired platform almost useless, leaving the Buyer with all the costs and none of the benefits of a pure build strategy.

For a Seller, it is important not only to consider all these issues but also to document them well. Technology platforms are complex, and, during the due diligence process, the Seller will have a small amount of time to demonstrate all these issues. Thorough planning and documentation can make a material difference in convincing the Buyer, particularly when the Seller convincing the Buyer of something fairly unproven, such as the fact that, though its systems have only supported 200 customers, they are well capable of supporting 200,000.

Going further, for a technology-driven company, it is worthwhile to build an infrastructure with these issues in mind. It is usually far harder to "retrofit" technology to new purposes and standards than it is to build it "to spec." For any company where sale is a serious possibility, it is well worth it to consider these issues and perhaps invest extra capital in building a platform that can fit well into a potential Buyer. This can include everything from choosing industry-standard protocols to building redundancy to ensuring scalability to very large volumes. Consideration should also be given to requirements that are often more stringent with larger companies, such as security, fraud protection, and data integrity. Most of these efforts will also be useful to the extent that the company stays independent but becomes highly successful.

Product

New product is one of the most common and appealing reasons to acquire a company. In its simplest form, this means taking the acquired product and selling it to one's existing customers, yielding almost immediate profit at little incremental cost. The challenge for a potential Seller is to consider the needs of a potential Buyer without substantially handicapping its own ability to sell as an independent entity. Certainly a company should not develop products that can be sold by a Buyer but not by itself. However, crafting products that could fit well into a potential Buyer's suite is a powerful way to make a company an attractive Target. Certainly, choosing pricing and delivery structures and other features that match well with a potential Buyer, and making other choices that will not damage the company's selling capability but would make product integration easier, would be wise. More broadly, the Seller should consider how its products fit into the product offering of various types of companies. This exercise will also help to identify potential Buyers. For example, a company that provides consulting services on advertising programs could be an attractive Target to both consulting firms and advertising firms, the former broadening its product offering horizontally, and the latter extending its product offering vertically.

One interesting way to both ease the cost of crafting products to the Buyer and also entice the Buyer is to develop cross-selling arrangements. Under a cross-sell partnership, the Buyer resells the Seller's products (and perhaps vice versa). This arrangement serves the dual purpose of effectively underwriting the Seller's costs of changing its product to match the Buyer's product suite and effectively providing the Buyer with advance due diligence as well as concrete evidence of the value of the Seller's product. It is common for large companies to acquire smaller product suppliers once the appeal of the product to the Buyer's customers has been demonstrated.

Customers

Acquiring customers is the simplest and most risk-free reason for acquiring a company. In effect the Buyer is simply buying revenue, so the purchase price pays for itself. There are some very notable pitfalls to this theory, and things that the Seller can do to address them in turn. The key issues with customers are going to be the value of the customer base, as measured by a variety of metrics, and the ability to retain that value through a deal.

Customers have value to a Buyer based on several factors. Since customer acquisition costs are significant, the longevity of customer relationships is a multiplier in the value of a customer. Short-lived customers are of little value. Again, this is true for a stand-alone company, but perhaps not as much as for a Buyer. The stand-alone company may be focused on growth and immediate revenue, and may be willing to accept high customer turnover, whereas a large, established Buyer will be more focused on customer longevity. Even where a Seller has focused on customer longevity, it needs to be able to document it effectively, to get the benefit of that value. Keeping detailed customer data is usually hard for smaller businesses, but in an industry where customer relationships are of significant value, it is wise to start keeping this data as soon as possible. This is particularly important to demonstrate the length and resilience of customer relationships.

Customer quality is another important variable. This can be measured in the customer's payment promptness, its creditworthiness, the growth in its purchases over time, or other variables. Again, the key is to capture this data in a way that can demonstrate this value to the Buyer. In some cases, the Seller may have a different type of customer base than the Buyer is familiar with, and demonstrating the value of new quality metrics to the Buyer can be a way to increase the implied value of the customer base. Such metrics could include referral of additional customers or perhaps currency used to make payment (e.g., cash versus credit where credit incurs a fee for the vendor).

Customer demographics can also be important. If a Buyer is particularly weak in a geographic, cultural, economic, or other sociological segment of the market, a Target with a strong customer base in that segment is particularly attractive. A Seller may want to consider analyzing its customer data along a wider variety of demographic factors. Even if a particular slice of the world is not important to a Seller, it may be very important to a Buyer, and demonstrating penetration in that slice can add value to a Seller's business. For example, a company offering Internet access may not be overly focused on the age of its customer base, but if a potential Buyer has an online music service, high penetration of the younger market segments will give it an attractive opportunity to cross-sell.

Good data on its customer base will allow a Seller to demonstrate the value of the customer base and tailor that demonstration to the business and needs of a potential Buyer. This is premised on an assumption that customers are easily transferable, which is not always the case. Beyond having detailed data on customers, a Seller needs to consider the potential for customer defection after a sale, because a Buyer certainly will. In fact, a Buyer will be inclined to assume the worst in terms of customer retention.

There are several factors that can influence the likelihood that customers will flee after an acquisition. To the extent that a primary driver of their patronage—such as the Seller's culture, focus, or role in the market—will be removed by the deal, the Buyer can expect to lose a lot of the Seller's customers. To provide a concrete example, consider that customers that preferred a small business focused specifically on their products would be inclined to move their business when the provider was swallowed up by a large conglomerate. In some industries, there is a particular distaste among customers for some of the large providers, and when one of them acquires a smaller player, it can see large-scale customer defections. In some cases, the acquirer may be a competitor with a customer in another area, and the customer will be hesitant to keep doing business with a company with which it competes. For example, if Citibank acquires an insurance company that has been selling its products through a network of banks, it is likely that many of those banks would take their business elsewhere, rather than continue to buy product from a direct competitor.

In many cases, a Seller may be able to do nothing to alleviate the danger of customer loss, but, in some cases, by proactively sending messages to customers, it can eliminate some of these risks. For example, if a small specialty provider is being acquired by a large conglomerate, reassuring customers by emphasizing that the level of service and focus they have received will remain unchanged might encourage many to stay on. The secrecy surrounding a deal may make it impossible for a Seller to make such efforts before a deal closes, but working with the Buyer to develop a proactive plan for reaching out to customers together, immediately after announcing the deal, can minimize the damage. When trying to manage customer perceptions of a deal, time is of the essence. Delaying the effort by even a matter of weeks can lead to significant customer erosion.

Even if the problem is not soluble, as perhaps in the Citibank example above, understanding these risks will help the Seller craft its value proposition to potential Buyers and, in fact, help it choose the more attractive Buyers. In some cases, the Seller may eliminate entire groups of potential Buyers because the acquisition by that type or set of Buyers would so damage the customer base.

Employees

The regulatory and compliance issues of employees have been discussed above, under "Human Resources/Compliance." Now, the discussion turns to employees as a valuable asset and resource. While not necessarily true in all deals, in many, employees will be a key or even primary reason for the acquisition of a business. As with customers, the loss of employees as a result of a deal can dramatically affect the value of the company. Buyers are so sensitive to this issue that they will often make contracts with key employees a part of the deal documentation that must be executed in order to consummate the transaction.

To the extent that employees are important assets in a deal, the Seller can take a variety of steps to ensure that the Buyer will be able to retain them, and to demonstrate this to the Buyer. The first step is to try to identify which employees are particularly essential in a deal. In some cases, this will be fairly clear and may derive from the nature of the core assets of the business. For example, the most important employee pool in a software development company might be the technology and software developers, while, in a consumer brand company, it might be the product development and marketing staff. This analysis will be muddied by the fact that different Buyers may view different employee groups as essential. If Brooks Brothers acquired a small chain of menswear stores, to expand its location network, it would be far less concerned with keeping store operations and real estate staff than Polo would be, if it acquired the same chain as a channel for its products.

Once key employees and employee groups have been identified, the challenge is to take measures to try to ensure that the Buyer will be able to retain them. In some cases, this is particularly difficult. Employees may flee a company after it is acquired, if they perceive a dramatic change in culture. This is a particular problem when small entrepreneurial companies, or those with a distinct culture, are acquired by much larger and more mainstream companies. One solution to this culture-shift problem is to try to moderate the culture in advance of a deal, to make the difference less stark. Of course, the Seller needs to avoid causing the damage it is trying to prevent, by driving key employees away as a result of these changes. A Seller can also work with the Buyer to try to retain key aspects of the culture, and communicate these agreements to employees. The Buyer will need to balance its need to maintain its own overall culture and gain the full benefits of integration, with the need to retain key employees.

Employees may also acquire so much wealth as a result of the transaction itself, if they have significant equity, that they are no longer motivated to work. This was a particularly common scenario during the technology boom of the late 1990s, when even midlevel employees were given such large pools of equity that, after an acquisition or an IPO, they were left with hundreds of thousands or even millions of dollars. It is difficult to offset the impact of massive wealth. One solution is to avoid giving equity to employees that vests on a change in control. This will ensure that the deal does not create a dramatic wealth event for the employees but rather continues to provide the same incentive structure in place before the deal. However, when senior management and founders are taking their money off the table in a sale, it is difficult to justify a structure where the rank and file cannot also get an immediate benefit. In particular, where the company is small and the founders personally hired these employees, founders may find it hard to give employees different terms than their own equity positions have. Additionally, the morale impact of such differential treatment can be damaging to the retention of employees.

Each Seller will have a unique set of employee issues related to a potential sale, but the need for an effective communications strategy is pretty much universal. As discussed below, managing employee expectations and perceptions of a deal can have a significant impact on the ability of the Buyer to retain employees. It can also help prepare the employee base for a potential deal. The process of "corporatizing" an organization, or shifting compensation structures to match better with those of potential Buyers, needs to be communicated effectively to employees, not only to be effective but also to avoid actually damaging the business in advance of a sale. Every company has growing pains, and, as companies get larger and their culture changes, there is often employee confusion, fear, and discontent. Crafting a message to employees that helps them understand the changes and demonstrates how the changes can accrue to their benefit is an important effort, not only after a deal is done but also well beforehand. The secrecy of deals may limit what can be communicated to employees before a deal is announced, but planning for that event is important. Communicating with employees at the time of a deal is crucial, to ensure that the company has the opportunity to "spin" the deal and manage employee expectations. Failure to effectively communicate with employees can dramatically affect performance prior to a deal closing, as employees are distracted and dispirited, and after a deal, to the extent that they flee the company. In most cases, it is good to try to get a communication to employees directly prior to the announcement of a deal. This is a delicate timing game. If this communication takes place too early, the news of the deal can leak. If the company waits too long, employees will end up hearing about a deal from the press or other outside parties. The former can damage the deal, and the latter can damage employee morale and retention.

Public Image Issues

Sellers need to consider the public image of their company for several reasons, when planning for a deal. Public image can help attract Buyers, enhance the value of the company, and prepare constituents, including employees, customers, and partners, for a sale. This is a particularly big change for privately held companies that may have given little or no thought to public relations and their public image. For private companies with a relatively small number of large customers, with whom they communicate directly, there may have been absolutely no thought or effort given to public image issues.

More importantly, a company's public image can be a positive or a very strong negative to a potential Buyer. Private companies often have the luxury of not being particularly sensitive to public image, especially if they sell to a small number of direct customers. Larger companies, particularly those that are publicly held and/or have developed a valuable mass market brand, do not have this luxury. In many cases, a negative public image can make a company not only less attractive but even "unbuyable." For an extreme example, consider the pornography industry. No matter how profitable and well run a pornography producer may be, most companies in the media space would not consider acquiring the business, given the public image of the industry. Even where the sector does not have a negative public image, individual companies can. If a company has been investigated for legal violations or been the subject of high-profile controversy, these issues can dog the company and affect its ability to be sold.

As a company considers a sale, it should examine its public image and consider how that may limit both its value and the range of potential Buyers. The Seller should also consider the potential to ameliorate these issues as it prepares to be sold. Reaching agreements over legal and regulatory conflicts, and working to improve its public image through public relations and industry press, may help enhance the company's value.

Financials

If notes are the language of music, financials are the language of business. Strategy, planning, and pitch work are all well and good, but at the end of the day, the buck stops with the financial results of a company. Following the language analogy, financials are also the most universal and precise way to describe a business. Universality is key, since the Buyer is challenged to try to get a deep understanding of a business in a very short time. Providing a potential Buyer with detailed, accurate, and complete financial statements is the single most important effort in completing a sale and maximizing the value of a business. This presents several challenges to a prospective Seller.

The rules regarding the preparation of financial statements are laid out in tremendous detail and governed by the Generally Accepted Accounting Principles (GAAP).[4] Some Sellers will already maintain financial statements in accordance with GAAP. In many cases, private companies are required to maintain GAAP financials by their investors. To the extent that GAAP financials are not already maintained, any company considering a sale would be wise not only to maintain its financials according to GAAP but also to restate its historical financials to conform with these accounting rules. Though there is no hard rule, a Buyer will often require three years of historical financials for review. How much historical data a Buyer will require will depend on the nature of the business. For example, when reviewing a company with a very stable business and modest changes over time, a Buyer may want to see a longer history, to confirm that stability. By contrast, in reviewing a company that has undergone dramatic change, a shorter historical period may be relevant, since the changes have made historical financials fairly irrelevant in predicting future performance.

Developing and maintaining GAAP financials takes some time and investment, and thus is a great example of an effort that should be started well in advance of a sale process. The company will need to retain an auditor, and a staff that can maintain the financial records required by the auditor. It is not essential to use one of the largest auditing firms, though it is advisable to use a firm large enough to have a national or at least regional reputation. The reputation and prestige of a large auditing firm used to be perceived as valuable in a sale process. However, in the wake of the accounting scandals of the past decade, there seems to be a trend toward midsized, but still large and reputable, accounting firms.[5] These firms may provide a combination of lower costs and greater focus by more senior staff. It is important to build a relationship with whichever audit firm is retained, since, in the event of a sale, this firm will be called on to provide a detailed explanation of its work to potential Buyers. Beyond the basic preparation of financials, it is useful for a potential Seller to begin preparing well-formatted and detailed financial reports. Once a sale process begins, a full set of historical financials will be one of the first requests from any potential Buyer.

There are two sides to the financial picture of a company: past and future. Buyers do not acquire companies for their historical financial performance but rather for their future financial performance. Historical financials are a valuable tool for a Buyer in predicting that future, since they are, by definition, factual and accurate. However, a Seller should also provide any Buyer with its own financial projections of future performance. Unlike the historical data, which will generally be taken at face value, projections will certainly be taken by the Buyer with a grain of salt, if not an entire shaker. However, they are the most direct and digestible way for a Seller to make the case for the value of its business. Financial projections also provide a platform for discussing the as-yet unrealized opportunities of the business.

Developing financial projections is also a time-consuming effort, and, since it is a blend of strategy and finance, it usually requires a series of iterations and constant adjustment. The most important step in developing financial projections, and one that will become essential content for a Buyer, is the development of assumptions. This is a very self-reflective exercise, since even determining what variables should be used in the assumptions requires a company to consider the core factors that influence its business. Once the company chooses a set of drivers and relationships between those drivers and financials, it can begin to make assumptions about those drivers. Consider the example of an auto manufacturer. Among the drivers that may affect the income side of its profit and loss statement (P&L) would be the demand for new vehicles and the purchasing power of consumers. Those drivers may in turn be affected by factors such as the cost of gas, the strength of the economy, and more indirect factors such as the strength of foreign automakers and the exchange rate between those countries' currencies and the U.S. dollar. On the cost side of the P&L, there are drivers such as the cost of labor, the cost of steel, regulatory requirements such as emissions standards, and even real estate prices. A strong set of financial projections lays out the key assumptions clearly and provides as much detail as possible justifying the assumptions made. It is also important to do a reality check on such projections. A good test is to look at variables such as growth rates and margins in other similar businesses. To the extent that a company's projection model shows a huge variance in key financial variables from those of other, similar companies, it needs to consider whether there is a reasonable explanation for these differences. For example, if a privately held trucking company developed projections showing a 20% growth rate and a 10% net income margin, where similarly sized publicly held trucking companies were projecting growth of 5% and margins of 3%, there would be good reason to question the accuracy of the model. This is where iteration becomes important, as the results of a model are questioned, which leads to a review and refinement of the driving assumptions.

Detailed, well-supported, and reasonable financial projections can be a powerful tool in convincing a Buyer that there is unrealized potential in a business, justifying a premium to the valuation that would be derived from historical financial performance. They can also help demonstrate that the management team has a well thought-out strategy for growth and profitability, as demonstrated through a review of the assumptions, which naturally leads into a discussion about how those assumptions will be achieved.

When developing both the historical and projected financials, it is important for a Seller to consider what metrics and line items to present and break out for review. While the Seller does not want this material to become overwhelming in detail, as a general rule more detail is usually better than less, since a Buyer will get a great deal of visibility into the business from the financials. That said, when the Seller is choosing which metrics to present, it is important to consider the needs and interests of a potential Buyer. Certainly, many of the same things that a business manager or owner will want to see will be of interest to a Buyer, but there may be some notable differences. A potential Seller needs to put itself in the shoes of the Buyer when considering how to present financials. For example, a Seller with a single product offering might only be concerned with fairly basic data on its customer base, but a Buyer who has plans to try to cross-sell multiple products to the acquired customer base would be interested in much more detailed metrics on the customers. A privately held company selling software or membership services might be required by GAAP to recognize revenues over a period of time based on variables including refund rights of customers and the length of contracts. While the company might only focus on cash flow, a public Buyer would be very concerned with understanding the details of how those revenue streams are recognized over time. Presenting the metrics and measures that a Buyer is interested in can not only enhance the Buyer's interest in the deal but also make the process more efficient, limiting the amount of additional financial data the Seller has to develop during the deal process.

Final Thoughts on Needs of Buyers

Investing in these various efforts before a deal is imminent may seem difficult to justify, particularly for a smaller company with limited resources. Staff who are focused on their primary job of growing and enhancing the business will be reluctant to be sidelined for work that has an air of defeatism to it. As discussed, the very notion of selling a business has a feel of failure, and preparing for a sale may seem almost like planning to fail. However, senior management and shareholders need to make this kind of preparation a priority.

The financial payoff for proper planning can be dramatic. Theoretically, a Buyer should only be willing to pay the future cost of making whatever changes the Seller has made to accommodate the Buyer. For example, for a Seller that implements a higher standard of quality controls, the Buyer should only be willing to pay as much as it would have cost to implement those changes themselves, after buying the company. In point of fact, the premium for these kinds of changes is usually much higher. There are several rational and less rational reasons that a Buyer is willing to pay a "premium to cost" for these changes. The value of these fixes is not only in the cost of making them but also in the impact on time to market. To the extent that fixing an acquired company takes time, it will slow the process of getting the value out of the deal that motivated it in the first place. The distraction can even reach beyond the acquired company's operations to those of the Buyer. For example, if an acquired company's product line needs to be upgraded to meet the standards of the Buyer, not only will the acquired product development team be sidelined making these changes, but a portion of the Buyer's product development team may also be distracted. To the extent the fixes improve visibility into the acquired company, they eliminate uncertainty. As discussed in Chapter 8, uncertainty is a key driver of the difference in price expectations between Buyer and Seller. The Buyer will naturally choose to take a worst-case scenario approach to any uncertainty.

Improving visibility into the Target company (everything including financials, operations, customers, etc.) can substantially increase the price the Buyer is willing to pay. Beyond these concrete reasons, there is also the broad matter of confidence and risk. The people driving a deal on the Buyer's side are staking their reputations on the success of a deal. Removing uncertainty in terms of performance and integration helps to alleviate their concerns about a failed deal. While, in a theoretical sense, a Buyer should be willing to pay a measured premium for the removal of risk, the potential downside to individuals driving a deal is often significant enough to increase that effective premium. The real estate analogy is somewhat relevant here. A real estate broker will tell a prospective buyer that certain improvements to a house will pay for themselves several times over, when selling it. The same can be said of some of these steps for which a Buyer will be willing to pay a premium well in excess of the costs of implementing them.

Thinking Like a Subsidiary

When a company begins contemplating a sale, it must not underestimate the cultural change inherent in shifting from an independent company to a subsidiary. Ironically, while greater integration into the acquirer usually translates into greater synergies and value for the business, it also translates into ever more dramatic changes in the culture that impact every employee, from the rank and file to senior executives. From specific metrics such as compensation and benefits to more amorphous matters of corporate culture, such as formality, congeniality, and career management, the change will be felt throughout the organization. Similarly, the shift from an independent entity to a subsidiary has substantial impact on the actual operation of the business.

A company planning a sale should consider starting the process of thinking like a subsidiary. This will mean different things for different companies. Aligning compensation structures and benefits plans with market standards is an obvious step. Another is to begin to professionalize the culture to the extent that it has been more entrepreneurial to date. One good example of this shift is to start to formalize approval processes. This will also help the company demonstrate formal compliance with regulatory structures. The stress of these changes is not limited to the junior employee base. As the programmer has to do without unlimited free snacks, the entrepreneurial founder has to get used to allocated responsibility and decision making throughout his or her organization. This brings up one important topic. While, in some cases, a Buyer may treat an acquisition as an asset sale, in most cases it will be concerned with retaining all or part of the management team. The most senior executives may not have a place in the new organization, but usually the core of the management structure is retained. Thus, creating an organization where managers have the right decision-making power and responsibility is extremely important. If all the key decisions are made by the seniormost executives, who are most likely to depart as a result of a deal, a Buyer can be concerned that the organization will falter right after the deal.

As with professionalizing the approval process and decision-making allocation, a company can begin to formalize a variety of other areas of the business. One of the hallmarks of this exercise will be forcing more extensive documentation through a variety of areas, including contracts and legal documents, product and technology development, and all areas of planning. The increase in formal documentation will fit better into a larger acquirer culture, and will also prove extremely valuable when various parts of the company are combed for material during the due diligence process.[6]

To the extent that they feel comfortable doing so, senior management may also want to start indoctrinating the employee base with the prospect of a Strategic Transaction. In some cases, secrecy overrules this approach, but, in other cases, particularly if the company is already rumored to be for sale, or if the company is planning an extended and fairly public auction process, it may be productive to start to communicate with employees. While it is almost impossible to guarantee anyone employment, there is much that the Seller can do to allay the fears of employees about this kind of dramatic change. Simply changing rampant rumors into clear fact will do much to provide calm in the workplace.

Market Reputation Building

In preparation for a sale, a Seller needs to consider its public image and develop a strategy for how to manage and project that image, to maximize the value of the business in a sale. The goal is to affect a variety of different potential constituents. The formula and focus will be different for each Seller, but few Sellers can entirely forgo considering this issue.

Public relations is often a powerful tool for attracting Buyers. Few Sellers have a complete image of all the potential Buyers for their business, and, even when they do, it may be hard for them to connect with those Buyers. This is particularly true for smaller private companies trying to deal with large Buyers. Developing a public image helps alert Buyers to the presence of a Seller. This may sound simplistic, but, given the huge number of companies in the market, it is often a particular challenge for Buyers to identify potential Targets. In many cases, Buyers will use such basic tools and news and web searches to identify small players in a niche.

Developing a user-friendly website, engaging a public relations firm to generate articles in industry press, presenting at industry conferences and meetings, and various forms of advertising are all tools for developing a public image. Of course, all these efforts do double duty. In addition to accomplishing some of the goals above, they can be leveraged to enhance customer relationships and strengthen brand.

Sellers can also develop their market reputation through a variety of "surrogates." Firms such as investment banks, consulting firms, industry associations, and law firms can help develop the reputation of a company, particularly among potential Buyers. The challenge is to manage these efforts, since there are often adverse incentives at play. For example, an investment bank may have an interest in using the fact that a company is considering a sale as valuable information to impress other clients, leading to a premature leak of the potential sale to too large an audience, or even the press.

A company can also build its reputation through its business dealings. Proactively maintaining strong relationships with potential partners and Buyers, even in the absence of an active deal, can be a good investment. Again, this effort does double duty, since the relationships developed can drive partnerships and other valuable business relationships. However, a Seller should not underestimate the impact that this informal networking can have, once a sale process begins. In a perfect world, a Buyer might do a complete industry study, identifying every potential Target, before making an approach. However, in practice, the Buyer usually has neither the resources nor the patience, and often falls back on its own network of relationships and those of its advisors to develop a Target list. Similarly, while formal due diligence allows a Buyer to vet any Target, having an initially positive view of a company often creates a predisposition to focus on it as an acquisition Target. As when choosing a restaurant for dinner, when faced with a dozen choices, people will often lean toward the familiar place with which they have already had positive experiences, or about which they have heard good things.

Press

The press is the most powerful way to develop a market reputation, but, of course, it is also the hardest to utilize. Particularly for smaller companies, it is hard to get the attention of the press, and, when they do get it, it is hard to manage the resulting message. Unlike the other surrogates that will be discussed, the press does not work directly, or indirectly, for the Seller. The challenge is to craft a message that is positive and also interesting enough to attract the attention of the press. This work is certainly not easy, and often it is valuable to hire either a public relations professional or an outside public relations firm. These professionals not only know how to craft the message but also have the network of connections to reach the right members of the press, and often the credibility to get their attention.

This book will not go into much detail about how to develop a public relations strategy but will note some particularly important elements. First, the Seller needs to remember that the press is like a bullhorn. Anything shared with the press must be assumed to reach anyone and everyone. The press is a blunt instrument, not a delicate tool, and thus if a company is seeking to send a message to one group but not another, the press is the wrong place to go. People often forget that the press reaches not only their intended Target, perhaps their shareholders and customers but also other Targets, such as the regulators or their competitors. There is also always the danger that the press will misunderstand or misreport the information, and that, before (and if) it can be corrected, the damage will be largely done. There are myriad examples of the financial press misreporting information and having a devastating effect on the stock price of the related company. Perceptions created by the press are not easily reversed, even if a correction is issued quickly.

Using the press in a Strategic Transaction is particularly risky. For the most part, people tend to avoid working with the press until a deal is done and they are ready to send a clear final message. The potential benefits are usually outweighed by the downside. Usually, the press is more valuable before a deal emerges, when a company is trying to create a more general public image. In particular, it is useful for Sellers trying to create a stronger awareness among potential Buyers. The only exception is when a Seller wants to create a formal auction process, and so is trying to attract as many Buyers as possible, and is comfortable with making its intention to sell public. In this situation, the press is a powerful tool for alerting as many Buyers as possible, and, since it is public knowledge that the company is being sold, there is no need to be coy with the press.

Investment Bankers and Lawyers

Unlike the press, investment bankers and lawyers are much more "friendly" surrogates that, to some extent, are controllable. It is important to remember that they are not entirely controllable, and that, particularly with investment bankers, there can still be adverse incentives. Both lawyers and investment bankers have networks of relationships they can call upon to try to identify potential Buyers. More importantly, they can serve as a surrogate in contacting these Buyers, allowing a Seller to go on a "fishing expedition" to try to identify levels of interest in a sale without identifying itself. Even before beginning a sale process, these surrogates can help a Seller develop a market reputation and become better known to the market of potential Buyers.

Both lawyers and investment bankers develop networks of relationships within an industry, particularly those with an industry focus. A lawyer or investment banker who focuses on a particular industry likely has had direct or indirect contact with senior executives of almost every player. Furthermore, by virtue of both their personal reputations and those of their firms, these professionals have credibility and more ready access to these executives. While the CEO of a small independent company might have difficulty reaching senior executives at a very large player, lawyers and investment bankers may have more ready access.

Bankers and lawyers are also excellent tools for gauging interest while remaining anonymous. The banker or lawyer will reach out to a potential counterparty and ask its level of interest on behalf of an unnamed client. Usually they have to give the counterparty some level of information to get a useful answer. For example, a banker might call Citibank and ask whether it would have an interest in acquiring a "midsized regional bank" or a "national mortgage lender." Obviously, the fewer direct competitors a Seller has, and the larger it is, the harder it will be to give the Buyer useful information while still masking the identity of the Seller. It would be hard for a surrogate to gauge interest in a company like General Motors or Motorola without giving away its likely identity. Imagine this call: "Would you have an interest in acquiring a U.S.-based auto manufacturer?" "Well, there are only two, so are you talking about Ford or General Motors?"

Sellers can also use these surrogates to become better known to potential Buyers. Lawyers can make introductions to other companies and arrange meetings. Bankers can do this as well. More importantly, bankers have access to the powerful venue of their analyst conferences. Most investment banks host annual industry-specific conferences for the investor community, largely research analysts that cover these sectors for large institutional investors or investment banks. These conferences usually attract senior executives from most of the largest players in the sector. Speaking at such a conference is a powerful channel to develop a company's reputation, both in the market and among potential Buyers. Of course, there is a lot of competition to get on the roster for these conferences, so it may be difficult for a smaller company to secure a spot.

While both lawyers and bankers can theoretically provide these services, it is far more common to use investment bankers. They tend to have more extensive networks and tend to have a greater industry focus, whereas lawyers are more likely to be generalists. More importantly, this is how investment bankers get paid, so they tend to be willing to exert far more effort. While lawyers get paid on deals, it is on an hourly basis, and generally they already have an established relationship with the Seller, ensuring that they will be retained when a deal happens. By contrast, investment bankers are usually retained in relation to a specific deal. They will usually pitch the notion of a sale, and part of the reason to retain them is their ability to leverage their network to test the market and develop interest in the Seller. Certainly, once a Seller is seriously focused on a sale, it is likely to turn to an investment banker to test the market. In some cases, Sellers will retain them to do this exercise, and in others, they will use the potential to be retained as a "carrot" to get the banker to assist them in testing the market.

It is important to remember the adverse incentive issue, particularly when using investment bankers to test the market and build a market reputation. A banker will always have an incentive to drive toward a live deal as quickly as possible. If a Seller is just trying to gauge the market, or just develop a reputation, it needs to be wary of a banker who may try to press toward a deal, or even trigger a process by trying to get a Buyer to make an unsolicited offer, hoping that this action will drive the Seller into initiating a sale process. Similarly, it is important to remember that bankers (and sometimes lawyers) trade on information. Information is one of the most valuable ways for a banker to differentiate herself to her clients, and the potential for a sale by another company in the space is a valuable tidbit to share with clients.

Other Industry Sources

Some industries are fairly tight-knit, and, in those cases, industry organizations, publications, and meetings can be a particularly effective tool for building a reputation and eventually networking with potential Buyers. Of course, the fundamental limit to this approach is that it only develops a network within a particular group of companies. It is important to comment here, since this is a common mistake on the part of Sellers. While competitors in a Seller's sector are an obvious source of Buyers, in many cases they are not the exclusive or even most attractive source of Buyers. When considering a sale, it is important to think broadly about the Buyer universe. That said, the most common source of Buyers is still other players in the sector, and thus, industry sources are a valuable tool.

Industry organizations bring together companies for a variety of purposes, including lobbying, setting standards, and exchanging information.

Active participation in these organizations can allow a Seller to develop an informal network with other industry players. In many cases, very large companies will be particularly active in these organizations, since the issues they address have a considerable impact on large companies, which have the resources to devote. For example, the largest companies are likely to devote the most resources to lobbying Congress for more lenient regulation, and to fund efforts to create industry standards.

Industry conferences and expositions are also an excellent opportunity to develop a reputation among other companies. This can be as simple as setting up a small booth, or as extensive as hosting a large reception or taking a speaking slot. As with investment banking conferences, there will be competition for these slots. Industry conferences also allow for more informal and efficient networking. Since these events bring together a large number of executives from many companies in one place, and since they tend to clear their calendars to accommodate meetings during these trips, conferences are an exceptionally good place to get a large number of meetings done and connections made. As a corporate Buyer, I have often used such conferences as a particularly efficient way to survey the players in a space and try to identify acquisition Targets.

In the final analysis, market reputation building is best done over a long period of time and with a concentrated effort. It may seem arduous, but consider that when a company finally undertakes a selling effort, its reputation can affect not only the number of potential Buyers but also the premium paid. Acquisitions are, by their nature, risky propositions. Buyers are desperate to minimize that risk, and will usually pay a premium for doing so. Developing good financials and taking other concrete steps are the obvious way to reduce risk and add certainty for a Buyer. However, building a market reputation is a more subtle, but nonetheless valuable, way of doing so. For a Buyer, acquiring a company that is totally unknown seems much riskier than acquiring a player with which it has had repeated interaction. Familiarity and market reputation can have a material, though perhaps hard to calculate, effect on the premium that a Buyer will be willing to pay. In some cases, they may even affect the willingness of a risk-averse Buyer to do a deal at all.

SETTING EXPECTATIONS WITH CONSTITUENTS

The sale of a company is a dramatic and often life-changing event for many of the people involved. For many smaller companies, a sale is a potential, if not likely, endgame, well before a particular deal goes live. The expectations of all the constituents need to be managed in this regard, probably more so than with any other single issue. For those constituents who have a say in the decision, it is important to make sure expectations are coordinated, or there is a danger of huge conflict. Even for those people with little say in the decision, it is important to manage their expectations or the company risks incurring damage during the course of a deal, to everyone's detriment.

The challenge here is that the sale of a company is usually done in secret, and so there are significant limits on how much information can be shared. Even so, it is important to manage everyone's expectations, so that, when a deal does get under way and begins to be exposed to people in the organization, little or no damage is done. In some cases, this is a matter of managing economic incentives to ensure that the transaction accrues to everyone's benefit. Beyond pure economics, there are emotional and personal factors at play, and so the company needs to think beyond simply financial incentives to the personal reaction people will have to a deal.

Owners

First and foremost, it is necessary to remember that there are usually several types of owners of a company, and each group, or even each individual, may have different goals. While a private equity investor may be focused on driving to a liquidity event in relatively short order, an entrepreneurial founder may be focused on building a great company. A strategic investor may be focused on steady continued growth to maintain the relationship that may exist between itself and the company.

One key here is effective communication. In some cases, a sale is planned well in advance, and a company is built specifically to be saleable. Presumably, in that simple situation, all the owners' expectations are somewhat aligned. In most cases, a sale is not the primary focus of the owners but rather an evolutionary outcome as the business grows. Even if a company is not being built to be sold, the owners need to recognize that this is a common exit event, and should begin to discuss it well in advance. They need to try to reach some level of consensus around how they will react to an unsolicited offer, or even to the emerging possibility of a sale (perhaps based on a pitch from an investment banker). It may not be possible to set specific metrics (e.g., "we will sell when we can get $50 million or more"), but gauging the level of enthusiasm for a sale will help ensure that potential conflict is anticipated and dealt with. One of the most damaging events possible in a business is outright and visible conflict between owners.

Keep in mind the silent owners. In many companies, a significant stake is held by people or entities that are not actively involved in the management of the company. Often, they are not considered when a company starts to plan for a sale. However, while they may not be actively involved in day-to-day management, the one event that will clearly arouse their attention and involvement will be a Strategic Transaction. Depending on how the legal structure of the company is defined, even a small group of minority investors may be able to block an acquisition. At the least, they can complicate the process and sometimes muddy the waters with a Buyer that may be hesitant to get involved in a conflict between shareholders, opening itself up to potential litigation.

Management

In some ways, management is a more powerful force on a deal than even the owners. In many cases, management will have a significant equity stake, particularly in a smaller company or a start-up. However, even when they are not significant shareholders, management can dramatically affect plans to sell. It is hard to sell a company and realize full value without the active and energetic support of management. They will not only likely be the managers of the process but will also be responsible for making the case for the value of the company, and, in fact, for developing that value in the months and years prior to a sale. If a CEO is not supportive of a sale, she can do much to slow or even stall a process and sour a Buyer on the company. In some cases, retention of the management team is an essential part of the deal.

One of the keys is certainly economic incentives. Whether this takes the form of an equity stake that will allow the management to realize a part of the sale price, or golden parachutes and other compensation structures that bring a windfall on a sale, much can be done to align management's incentives financially. However, management is not motivated by wealth alone. Often, the sale of a company means an effective demotion, or even termination, of many members of senior management. Even if there is a role for the executives within the bowels of the acquirer, it is usually far less motivational to be a unit head or business manager within a larger company than to be the CEO of one's own business.

As with owners, one of the keys here is communication. While owners may not want to share the details of their plans with management, and will sometimes even negotiate a sale without their knowledge, it is probably a good idea to have at least general discussions with top executives about the potential of a sale. Certainly, setting expectations when hiring a management team is important. Being hired with the explicit plan of growing and selling a company is far different from being hired with the expectation of growing a company for years and taking it public, only to have it sold without warning, a year or two later. Executive egos can be sensitive, and setting expectations about a potential sale may help those executives to see it as a win rather than a failure.

Employees

If the potential of a sale is public information, or at least widely understood, the Seller may be able to communicate with employees in advance of a deal announcement. This gives the Seller a great opportunity to prepare employees for a sale and manage their expectations. More importantly, it gives the Seller a chance to calm their fears. Unlike management, who will likely see a financial windfall from a deal, most employees will see modest financial returns, if any, from the sale of a company. Nearly all of them will need to keep working for a living, and a sale undoubtedly creates a risk of losing their jobs. Different types of deals can increase or decrease that risk, but, regardless, the fear will likely be there. If the deal is public, it is important to address those fears and concerns as well as possible. Even if the company cannot provide certainty and guarantees, it can often moderate the most hysterical fears.

If a deal is not public, or if one has not yet come to light, it is difficult to communicate with rank-and-file employees. However, if a sale seems like a likely result in the next few years, it may be worthwhile to begin to educate the employee base and try to get them used to the idea. The challenge here is to avoid creating a sense of dread or insecurity, since this can damage the workforce, as people are more likely to consider leaving, and turnover can increase. Certainly, once a deal is live, this risk increases dramatically. If the employees hear about a live deal in progress, they may scramble to secure new jobs, for fear of being cut in the resulting postdeal integration, the victims of the dreaded "cost synergies." This can cause substantial damage to a company, as the best talent easily finds other jobs, and the remaining staff is distracted, and morale drops.

In the end, the Seller must balance the need to maintain morale with the need for secrecy. In most cases, secrecy will win, and employees will be told little. The best the Seller can do in this case is try to create a perception among employees that they are unique, with the implication that they would not be shed in a deal. However, the Seller also needs to plan carefully for the message that will reach the employees once a deal is announced. Failure to act quickly and clearly can still damage the company, even in the late stages of a deal.

Conflicts in Plans

When starting up or investing in a business, few people, even professional investors, spend much time thinking about exit options and liquidity events. The focus is usually on drivers to making the business successful. In some cases, this may be the hubris of thinking that they are "the next Bill Gates and Microsoft," while in others, it is simply a prudent focus on the near-term goals of moving the business to profitability and early success. The logic is that if they do their work well, the business will be successful, and if faced with more than one option—sale, public offering, or continued profitability—they will have a "high-quality problem." This is true to some extent. Certainly, it is silly to spend a great deal of focus worrying about liquidity events when the company is not yet worth buying or taking public. However, failure to discuss or consider these eventual events can plant the seeds for some major conflicts. Running and owning a business is like a marriage. While children may be years in the future, the topic should certainly be at least raised before the marriage takes place. The couple may not be able to make detailed plans, but they can at least try to ensure that everyone has generally similar expectations. Otherwise, they may create a wonderful child and then find themselves traumatizing it with vitriolic arguments over how it should be raised.

NOTES

1. Much has been written about the failure of Strategic Transactions. One recent article cites studies showing that 64% of the M&A deals done in the United States between 1985 and 2000 destroyed value. "The Return of the Deal," *The Economist* (July 10, 2003). Another article argues that, when properly measured, the number is closer to 30%. Robert Bruner, "Does M&A Pay? A Survey of Evidence for the Decision-Maker," *Journal of Applied Finance*, vol. 12, issue 1 (Spring/Summer 2002), p. 48.

2. "Integration failure is the most frequently cited reason for unsuccessful acquisitions." Haig R. Nalbantian, Richard A. Guzzo, Dave Kieffer, and Jay Doherty, *Making Acquisitions Work: Human Capital Aspects of Due Diligence and Integration* (Marsh & McLennan, Fall 2003).

3. McKinsey & Co. provides a good overview of the issues in Lisa Aberg and Diane Sias's article "Taming Postmerger IT Integration," *McKinsey on*

Finance (Summer 2004). Other useful texts include Alexandra Reed-Lajoux, *The Art of M&A Integration: A Guide to Merging Resources, Processes and Responsibilities* (New York: McGraw-Hill, 2004) and Timothy Galpin and Mark Herndon, *The Complete Guide to Mergers and Acquisitions: Process Tools to Support M&A Integration at Every Level* (San Francisco: Jossey-Bass, 1999).

4. Outside the United States, there are sometimes other accounting standards maintained by local accounting authorities, although GAAP or a variation thereof is used in many countries beyond the United States. When developing financial statements for a transaction where one or both parties are non-U.S. companies, the Seller needs to consider not only the accounting rules that govern it but also those that govern the Buyer, since, once acquired, those are the rules by which the Seller's business will be judged and the lens through which a prudent Buyer will view it.

5. For example, in 2003, 55% of the companies that shifted from a "big four" auditing firm chose a smaller firm for their audit work. The trend has continued in 2004. Jill Lerner, "Rollins Dumps E&Y in Favor of Grant Thornton," *Atlanta Business Chronicle* (September 17, 2004).

6. This is particularly true if the deal is being negotiated secretly. One of the biggest challenges of running a secret process within an organization is surreptitiously gathering documentation from across the business, to provide the Buyer with due diligence material. If more of the business is formally documented as part of regular operations, most of this material can be assembled quickly and quietly for due diligence. Of course, it is also far faster to gather reports and material previously developed in the course of standard operation than to ask staff to develop it from scratch, during the heat of a deal.

CHAPTER 6

Deal Process

This chapter will provide a step-by-step review of each stage of the deal process, from the basic form of the process to each stage, including due diligence, valuation, integration, negotiating, financing, closing, and postclosing issues. At each stage, this book will identify key issues and potential challenges to the deal and each participant. This book will provide tools to ensure a smooth process and avoid dangerous missteps, notably weak marketing of a deal, inaccurate valuation of a company, insufficient due diligence, weak or lacking integration preparation, and some of the most difficult negotiation points. This critical chapter will provide a road map to the core deal process and try to highlight the most common and significant points of failure. Anecdotal "war stories" will be used to illustrate pertinent points.

Once a company has made the critical decision to sell, it needs to decide how it is going to manage that process. Before deciding on a process, there are several critical steps that a Seller needs to take. Not only are these steps important to ensure an effective sale at the best possible price, but they will also help the Seller determine the best format to use in the sale process.

As discussed in Chapter 5, the Seller needs to complete a valuation of its own business. The valuation will help the Seller set expectations with its owners and confirm the decision to sell. The valuation can also help determine who are viable Buyers for the business. For example, the company that determines its value to be between $300 and $500 million will likely not consider Buyers with a value substantially lower than that, unless they have some unusual sources of capital. In determining what kind of companies will have the financial resources to acquire it, the Seller will need to consider not only its valuation but also the nature of its business. For example, companies with strong cash flow are more likely Targets for private equity for LBO Buyers, who can use that cash flow to lever the business and finance most of the acquisition with debt.

DETERMINING THE UNIVERSE OF BUYERS

As discussed above, there is a variety of reasons for a company to choose to acquire. When a company is considering a sale, it needs to broadly define the universe of potential Buyers. A company considering a sale will naturally first turn its eye to its direct competitors. However, the most attractive Buyer may turn out to be a company in a completely different business or a completely different geography. When considering a sale and trying to define potential Buyers, a company needs to think like a Buyer. The potential Seller needs to consider all of its assets and resources, and then think about who is likely to get the greatest value from them.

Establishing a list of potential and likely Buyers can be a lot of work. The Seller will need to consider many industries, spaces, and companies with which it is not necessarily familiar. This is one of the areas where outside advisors and consultants can often add value. Not only are they more familiar with other industries and players, but they bring an "outside view" fresh approach to the question, and may identify Buyers whom the company would not have considered, otherwise. When trying to develop a list of potential Buyers, a Seller needs to consider all the different reasons that a company may want to acquire its business. It also needs to consider the financial capabilities of the Buyer, as well as the broader question of whether the company uses acquisitions as a strategic tool. While it is always possible to do a deal with a first-time Buyer, it is far more likely that a Seller will be able to entice a company that is familiar with using acquisitions to grow. Current market trends and market cycles should also be considered. At different points in their business cycle, companies will be more or less likely to acquire.

Another factor that the Seller may want to consider, when developing a potential Buyers list, is the way a Buyer will integrate the Seller's business. In theory, a company concerned only with maximizing shareholder value will simply look to the Buyer who will bring the best price. However, many companies, particularly those owned by founders in management, will be concerned with how the acquirer will integrate the business, whether the Seller's employees will be retained, and even how much the brand and "vision" of the Seller's business will survive.

Once a Seller has made the strategic decision to sell, determined the likely valuation it is expected to receive, and developed a list of likely Buyers, it needs to consider how it is going to run the sales process. There is a variety of different process structures that can be used in selling a company, and each has its own advantages and disadvantages. The Seller needs to choose a process that matches its particular goals, identified Buyers, timing, and other factors. Choosing the right process is important, not only to maximize the value received in a sale but also to maximize the likelihood that the sale will actually close. It is important to remember that, while launching a sale process makes the sale of a company likely, it does not guarantee it. On many occasions, a company will launch a sale process but not end up selling the company. Sometimes, this is inevitable—the result of unrealistic expectations or outside market forces—but sometimes it is the result of choosing the wrong process and managing the sale badly.

MAKING THE APPROACH

As discussed later in this chapter, in "Direct Versus Proxy," both the Buyer and the Seller may choose to use proxies or representatives, or to act on their own behalf. In either case, in order to start the ball rolling on a deal, one side must first make the initial approach. In theory, the initial approach should be a simple and perfunctory event, where one side suggests a potential transaction, the other side expresses interest, and then they get down to the business of trying to craft a deal. However, in most cases, the character and nature of the initial approach can do a lot to set the tone for the subsequent negotiation, and, in some cases, even determine if a negotiation ensues. It is human nature to establish initial perceptions and impressions that are later hard to dislodge. As with dating, the first impression can often be important, if not crucial, in a deal. The party making the initial approach needs to try to "telegraph" the right impression to the counterparty of both itself and the deal.

While it might seem obvious, there is a variety of methods for making an initial approach. When using a proxy, one would hope that the proxy has a direct or indirect personal relationship that makes the medium of approach less important. A direct approach can be more formal, by letter, or less formal, by email or a direct call. It is important to keep in mind that a written approach is not only more formal but also potentially more intimidating. For public companies with disclosure requirements, the more formal the approach (on either side), the more likely it is to trigger a requirement to make some kind of statement to investors. The other danger with a written approach is that it does not give the author an opportunity to clarify meanings and intents—it stands on its own. A phone call can be less intimidating and allow a freer give and take of questions and clarifications. However, it is often hard to make a live conversation happen. While a written approach will eventually reach its intended recipient, it is often hard to actually connect with a counterparty, particularly a senior executive in a large company. When making a phone approach, one is likely to encounter either voicemail or an intermediary, such as a secretary, and only be able to leave a message, to which one hopes the counterparty will respond. This leaves the caller in the same situation as with a written approach—that is, the message must be crafted carefully. In either case, the intermediary's job is to intercept and filter messages to the executive, and the message must be crafted carefully, to ensure that it does not get discarded. At the same time, it is necessary to maintain substantial discretion.

This leaves the challenge of communicating the importance of the approach, while not giving away details that might not be appropriate for the intermediary. In most cases, a message like "Please tell the CEO to return my call so we can discuss my acquisition of his company" will not be well received. By contrast, simply asking for a return call may not be sufficiently serious and clear to get the message to the executive. Coded language like "strategic transaction" or "strategic alliance" are helpful in communicating seriousness to the executive, while not giving too much specificity to the intermediary.

When a Seller makes an initial approach to potential Buyers, it faces a fundamental Catch-22. It must somehow communicate the inherent value and strength of its business, even as it is initiating a process to sell it. The first reaction of any Buyer to an unsolicited offer may be, "If it's so good, why do you want to sell it?" or "What's wrong with it?" One valuable tool for explaining this perceived inconsistency is to quickly identify the reason for the sale. In the absence of a clear reason for a sale, the Buyer will likely assume that something is wrong with the Seller's business. As discussed in Chapter 3, there is a variety of reasons that a Seller could choose to sell a perfectly good business. Telegraphing this reason to the Buyer upfront may help to allay fears. The Seller also needs to try to communicate that it will be a reasonable and accommodating negotiating partner. Particularly in the case of selling companies controlled by founders or other individuals, a Buyer may be concerned that negotiating with these individuals will be complex and difficult, and be concerned that people with an emotional interest in the business may have irrational or unreasonable expectations.

When a Buyer is making an initial approach, it also needs to try to communicate certain things. First, it needs to communicate its seriousness.

Since Strategic Transaction negotiations usually require a Seller to expose confidential and valuable information about its business, it will be concerned about Buyers going on a "fishing expedition" by proposing a deal simply to get access to competitive information. Deal negotiations also take a high toll, particularly on the Seller, in terms of distracting senior management and employees from the core business. For both these reasons, it is important that a Buyer communicate a significant level of seriousness about the deal. Like a Buyer, a Seller also has concerns about dealing with an unreasonable or irrational counterparty. While Buyers may be less prone to personalizing a transaction, since, unlike Sellers, they are not founders selling off their life's work, they can still be difficult negotiating partners. For example, some Buyers develop a reputation for making high initial offers to stimulate a discussion, and then drastically reducing their bids once they have gotten a Seller in "sales mode." A Buyer making an approach also needs to try to anticipate some Seller-specific needs and concerns, and address them during the approach. For example, some potential Sellers will be particularly concerned with protecting their employees in any deal. In this situation, making a point upfront that the Buyer expects to retain all or most of the Seller's employees can be a strong motivator for the Seller to begin discussions. A Buyer can also try to play on a Seller's fears, though this is a risky strategy. For example, a Buyer can signal that, in the absence of a deal, it plans to launch a business that competes directly with the Seller. This may drive the Seller to the negotiating table but may also harden it to any approach.

ONE-ON-ONE NEGOTIATION

The most basic form of sale process is a simple one-on-one negotiation. Here, Buyer and Seller come together in a direct negotiation and try to reach mutually accepted terms. Immediately moving to a one-on-one negotiation has some distinct advantages. This simple process appeals to the Buyer, because it eliminates the danger of a competitive bidding process. This is not to say that the Buyer has all the power. The Seller always has the option to break off negotiation and enter a competitive process with other potential Buyers, but as long as the one-on-one negotiation continues, the Buyer simply has to reach a set of terms that is acceptable to the Seller, without the constant risk that another Buyer will outbid it. A one-on-one negotiation also offers benefits to the Seller. Direct negotiation with a potential Buyer is usually a fairly fast process, and one that increases the likelihood of getting a deal done. Once direct negotiation starts, the

Seller can quickly ascertain whether a deal is likely to happen, since both parties will quickly put their proposed terms on the table. If those terms are not far apart, the Seller can have confidence that the deal is likely to get done. That said, one-on-one negotiation is usually the preferred form for a Buyer. The Seller will be hesitant to get into a one-on-one negotiation, since it eliminates the opportunity to do exactly what the Seller is trying to do—play off one Buyer against another, to maximize value. The one-on-one negotiation also creates a risk, for a Seller, that if it does not reach terms with the Buyer, it will have to go back to step one and try to find another Buyer.

It is important to note that eventually all negotiations come down to a one-on-one relationship. The key question is whether the Seller chooses to start there or to use a more complex process that eventually winnows down multiple Buyers to a single one.

A one-on-one negotiation is particularly common when a Buyer makes an unsolicited approach to a Seller. In this situation, while the Seller may have been considering a sale, it has not initiated a process but rather has been approached by a potential Buyer. This approach, if it is not rebuffed, can often trigger a one-on-one negotiation. The Seller is certainly not required to immediately enter into a one-on-one negotiation with the Buyer, if it is approached. It can always choose to use that initial bid to build a larger sales process, and use that Buyer as a "stalking horse." However, this is a risky maneuver. If the Seller does not immediately enter into one-on-one negotiations with the Buyer, it risks losing that "bird in the hand" offer from the Buyer. When considering any one-on-one negotiation, and in particular an unsolicited offer from a Buyer, the Seller needs to balance the goal of maximizing the price it gets against the risk of not doing a deal at all.

As with any sale process, there are no hard and fast rules about how it needs to be conducted. This is particularly true of a one-on-one negotiation, where the Seller does not have to be concerned about maintaining an even playing field between different bidders. That said, this discussion will try to lay out what a standard, or at least common, one-on-one negotiation process looks like.

The first step is to establish contact and determine a level of interest. In some cases, the parties will deal with each other directly. A Seller may reach out directly to a Buyer, or a Buyer may make an unsolicited offer or indication of interest to a Seller. In many cases, one or the other party will use a surrogate to make this initial approach. While investment bankers are perhaps the most common surrogate, Buyers and Sellers may also use lawyers, consultants, or other advisors. The party who is making the initial contact will usually propose very general and rough terms, to attract the interest of the other party. When the Buyer makes the approach, this may be as simple as communicating an interest in buying the company. When the Seller makes the approach, it usually means coupling an interest in selling with some basic information about the business. If the business is public, this may not be necessary, but for a private company, a "teaser" is often used. A teaser is usually a one- to two-page document that gives a very high level description of the business that is for sale.

Once the two parties have established that there is a mutual interest in discussing a transaction, they usually exchange basic nondisclosure agreements (NDAs). This document primarily protects the Seller but also provides some protections for the Buyer. In general terms, it provides that neither party will share the information it gets during the process, and often includes other clauses, such as a bar on actively recruiting the employees of the other party. Once the NDA has been signed, the Seller will usually share more extensive information with the Buyer, including more detailed financial data and an overview of the business and operations, as well as key assets. This information is usually in the form of an information or offering memorandum. This document is basically a precursor to full due diligence. After providing an information memorandum, the Seller will often provide the Buyer with an opportunity to meet with members of its senior management team and receive a management presentation, which provides more detail and color on the business. This also gives the Buyer an opportunity to meet the management team, the quality of which may be a factor in the Buyer's decision. At this stage, there may be some informal discussion of price, but usually the Buyer will view all this data before coming to an initial view.

Once the Buyer has been given this basic information, it will usually be asked to provide an indicative and nonbinding price. The focus of this exercise is to make sure that, after the basic review of the business, the Buyer is still interested, and is still willing to offer a price that might be sufficient to the Seller. In some cases, this is as simple as a conversation between the parties. In many cases, the Seller will ask the Buyer to provide a more formal indication of interest. This usually takes the form of a letter of intent or indication of interest. These documents are almost always legally nonbinding but provide greater detail on the price the Buyer is willing to pay, the currency and form it intends to use, the structure of the deal it envisions, the assets (if not all) it is seeking to acquire, and the process by which it would propose to complete the transaction. In some cases, this latter item, as well as some of the others—such as the structure of the deal—may be dictated by the Seller. In many cases, the letter of intent will assume an exclusivity period, during which negotiation will take place. Usually the letter will require the Seller to sign a commitment to exclusively negotiate with the Buyer for a period of time. While they vary, exclusivity periods are often in the range of one to two months. The goal is to give the parties enough time to completely negotiate a transaction but not block the Seller from beginning negotiations with another Buyer, if it becomes apparent that the deal is not going to go through.

Once the letter of intent has been accepted, and, in some cases, an exclusivity period has begun, the Buyer and Seller will begin active negotiation. In most cases, they will pursue a dual-track process, whereby the Buyer simultaneously completes full due diligence and negotiates the agreements. As discussed in Chapter 7, due diligence can be an extensive process of reviewing the details of the business, and can involve dozens of people from both the Buyer's and the Seller's staff, as well as outside consultants and advisors.

If the two parties are able to reach agreement, complete due diligence, and finalize legal documentation, they will then move to consummate the deal. In some cases, a deal is closed all at once. In this situation, the Buyer and Seller come together and execute all the legal documents necessary, and payment is made, all at the same time. In many cases, however, there is a need to separate the transaction into two events, the signing and the closing. The signing will usually involve executing all the legal documents necessary but will make final completion of the deal subject to some small list of discrete events. The closing will occur as soon as those events have happened, or those conditions have been met. At the closing, the definitive set of documents will be signed, and payment will be made. The idea behind a separate signing and closing is to lock down as much detail of the agreement possible, subject to only those things that cannot happen immediately. A common example is the need for regulatory filings and regulatory approvals. In that situation, the two companies may have a signing where the only condition to closing is government approval of the transaction. Usually the Buyer will also require that there be no "material adverse change" in the business. The point here is that if the Seller substantially damages the business during the period between signing and closing, the Buyer does not want to be bound by the agreement. Other conditions to closing might include the Seller completing some changes or actions within the business. One example would be the need to wait for a particular product or technology to receive a certain certification. Another would be a drug company awaiting FDA approval of a drug. The idea here is that the Buyer and Seller have reached agreement, subject only to one single future event, and want to lock in the deal and simply wait for that event to happen. From both parties' perspectives, this structure allows them to limit the chance that the deal will unravel, or that another party will come in and offer better terms.

In some cases, the closing is a singular and definitive event, leaving the selling shareholders totally disengaged from the company and holding a full purchase price in their bank accounts. In other cases, there may be a "tail" to the transaction. For example, as discussed further in Chapter 8, the purchase price may be paid in part at closing and in part months or even years later, based on an earn-out provision. In other cases, the Seller may have continuing obligations to the Buyer after the closing date. For example, the Seller may often be required to complete postclosing regulatory filings or take other actions.

This discussion has described the way all transactions will end; however, the process that a Seller chooses will affect how the transaction begins. In many cases, a Seller will choose not to go to direct one-on-one negotiations but rather to conduct a more complicated process.

FORMAL AUCTION

A Seller can choose to run a full formal auction, to narrow the field down to the best Buyer. In theory, this process should end with a one-on-one negotiation with the best Buyer, who will give the Seller the best terms. In addition to maximizing purchase price and other terms, an auction can help a Seller to identify potential Buyers and test their level of interest. If a Seller enters into a one-on-one negotiation immediately with a single Buyer, it not only risks getting a low price but also risks having no deal at all. The auction process can not only push up the price but also, through its various hurdles, test the sincerity and level of interest of the Buyers.

A full formal auction process is the most likely sales strategy to acquire an investment bank advisor. This is, in part, because it requires a lot of networking and communication with potential Buyers but also because of the complexity and inherent workload of the process. One of the downsides of a formal auction process is the risk to secrecy. While a Seller can certainly try to run an auction confidentially, the fact that so many different parties are involved—and the fact that, at one or more stages, some of them will be rejected—makes it far more difficult to keep the process and the potential of a sale secret.

The first step in an auction process is to identify potential Buyers, who will be invited to bid. In an extreme case, this can be done through a public announcement welcoming all bidders. This is a fairly rare occurrence, and is usually limited to court-managed sales (most notably the bankruptcy process; see the "Bankruptcy Auction" section). Far more common is to identify a list of potential bidders, and then to make contact, either directly or through a surrogate. In most cases, a potential bidder is provided with the teaser document discussed above. In some cases, the potential bidder is told the identity of the Seller, and, in other cases, that information is kept confidential. Note that the further along the process goes, the more difficult it is to keep the identity of the Seller confidential. Even if the identity of the Seller is not disclosed, with a modest amount of information, most Buyers can ascertain what company is being discussed.

Bidders in an auction process are usually given a formal timeline and outline of the process. While the Seller is not usually legally bound to maintain a fair and balanced playing field, failure to do so risks alienating the Buyers and damaging the auction. There is no magic structure to an auction process, and each sale may introduce its own unique aspects; however, there are some fairly common steps. After bidders receive a teaser, they will usually be asked to confirm their level of interest. Bidders will then be asked to sign an NDA, and will receive a full information memorandum. In some cases, they will also be given access to a management presentation. Obviously, if there are a large number of bidders, coordinating all this documentation and all the management presentations can be a significant amount of work. The bidders will usually then be asked to submit a nonbinding letter of intent. In some cases, the bidders will also be provided with a form of the legal purchase agreement, and be asked to provide a marked-up version of this agreement as part of their nonbinding bid. In some cases, the Seller will choose a single bidder, based on the letters of intent, and enter into exclusive negotiations with that bidder. In other cases, the Seller will carry out a two-stage process, in which it will use the letters of intent to winnow the group of bidders down to a smaller number. That smaller group of bidders will be given access to more extensive due diligence information, and then be asked to submit a refined bid. In some cases, the second bid may be a "binding" offer. In that case, it will certainly need to be accompanied by a markup of the purchase agreement. After the second round, the Seller almost always chooses a single bidder with which to negotiate. However, in similar cases, the Seller may choose to simultaneously negotiate with multiple parties. Throughout this process, the Seller is balancing the advantage of having multiple bidders putting pressure on each other to raise the price and better the terms against the risk of losing the interest of a bidder.

The letter of intent or indication of interest is a misunderstood and often misused document. In basic terms, this is a short letter delivered by a potential Buyer, outlining the key terms of its proposed acquisition. Letters of intent (LOIs) serve a valuable purpose in the negotiating process. Presenting an LOI requires the Buyer to lay out the high-level terms of its proposal. This ensures that the Buyer and Seller are "in the same neighborhood," and, if they are, substantially increases the likelihood that they will be able to cut a deal. Actually producing a signed LOI is valuable, since it usually forces a Buyer, particularly a large corporate Buyer, to review key terms of the deal with fairly senior managers, as well as lawyers. In a sense, producing an LOI ensures that the Buyer is not simply acting on a whim but is taking the transaction very seriously. Having said this, it is important to point out what an LOI is not. In most cases, an LOI is a nonbinding document. What this means is that lawyers will insert language that explicitly says that the offer is only an indication of a potential deal but is in no way legally binding. While the Buyer may try to lay out the key issues and areas of due diligence that stand between this letter and a binding commitment, in reality the Buyer can use almost any excuse to avoid consummating a deal. Many people take too much comfort in an LOI, believing that it somehow creates a legally binding obligation. In reality, an LOI is usually simply a demonstration of good faith in the negotiating process and evidence of sincerity and senior-level focus. The LOI is a valuable tool to try to filter down a bidder population to those that are particularly serious, and get a good idea of the general terms on which they are willing to do a deal. However, an LOI is not a necessary component in every transaction. When a Seller is running an informal process, and has particularly good communication with potential bidders, it may be able to gauge both the level of interest and the indicative terms without requesting a formal LOI.

In some rare cases, Sellers will request a binding LOI. I have always thought this is a particularly odd document. Technically speaking, a binding LOI is never really fully and completely binding. No short document can ever reflect the full range of legal terms that need to exist in a purchase agreement. A binding LOI simply tries to tighten the range of excuses a Buyer can use for walking away from a deal. In a sense, a binding LOI simply creates the opportunity for a spurned Seller to sue the bidder, claiming damage for not completing the transaction. Given the difficulty of nailing down this level of commitment from a bidder, binding LOIs are fairly rare. They will be most common and most effective in deals where the asset or company being acquired is extremely simple and easy to value, and where the terms are likely to be very concrete and not subject to much debate.

However the process is structured, the end goal is to enter into detailed negotiations with the most likely Buyer, and then follow the process discussed above. One advantage of the auction process is that, in the event that negotiations with that Buyer break down, the Seller has the option of returning to the pool of other Buyers involved in the auction. While there is no guarantee that they will remain interested, the Seller likely does not have to start from scratch, and, at the very least, it has identified the most interested Buyers and set the level of likely pricing. Of course, returning to the pool sends a strong signal to the other Buyers that the Seller may be weak, since it was not able to cut a deal with the lead Buyer. This may damage the Seller's negotiating position.

One other advantage of a formal auction process is that it allows the Seller to introduce more complex structures potentially involved with multiple Buyers. For example, a Seller with two divisions can run a process whereby bidders can bid on one or more of the divisions. This allows the Seller to maximize the value of the whole company, in situations where the most attractive Buyer for one division may not be the most attractive Buyer for another. Of course, with complexity comes risk. Negotiating a deal with multiple parties creates a greater risk that at least one of the two negotiations will break down. However, in some cases, the risk is worth taking, since it can substantially increase the price the Seller receives.

One nuance to the auction process is the delicate exercise of signaling. In theory, a Seller wants to run a fair and balanced auction process. However, the Seller also has a powerful incentive to try to drive the Buyers to increase the value of their offers. The Seller can take advantage of the competition between the Buyers, and can also make use of the multiple stages of bidding to try to drive the price up. As the auction proceeds, the Seller can formally signal by actually telling all Buyers that there are minimum terms necessary to reach the next round. The Seller can also more informally signal Buyers in one-on-one conversations, to try to coax their bids up in various ways. For example, a Seller might approach one Buyer, who had put in the highest purchase price but offered to pay most of that purchase price in stock. The Seller might tell this Buyer that, in order to be competitive, it needs to increase the cash percentage of its bid.

Formal auctions also provide a certain amount of "cover" for the management and board of directors. They provide a clear demonstration that the board made every effort to maximize the value received for the shareholders. It is not entirely clear that a formal auction always maximizes price, but it is much harder to argue that a board failed in its duty by running a formal auction than it is to argue that it somehow missed the potential for a higher bid by going directly to a one-on-one negotiation with a single party. Formal auctions are thus more likely in the sale of companies that are not closely held, while those running the sale process are not those who own the majority of the shares. Formal auctions are also more common in the sale of larger companies, where the expense and time commitment of this more complex process are justified by the size of the deal. For the same reason that a board of directors conducts a formal auction, they often are used in the divestiture of subsidiaries, where the managers making the sale want to demonstrate that proper care is taken to maximize the value received by the company.

INFORMAL AUCTION

Sometimes there is an attractive midpoint between the simplicity of a one-on-one negotiation and the complexity of a full and formal auction. Informal auctions often provide the Seller with many of the benefits of competing bidders and more of the certainty of a direct and quick one-on-one negotiation. In basic terms, an informal auction simply means that the potential Seller is talking to multiple parties at the same time. The challenge for the Seller is to manage both the expectations of the counterparties and the timing of the process. In an ideal world, the Seller will be able to time the process so that it gets responses from all of the potential bidders simultaneously, and can make an "apples to apples" comparison. Managing expectations of potential Buyers is important, since there may be an expectation or a demand for exclusivity. Each Buyer will try to press the Seller into an exclusive negotiation.

Informal auctions are most common with smaller deals, and deals where nonfinancial variables are important. In the case of smaller deals, the complexity and logistics of a formal auction may be expensive and excessive for the size of the deal. When selling a small business or a small subsidiary, the Seller may want to test the market and ensure it is getting a good price, by talking to multiple bidders but not feel the need for a full and formal auction process. An informal auction process also makes it more likely that the Seller can maintain confidentiality, since it will involve a smaller number of people and will probably move more quickly. This can be particularly important if the Seller is worried about either public market reaction or reaction of employees.

Informal auctions are also very useful where nonfinancial variables are important. In many cases, the Seller is not only concerned with maximizing the price but also with other variables, such as the fate of employees, or, in the case of a partial sale or the sale of a subsidiary that works with the parent business, the nature and the reliability of the Buyer. For example, if the Seller is looking to sell only a minority stake in its business, it will presumably be concerned with finding a Buyer that is going to be a good partner and productive investor. If the Seller is selling a subsidiary with which it will continue to have ongoing business dealings, it will want to ensure that the Buyer will run the business and maintain the relationship well. For example, if General Motors (GM) sells a division that manufacturers a part that it will continue to use in its cars, it will be extremely important to GM that the Buyer be a reliable company. Reliability can include such factors as financial stability and capitalization, good business practices, and a good overall reputation. Informal auctions allow the Seller more leeway in communicating one-on-one with Buyers about such nonfinancial issues, and do not hold them to strict timelines and processes.

BANKRUPTCY AUCTION

In very simple terms, U.S. bankruptcy law provides that a company that files for bankruptcy can either be reorganized or sold.[1] When a company is sold out of bankruptcy, a variety of new and interesting issues arises. The bankruptcy auction process is usually far more formal, structured, and time-consuming. In simplest terms, the Bankruptcy Court will appoint a trustee, who will then conduct an auction. Again, in simple terms, the goal of the trustee is not only to maximize the money recovered through the auction—which will be used to pay out creditors and, if anything is left, equity-holders—but also to consider such issues as the continuation of the business and the effect of the bankruptcy on employees, customers, and other related parties. In a bankruptcy auction, the trustee will usually organize a very formal process, similar to the one discussed above but with even more complexity. Once the trustee has conducted the auction and determined a winning bidder, the terms of the sale will have to be submitted for approval to the Bankruptcy Court. Creditors and other related parties will have an opportunity to object to the transaction, and the bankruptcy judge will have to make a final ruling, approving or disapproving the transaction. While a traditional formal auction may lock a Buyer into a binding bid, with little room to maneuver after the bid is accepted, the situation is even more extreme in a bankruptcy proceeding. In most cases, the bidder in a bankruptcy auction will have submitted a complete and final purchase agreement with all terms filled in. Once the bankruptcy judge has accepted the agreement, there is usually no room to make any changes.

The bankruptcy auction process usually takes months and requires far more resources and effort. It also subjects the Buyer to a lot more publicity, since the process is usually quite public. Finally, it subjects the Buyer to the judgment of the Bankruptcy Court, which is in effect yet another counterparty, beyond the trustee. Offsetting all these issues is the value usually found in a bankruptcy proceeding, because companies in bankruptcy are usually "fixer uppers." Acquisitions out of a bankruptcy auction may often be at a deep discount, and Buyers may receive the opportunity to acquire the assets very cheaply.

DIRECT VERSUS PROXY

One side issue in any sale process is the question of whether the parties deal with each other directly or through proxies. The most common proxies are investment bankers and lawyers, but a variety of other advisors can serve as proxies. There are several key advantages to using a proxy. In more complex negotiation processes, proxies are particularly valuable. Proxies are usually expert at running and participating in complex sale processes. They understand the strategy of how to maximize the value of their position for their client. In some cases, a proxy can be used to mask the identity of a party. This is particularly true in the very early stages of a transaction. Either a Buyer or a Seller may not want the other party to know its identity, and it can use a proxy to make initial inquiries or indications of interest. Deeper into the process, proxies also provide an unemotional negotiating voice. By their nature, Strategic Transactions can be very emotional and adversarial events. Since proxies are professional negotiators and counterparties, they can take a very unemotional stance. Proxies in this role also create a buffer between the two counterparties, allowing them to distance themselves from the more argumentative issues. This allows the principals in both the Buyer and Seller to remain friendly and congenial, leaving their proxies to argue and debate over the more difficult points. If the two parties are likely to have to do business in the future, this is a somewhat esoteric, but particularly valuable, function.

RELATIVE POSITIONS OF POWER

When crafting and running a sale process, or participating in one, both Buyer and Seller need to keep in mind the shifting relative power of each party. During the course of a sale process, negotiating power can shift from Buyer to Seller once or more than once. Understanding when each party has more relative power is an important part of negotiating effectively and maximizing one's position. Obviously, each party wants to try to press for concessions when it has the most power, and limit its need to concede points or issues when it has the least power. While relative power positions will vary from situation to situation, some broad generalizations can be made.

Outside factors can affect the relative power held by each party. Events such as changes in the economy or the industry, or the actions of other companies, can all shift the relative power of the parties. For example, if an airline is engaged in being sold, and fuel prices drop, the value of its business as well as the potential for it to continue to operate independently (and thus defer a sale process entirely) will likely increase.

The process itself can shift power from one party to another. As a general rule, at the beginning of a sale process, the Seller will have more power. It usually defines the terms of the process and can set the tempo. A Seller always has the option of bringing additional Buyers into the process. However, as the process progresses, and the Seller begins to negotiate directly with a single Buyer, the power will tend to shift to the Buyer. As a general matter, the failure of a deal at this stage will do more to hurt the Seller than the Buyer. Generally, the Seller will use the early stages in a sale process to try to extract the best terms from the Buyer, and, during the later stages, the Buyer will return the favor by trying to extract better terms from the Seller. For example, a Seller might use an auction process to get the highest possible bid from a Buyer, but once the parties enter into exclusive final negotiation, the Buyer may extract better representations and warranties, and perhaps an escrow agreement, from the Seller.

NOTE

1. There is a rich literature on U.S. bankruptcy law. For a definitive treatise, see Douglas Baird, *Elements of Bankruptcy* (Westbury, NY: Foundation Press, 1993) or Jagdeep S. Bhandari and Lawrence A. Weiss, eds., *Corporate Bankruptcy: Economic and Legal Perspectives* (Cambridge, UK: Cambridge University Press, 1996)

CHAPTER 7

Due Diligence

Due diligence may sound like an obscure legal term, but it is really fairly straightforward. It simply means that a Buyer has been duly diligent and careful in its review of a potential acquisition. Due diligence is basically the process of digging deep and ensuring that one is buying what one thinks one is buying. Put another way, due diligence is like checking the fine print on a contract, or testing out a computer to make sure it actually works before buying it. In some sense, due diligence is an exercise in confirming a negative. In a perfect world, during due diligence a Buyer would discover that its initial impressions of a Target company and its initial financial projections were exactly right. In reality, there is always almost some difference, some unexpected finding. These differences usually do not doom a deal, although they sometimes can lead to an adjustment of terms. However, in rare but important cases, due diligence uncovers facts that dramatically change a Buyer's view of a Target company and can derail a deal. Rather than a negative event, for a Buyer this is a huge relief, since it means that the Buyer averted a disastrous deal.

Due diligence also has an impact on the negotiation of the legal documents and on integration planning. Since due diligence exposes the details of a company and how it operates, it will inform the lawyers on the drafting of a variety of parts of the contract, including the representations and warranties, and even the details of what is being purchased. Due diligence is also an essential source of data for the team planning the postclosing integration of the two businesses, since it helps identify the key areas and pieces that will need to be integrated, and the challenges that will have to be overcome in that integration effort. The integration effort is discussed in more detail in Chapter 9.

BUILDING A TEAM

The first step to acquiring a company, or at least one of the first steps, is to have a team that can lead the transaction. The Buyer begins with a Corporate Development team, or at least with a person who is designated to lead the effort to acquire a business. Similarly, the first thing a Seller will need to do is to designate a team responsible for putting together the process in selling a company. Chapters 2 and 4 have discussed the details of the Corporate Development team and how one is formed. But it is important to note that, like a quarterback, the Corporate Development team is useless without the larger team around them. If it is just a quarterback on the field, he will get clobbered. When it is time to do a deal, a Buyer needs to form a due diligence team. For Sellers, there is a slightly different exercise of forming the team that is going to provide the due diligence material, but, for purposes of this section, it will be assumed that the teams look fairly similar, and that everywhere that Buyers are looking for information, Sellers will be looking to provide it. First, a due diligence team can be separated into people from staff functions and people from line management. Staff functions are those functions that exist at the corporate level. They include areas such as human resources, legal, real estate, regulatory and compliance, public relations, and finance and accounting. In some cases, some of these functions will exist within a business unit, but, for the most part, in all but the largest companies, they are likely to exist at the staff level. For a Buyer that does deals repeatedly, it makes a lot of sense to try to designate specific people from each of these areas to be involved in due diligence teams. This will reduce the start-up time and the challenge of training up a due diligence team. If a Buyer has a human resources person or a lawyer who does deals with a Corporate Development team regularly, it will be much more efficient at gearing up for every new deal. This does not mean that due diligence and M&As must be a full-time occupation for people in these specialty areas. In some cases, the amount of deal flow that a Buyer is doing will support a fully dedicated lawyer or a fully dedicated human resources person. But, in most cases, simply having someone who is dedicated to spending part of his or her time doing deals will suffice. The key is continuity between deals. This is not only important for efficiency but also for ensuring that the same mistakes are not repeated, and that standards are established and maintained.

In addition to line functions, a Buyer will need staff from the relevant business units dedicated to due diligence. In most cases, a Buyer is looking to acquire a business and integrate it with an existing part of its company. However, in some cases, a Buyer may be looking to acquire a wholly new business in a wholly new area, where there will be no integration into an existing business unit. Even in those cases, the Buyer needs experts from line management, and will simply have to find them in existing business units. Of course, this is more challenging politically, since the manager of that business unit does not get the direct benefit of acquiring and growing her business through the acquisition, but it is essential to have all these skills in place, even when buying a business that will stand on its own inside the Buyer. This brings up the key issue of management commitment. Whether the Buyer is building a due diligence team from a line unit that will own the acquired business, or seeking resources from business units to do due diligence on an acquisition that will stand alone, it is going to need management buy-in to get those resources and get them properly dedicated. The manager of the relevant business unit needs to be committed to the exercise and willing to dedicate the resources. Unless she is, her subordinates will be hesitant to dedicate their time to the project and to give it their attention. This is reasonable, since, in the absence of direction from their manager, there is no upside to working on a due diligence project, and only downside to the extent that it distracts them from their "day job." Thus, the first step in organizing a due diligence team is to involve the manager of the relevant business unit and ensure that she is committed to the effort and communicates that to her team. In some cases, members of the line management team will be able to continue at their current jobs and work on the due diligence project. In other cases, they will need to be taken "offline" during the due diligence process, or at least in part relieved of their regular work obligations. The cultural challenge is to ensure that these staff members do not view doing due diligence on a deal as a tarnish or unrewarded extra work. It is important that line management communicate to them that this is an important project, and that they will be recognized for the work on it. Due diligence teams work best when the project is perceived as high profile, important, and in fact an opportunity to showcase their skills in front of senior management. One of the best ways to motivate the managers of a business unit to be involved in a deal is the appeal of growing their business through acquisition. Similarly, one of the best ways to get members of the line management business involved in the deal is to show or ensure that they will be given a lot of visibility to their managers and senior executives in the company.

Staff Functions

Lawyers are the single most critical element in a due diligence team. At the end of the day, an acquisition is the purchase of a pool of legal rights and obligations, in addition to assets and a brand. Lawyers ensure that a Buyer is getting what it thinks it is getting when it buys a company.

There are two places to get lawyers for this exercise: (1) in-house and (2) outside. In-house lawyers work for the general counsel, while outside lawyers are employees of law firms that can be hired to work on a deal or project basis. For most deals, or at least larger ones, some combination of inside and outside lawyers is optimal. Each has distinct advantages and disadvantages. In-house lawyers will be much more knowledgeable about the business and the ways the Buyer's management team view the business, as well as their priorities, preferences, and particular "hotspots." To the extent the Buyer does deals on a regular basis, they may also be fairly expert in doing acquisitions, but, for the most part, they will be less experienced than outside lawyers in doing deals, since they are more likely to be broad generalists. In-house lawyers also have an innate limited capacity. Usually an in-house legal group is a fairly small team. By contrast, outside lawyers, to the extent that they are part of a large law firm, have almost unlimited resources at their disposal. While in-house lawyers are generalists with a deep knowledge of the business, outside lawyers will be specialists with only a passing knowledge of the specific business. As a result, in-house lawyers usually serve best as leaders of the legal negotiation team and the legal due diligence team. They have final responsibility for reporting to management, and, since they understand the business better, they are more likely to spot Buyer-specific issues. By contrast, outside counsel are valuable as experts in specific fields, including the more complex issues of M&As, tax, intellectual property, environmental law, and litigation issues. Outside lawyers also provide extra "fire power," since they can draw on a large pool of lawyers for the occasional peaks of workload that are inevitable in a Strategic Transaction. In practice, an in-house lawyer will usually lead the team, with a combination of a senior outside counsel to advise on the complexities of deal structuring, and a larger number of junior outside counsel for the "heavy lifting" of reviewing large amounts of due diligence material and drafting the large number of ancillary documents related to a Strategic Transaction. The outside law firm also brings additional resources for things like drafting and revising documents, distributing documents, meeting facilities, and other "infrastructure."

Finance and Accounting

If the legal due diligence team tells the Buyer what it is buying, the finance and accounting staff tells it how much the acquisition is worth and what it really does for the Buyer. As will be discussed in Chapter 8, the work of developing valuation and financial models is usually split between the finance staff and the Corporate Development team, with occasional support from outside advisors. In the final analysis, however, the finance and accounting staff must be responsible for the job of, in turn, interpreting financial statements and making determinations about accounting treatment. Generally, members of the finance and accounting staff will be brought into the due diligence team to review not only the main financial statements of a Target company but also underlying data such as pricing.

Finance and accounting due diligence is a lot of work and generally requires fully dedicated resources. Like lawyers, these resources can be found both inside and outside the company. Inside finance staff will have the advantage of understanding the Buyer's accounting policies and procedures, as well as being familiar with the financial structure of the business that the Buyer is in. Outside accounting staff, like outside lawyers, have the advantage of being able to pull large resources and numbers of people on short notice. In general, the finance and accounting due diligence team will be led by somebody internal, since they will have final responsibility for the financial statements of the Buyer, once the acquisition is complete. In most cases, this team is bolstered by outside resources that provide the extra head count needed to accomplish financial and accounting due diligence quickly. The addition of members of the outside accounting firm may add expertise, if the Buyer is buying a company in a new area of business, with which it is not familiar. In most cases, these outside resources come from the Buyer's audit firm. This serves two purposes. First, this is a firm with which the Buyer already has an ongoing relationship, and it usually can field the team more quickly and efficiently. Second, at the end of the day, this is the audit firm that will have to opine on the combined financials, and so it is important to have its input, to make sure there are no surprises when it does its audit.

In some companies, the finance and accounting team is brought in early, to do the initial models of a potential Target; in others, it is brought in only when negotiations get serious, and a full and final model needs to be done. Early discussions with the finance and accounting team are very important, particularly when there is some question as to how financials of a Target will be treated and what they mean.

Human Resources

Human resources staff are usually brought into a transaction later in the process. They are usually brought in less to evaluate the potential of a deal, and more to plan for integration and confirm that there are no "deal breakers." As a result, they tend to join the deal team late in the process but be much more heavily involved in integration planning and postdeal integration. Usually, the human resources team is limited to internal staff, members of the Buyer's human resources group. In similar exceptions, the human resources team may call on outside consultants for unusual situations where they do not have enough experience. One example could be the acquisition of a company with a large number of employees, in a country in which the Buyer does not currently operate. Here the human resources staff may need outside expertise in terms of standards for compensation and benefits, and the local regulations governing those compensation and benefits.

In similar cases, human resources staff may be much more extensively involved at a much earlier stage in an acquisition. These are situations in which the human capital of the Target company is a more important and essential part of the acquisition strategy. In these situations, retaining the employees of the Target is of paramount importance, since without them a significant portion of value of the Target company disappears. Law firms and other private partnerships are an excellent case in point. While a law firm does have a brand name and does have some hard assets such as desks, chairs, computers, books, and potentially real estate, the vast majority of the value of a law firm is found in its employees and the relationships and reputations that they have individually built. If a Buyer acquires a law firm but loses all or even significant portion of its employees, it has basically paid a massive premium for a lot of office equipment and business cards. In situations like this, human resources staff are essential. In the due diligence process, they will try to ensure that the staff can be retained on reasonable terms, and, in the integration process, they will ensure that this happens.

Real Estate

Like human resources, the real estate staff is usually brought in less to assess the value of business, and more to ensure there is nothing rotten in Denmark. Real estate staff usually play a relatively small role in an acquisition, largely ensuring that real estate valuations are not entirely out of whack, and beginning the integration planning for how to deal with the additional locations and, potentially, how to consolidate them. Again, the notable exception is a company where real estate represents a significant portion of the value of the business. Here, the real estate staff will be much more heavily involved. Most large Buyers have internal expertise in real estate that is sufficient for a deal. In some cases, outside consultants with this expertise will be brought in. The notable example is the crossover between real estate and regulatory compliance work—environmental issues. This is the one area of real estate where an outside consultant is almost always brought in, if owned real estate is part of the deal.

Regulatory and Compliance

The involvement of regulatory and compliance staff will vary dramatically from deal to deal. It will depend on how heavily regulated the Target's business is, and how familiar the Buyer is with those regulations. At the extreme, the Buyer is acquiring a Target in a new industry that is very heavily regulated. It will likely combine the team of its in-house lawyers with outside regulatory and compliance experts, who can help them understand not only what they are getting into but also how they are going to have to deal with it. Regulatory experts are usually lawyers who have a deep understanding of the regulatory structure and the regulators "in play" for a particular company. An example would be banking lawyers who understand both the banking regulations and the various regulatory entities, including the Office of Thrift Supervision. Such lawyers deal with these regulators on a regular basis to ensure their clients are in compliance. Compliance experts may be lawyers, or in some cases nonlawyers, who have a deep understanding of how to actually comply with the regulations. This will include not only an understanding of the regulations but, more importantly, an understanding of the compliance procedures, policies, and records that need to be maintained.

Public Relations

Any large Buyer will usually have at least one public relations staff member whom it can involve in transactions. Public relations staff are usually brought in near the very end of the deal, largely to manage the eventual press coverage and public reaction to a transaction. The notable exception here is transactions that are likely to cause significant controversy or require significant public relations work. In those cases, Corporate Development staff should bring public relations staff in early, not only to plan for such eventuality but also to consider whether such issues should be deal breakers.

An excellent example here is the online payments industry in the mid-1990s. On the surface, this industry was a growing and attractive sector of high technology, whereby companies provided a method for online retailers to take credit card charges from their customers. A large number of small players emerged in this space, and, by the late 1990s, were growing rapidly and were mostly highly profitable. However, most of them remained private, even during a flurry of acquisition activity in the sector. One reason, though by no means the only one, for this is public relations. A close look at these businesses reveals that, even by the late 1990s, the vast majority of revenue for these companies came from processing payments made for two large online industries: pornography and gambling. Most large financial institutions would shy away from acquiring even a highly profitable business like this, for fear of the public relations impact. Many people call this "the *Wall Street Journal* test." They ask themselves, "How would we feel if this deal appeared on the front page of the *Wall Street Journal*?" For a company like Citibank, even the risk of a front-page *Wall Street Journal* article discussing Citibank's involvement, even tangentially, in the pornography and gambling industries would be too great a risk to justify even an attractive small acquisition.

Companies will often use outside public relations firms, either in place of, or to supplement, internal public relations staff. In particular, when the company is seeking not only to predict media reaction but also to actively manage it, it will use an outside public relations firm. While most of a deal process is shrouded in secrecy, public relations staff are still brought into a process early, to provide an assessment of the likely public relations impact, and plan accordingly. In some rare cases, the analysis of likely public relations impact can actually derail a deal. Thus, getting an initial read of public relations issues is a good idea.

Line Functions

Key members from various line functions will be essential to effective due diligence and integration planning. Line functions provide crucial specialty expertise in a variety of areas. They are essential to developing a detailed and accurate understanding of the business being acquired. There are two key areas of challenge in using line function staff in a Strategic Transaction. First, line staff need to be chosen and utilized well to focus on the specific issues and problems of a particular acquisition. Which staff are needed and how they are used will vary from deal to deal. Second, Buyers also need to be cognizant of the political and human resources issues inherent in using line staff in an acquisition.

Corporate staff, and particularly the Corporate Development team, can maintain a certain amount of distance from the results of a Strategic Transaction. On a personal level, they are unlikely to be directly impacted, and on a professional level, simply completing a deal usually translates into success for them. By contrast, a Strategic Transaction can have long-term and significant impact on the careers of line staff. It is important to understand how line staff will be impacted by a deal and how they perceive it, when managing and during a Strategic Transaction. The first and most obvious impact is redundancy. In many cases, an acquisition brings on staff who are duplicative with the Buyer's existing team. While it is more common for the Seller's staff to be laid off, sometimes the Buyer's staff can be impacted as well. If a company acquires a Target with a particularly strong marketing and sales team, it is possible that it will be the Buyer's marketing and sales staff who are laid off, in resulting integration. Even if line staff do not lose their jobs as a result of an acquisition, the deal could impact their jobs going forward. An acquisition can signal a shift and focus away from the business on which they work, into a new direction. An acquisition can also signal a shift in resources away from what they do. Like a second child, an acquired business can often leave the staff of the "older sibling" jealous and frustrated. Line staff also have to deal with the challenges of integration, while corporate staff are usually allowed to partially or totally distance themselves from these challenges. Where a Corporate Development leader may see an opportunity to acquire great new technology, a line manager or engineering manager may see a huge headache of integrating the new technology with the existing operations. This latter issue is often exacerbated by the fact that corporate staff will sometimes, if not often, minimize the challenges of integration.

The key to managing this range of political issues is to understand in advance the likely impact of an acquisition on line staff. In some cases, this impact cannot be avoided. Certainly, integration can have its challenges, and an acquisition often results in staff redundancy and layoffs. However, by understanding the likely issues, a Buyer can at least help to moderate them. First, it can alleviate concerns that are not realistic. In many cases, line staff are not privy to the detailed plans of senior management. It may often make sense to share at least some of those plans, to alleviate unfounded fears. If senior management has decided that no layoffs are planned, it may make sense to tell at least the line staff involved in the deal that this is the case. Even when it is not possible to alleviate the fears, understanding what they are and managing them may be possible. If a Buyer recognizes particular issues of concern for line staff, it can try to manage around them

For example, if a Buyer is worried that line staff are likely to be overly negative on the product of the Target, because they fear the impact it would have on their own product line, the company can take that into account when assessing their views. More concretely, if the company suspects a bias in their analysis, it can demand a more concrete and quantitative approach, to try to weed out that bias. For example, instead of asking for a general evaluation of "how good the technology is," the Buyer can ask for a detailed comparison of quantitative metrics between the Target's technology and the company's technology—speed, accuracy, and other such measurable variables. In some cases, such concerns may lead the Buyer to make use of outside advisors and consultants, to confirm or even replace the work of line staff.

The second challenge in using line staff for due diligence is to identify clearly what resources and expertise are needed, and then to leverage them effectively. As will be discussed shortly, depending on the nature of the Target, the Buyer will be more or less sensitive to different issues. In order to effectively use line staff, a Buyer first needs to identify what the critical issues are. In simplest terms, the Buyer needs to identify what it really values in an acquisition, and then make sure to have sufficient staff with the right skills to assess whether it really is getting what it thinks it is in the deal. The first step in assembling an effective due diligence team is for the Buyer to identify what it really wants to know about the Target's business. This will in turn drive the resources that it needs from the line, to assess the Target effectively. The Buyer then needs to work with line management to get those resources allocated. This is, itself, a challenge. Unlike Corporate Development staff, for whom deals are the primary function of their job, for line staff, deals are usually a distraction. Lack of familiarity aside, line staff are rarely compensated financially or promoted for their role on acquisitions. That is why Buyers will usually find them hesitant to devote effort and time to a deal, and exceedingly hesitant to put the deal ahead of their regular responsibilities. Line management is the key to overcoming this challenge.

Every deal has different due diligence requirements, and almost any imaginable area of expertise will be required in one deal or another. Not only the nature of the Target but also the nature of the business itself will drive the Buyer's needs when building a due diligence team. Different businesses require different skills to assess and diligence properly. Rather than try to catalog the complete list of different specialists and line functions that may be called on in a deal, this section will discuss some of the most common functions that are needed in a due diligence effort.

Management

Involving line management early is often the key to developing an effective due diligence team. Line management can be thought of as the gatekeepers. Without line management's support, it is difficult, if not impossible, to get line staff to focus on the deal. The reason for this is obvious. When the dust settles, the careers and compensation of line staff are driven by line management. It is rare to find a company where line staff bonuses and promotions are driven by their involvement in due diligence efforts.

This brings up an inherent challenge for the Corporate Development team. As discussed in the previous section, line management incentives with regard to a Strategic Transaction can vary. In some cases, an acquisition can be a tool to help management grow its business dramatically; in others, it can create a rival business or even a larger unit that ends up gobbling its own business up. When line management is supportive of a deal, they will usually be very helpful in providing resources and motivating their staff to assist. However, when line management does not support a deal, they can often create a substantial roadblock to success. Even if line management does not openly oppose a deal, if they are not enthusiastic about it, that hesitation can get communicated to their staff, making it difficult to effectively marshal resources for due diligence. In some cases, a Corporate Development leader may need to get executive management to exert pressure on a line manager, to ensure effective support. In addition to providing resources, line management also provides judgment and business expertise. If the Target operates in a similar or related business area, the line manager may have the single greatest level of expertise in the company on how to assess that business. As with staff in general, it is important to keep in mind the biases of line management. It is not uncommon to see line managers who do not support a deal damning it with faint praise or being overly negative about it. Given their position of authority and expertise, this is a particularly dangerous and insidious bias. One challenge of the Corporate Development leader and executive management is to differentiate between the reasons and expert views of line managers, given their inherent bias. This is probably a more common problem on the positive side than on the negative side. It is not unusual to see line managers aggressively lobby for an acquisition that will substantially grow their business. The key with all staff, but particularly with line management, is to try to tie the judgments they make on a deal to the eventual result of the deal. With the rest of the staff, this is usually best done by making those who do due diligence assessments in their particular area also be responsible for the subsequent integration and performance in that area. In the case of line management, there is a more obvious and direct way to tie assessment to results. It is very important to ensure that whatever predictions and projections line managers make about an acquired business are then reflected in their goals and targets going forward. If a line manager asserts that an acquired business can grow at 50% a year, the Buyer needs to be sure that, once the business is acquired, that part of the line manager's business is still held to those same growth targets. This is particularly challenging when the projections for a Target look rosiest from a distance. The further into the distance the performance is projected, the more likely it is that the line manager will have moved on before his or her optimistic "chickens" come home to roost.

Other Line Staff

Once the Buyer has determined the key issues and assets that are driving a deal, it needs to identify the relevant line staff who can perform effective due diligence. Marketing and sales staff are particularly valuable for assessing retail and heavily branded businesses. Product development staff can help the Buyer assess the value of not only the products the company has launched but also those it has in the pipeline. Operations staff can assess not only the challenges of integration but also the efficiency of current operations. This analysis can help the Buyer identify places where increased efficiency after integration will drive additional cost savings. Customer service is another area where staff can help identify not only integration costs and opportunities for efficiency but also issues of compliance. When the Buyer is acquiring a technology company, engineering and development staff will be particularly important in assessing the value of the technology, including such issues as its scalability, security, and flexibility.

In all these areas, line staff will help the Buyer identify several different things. They will assess the value of what is being purchased, including consideration of the "build" alternative. Not only will they assess the value generally but also the value to the Buyer's company in particular. For example, any technology may be very valuable, but, if it does not operate on the same standards and protocols as the Buyer's core technology, it may be far less valuable to the Buyer's company in particular. Line staff will also assess potential pitfalls, including weaknesses in quality, standards, compliance, and operation. For example, marketing staff might identify that, while a brand is very powerful among its target demographic, it has also developed a very negative image in other market segments, thus limiting its expandability. Line staff can also start to consider the costs and challenges of integration in each of their respective areas.

One of the key factors in effective due diligence from line staff is clear direction and deliverables. The Buyer needs to remember that line staff are usually not familiar with the due diligence process. It is important to lay out the goals and purposes of the deal and of the due diligence effort. Line staff need to understand the big picture, at least in general terms. It is then important to lay out very specific deliverables and a clear timeline. Again, line staff are unlikely to have a good feel for the scope of work necessary or for the time in which it needs to be done. Setting expectations with line staff upfront will ensure that they devote the right effort to getting the work done on time and providing the right results. Giving even the smallest or tightest specialties a broad view of the Target will help them frame the issues. All members of a due diligence team should have a general understanding of the overall business of the Target, and a general concept of how it might be integrated into the Buyer's business and operations. Each member of the due diligence team should be given specific goals and specific deliverables. In most cases, it is useful to produce a template of a due diligence report for each major area or specialty. See Appendix B for an example of the table of contents for a due diligence report. It is also important to set out a clear timeline for the process and for each deliverable. Line staff also need to have a clear idea of their sources of data and potential need to travel. This is particularly important, since line staff usually have to maintain their "day jobs" while doing due diligence. They will need fair warning if they are going to be required to fly across the country and spend a week in a due diligence room, reviewing documentation and doing interviews. Finally, it is important to educate line staff on the unique and particular sensitivities of a Strategic Transaction. It is often useful for the Buyer to have its lawyers present some of these issues. Not only are Strategic Transactions subject to legal confidentiality requirements, but they are also sensitive issues even within the Buyer's own organization. Line staff need to be made aware of limits on whom they can discuss the deal with, and what topics they can discuss. Unlike Corporate Development staff and some corporate staff functions that do deals regularly, it is not safe to assume that line staff have a clear understanding of these issues.

Regular communication is also an important tool for managing the due diligence process with line staff. Regular conference calls and meetings will help to monitor the progress of line staff, and quickly identify any misunderstandings or slowdowns in the process. Regular meetings also help line staff to feel more involved in the deal, and give them a sense of ownership. In some cases, the Buyer can also develop this sense of owner-ship by allowing line staff to present the results to line management. Giving line staff visibility with their managers will help drive positive incentives.

WHAT THE BUYER WANTS TO KNOW

As described earlier, every deal is different, and every Target is valuable for different reasons and for different assets. Effective due diligence is not simply a matter of reviewing every bit and piece of a company but rather of identifying what really matters and focusing largely on those issues and assets. While a Buyer may do a cursory review of every issue, it should likely be focusing the vast majority of its efforts on the few issues and top-ics that really drive the value of the acquisition. For example, if Microsoft were to seek to acquire a company with a small technology that it intended to integrate into its Windows platform, it would likely focus almost all its efforts on assessing how that technology was built and how it operates. It would likely focus only a modest amount of effort on the current customer base of the company, and almost no effort on assessing the brand, since this latter piece would likely be thrown away.

Once the Buyer has determined which particular areas drive the value of an acquisition for its business, it needs to delve deeply into these topics and understand them, not only in the context of the Target company but also in the context of an integration with its own company. In many cases, there are particularly common pitfalls that need to be avoided. In this section, some of the most common areas or issues that focus atten-tion during a Strategic Transaction are discussed. Keep in mind that this is not an exhaustive list, and that in each deal a Business needs to do a fresh assessment of where focus should lie.

Business Issues

Almost any Target company will have a fairly complex set of core business and operational assets and processes. From the manufacture and product development to marketing and sales, these are the heart of what makes the company tick. In most cases, understanding these areas will be the key to understanding how the company works, why it is successful, and how well it can be integrated into and add value to the Buyer's business.

Operations

To understand how a business makes money, a Buyer first needs to under-stand how it executes on its product or service. Operations are a "behind the scenes" part of the business that is often ignored or given short shrift during a due diligence process. In some businesses, operations are a key part of the value proposition. For example, operations are the core to the Federal Express value proposition, enabling it to deliver packages so quickly. For a services business like Federal Express, it is hard to separate the product from operations. Even for businesses where product can be separated more discreetly from operations, how a company operates can be key to its profitability and success. The Buyer needs to understand operations in order to understand how a company is able to deliver a product or service in profitable ways and how/whether the model is expandable.

Understanding operations is also key in determining whether the business can be integrated into the Buyer's business, and how this will need to be done. In many cases, a stand-alone business may be highly successful, but it may be very difficult, due to the nature and design of its operations, to replicate that success after it is integrated into a parent business. For example, consider a designer manufacturer of very high-end men's fashions. Assuming that the suits are handmade and hand-tailored, then, while the business may be highly profitable at low volumes and high prices, it would be very difficult to expand down-market into higher-volume and lower-priced lines, without dramatically changing the nature of the operations. Another good example is the airline industry, where some carriers operate a hub-and-spoke model utilizing a few large hub airports, while other carriers operate more of a point-to-point model with fewer stopovers through hubs. Integrating a carrier with one model into a carrier with the other model could be difficult.

It is also important to understand that the standards and procedures used in operations may vary between Target and Buyer. If the two companies have similar operational platforms that will be integrated, the integrated business will need to conform to a single set of standards, and this can be a costly and challenging endeavor. In many cases, smaller companies are able to operate at lower levels of compliance and lower standards of quality or accuracy. One major cost of integration can be the need to upgrade those operations to match the standards of the Buyer.

Understanding operations can also give the Buyer the right insights into the business of the Target. A company's operations are usually constructed around its priorities and strategies. Examining a Target's operational structure can help the Buyer to understand whether the company is focused on product integration, customer service, low cost, high efficiency, or a combination of these goals.

Doing due diligence on operations usually requires the Buyer to "get its hands dirty." Unlike some other areas of due diligence, where a review of documentation and files is often sufficient, understanding operations usually requires in-person review. Sending due diligence staff to plants, service centers, and other locations to review operations in person will give the Buyer a substantially better and clearer view of the Target and its operations.

Technology

For some companies, technology is the core of their business, and it is rare that technology does not play a significant role in the success of the company. Technology can also be a huge pitfall during the integration process. Since the details of technology are often hidden, it is important for a Buyer to "get under the skin" of a Target company's technology platform and systems, to make sure it understands not only what the technology does but how it is done and what its inherent limitations are.

In some cases, technology may be the primary or even the only important asset of a company. In those cases, it is essential that the due diligence team do an incredibly detailed and thorough review. However, it is important to remember that even where the technology is the primary goal of the Buyer, other parts of the business may be essential to support that technology. In particular, a technology cannot be separated from the people who built and operate it. Even the most sophisticated engineers or software developers will take time to familiarize themselves with a new technology. Retaining the right talent can often be as important as buying the technology itself, if a Buyer wants to use it effectively.

The first step in doing due diligence on technology is to understand exactly what it does and how it does it. Whether software, hardware, or other engineered systems are at issue, the Buyer must be able to dissect the technology and understand how it works. This exercise usually requires not only a review of the technology and its specifications but also detailed discussions with the Target's staff who operate and built it. More so than other parts of the business, technology is particularly difficult to understand just by looking at it. One of the challenges in due diligence will be getting access to the right staff, since the Seller will be naturally reticent to expose potential Buyers to large numbers of its staff. This is a particular problem in technology-driven companies, where the people who developed the technology are also a valuable asset of the company, and the company may have concerns about those people being hired away. When reviewing the Target company's technology, it is important for the Buyer to consider not only how the technology works but also how it will be used once it has been bought. There are several factors to consider here.

Scalability and growth is an important variable, particularly when the Buyers are planning to leverage the technology across a much larger, new customer base. It is not uncommon to find technologies that work well in small volumes but are not easily scalable. This is a particular concern with small and start-up companies, which may have cut corners in the technology design in order to rush to initial revenue. Compliance and reliability is another important variable to consider. If the Buyer maintains a standard level of quality and security, any acquired technology has got to be brought up to spec on those standards. Security and regulatory compliance is a related and significant issue. In this day and age of concerns about identity theft and personal data, a Buyer needs to carefully assess whether a Target's technology meets its own standards, and be prepared to make adjustments if it does not. Infrastructure reliability is also a big concern. Many smaller companies may not maintain the kind of redundancy and secure infrastructure that would be expected for a large company. Particular examples include redundant locations, access to power backup, dedicated data lines, and secure facilities. As will be discussed shortly, under "Legal Issues," the Buyer also needs to carefully consider the issue of actual ownership of technology. In particular, the Buyer should consider whether the Seller has properly protected its rights to any intellectual property embedded in the technology.

The second key issue with technology is the challenge of integration. Even if a technology is well built and well designed, it can still be difficult to integrate. Technology is built on a variety of platforms, standards, and protocols. In many cases, there is no "right" standard to follow. When a Buyer is acquiring a technology that it plans to integrate into its operations, it needs to consider the full cost of integration. When acquiring a large software platform, for example, a Buyer needs to consider whether the software runs on the same operating system and the same hardware that the Buyer uses for the rest of its infrastructure. If this is not the case, the Buyer will be faced with the challenge of either rewriting the software to comply or maintaining a dual set of operating systems and hardware to run it. Keep in mind that not only will this require the Buyer to purchase additional software, operating systems licenses, and hardware but, far more importantly, to maintain staff with two different sets of expertise. Even the simple matter of integrating two technology platforms that run on the same protocols and standards can still be significant. Transitioning from two different operating centers and two different infrastructures to a single one can be a source of substantial cost savings but also an integration challenge in the short term.

When acquiring technology. a Buyer also needs to consider intellectual property. For technology that is core or essential to a Target business, the Buyer must differentiate between technology that is owned and technology that is simply being licensed. For owned technology, the Buyer needs to be concerned about whether the company has protected its intellectual property rights effectively. For technology that is licensed but is not owned by the Target, the Buyer must establish not only whether the Target has sufficient rights to use it but whether the Buyer will be able to secure a continuation of those rights, after the acquisition.[1]

Employees

For many companies, employees are the single most valuable asset, and there are very few businesses where employees are not an essential ingredient for success. At the same time, employees are one of the hardest parts of a business to assess and diligence properly. Understanding the strengths and weaknesses of an employee base, as well as challenges to retention after a deal is done, is one of the most challenging parts of the due diligence process. A Buyer needs to assess the strengths and weaknesses of the employee base, its ability to retain those employees, fees of integration into its own organization, and the risks associated with failures on any of these fronts.

The first step in doing due diligence on an employee base is to understand the different employee populations in a Target company. The most common differentiation is to separate employees based on function. Employees may also be separated based on division or business unit. The Buyer then needs to try to establish how valuable each of these different groups of employees is to the Seller's business. In some cases, groups of employees may be absolutely essential to the success of the business, while, in other cases, they may be easily replaceable or not particularly critical. For example, at a company like Microsoft, software developers and engineers are likely among the most essential and valuable group of employees. While there is usually no group of employees that is entirely replaceable, at a company like Microsoft, one might argue that marketing and sales staff are less core to the business. By contrast, in a more commoditized business, such as steel manufacturing, operations and plant management staff might be the key to success. Which employees sit at the core of a business's value proposition will vary from company to company.

There is a second step to assessing the value of groups of employees. The Buyer needs to look at how it plans to use the business and operations once they are integrated into its own business. In some cases, a group of employees that is essential to a Seller's independent operation will become much less essential, once the operation is integrated into the Buyer's. For example, if Wal-Mart were to acquire a small department store chain, one might assume that it would replace that independent company's distribution network with its own much larger and more complex distribution network. In this situation, the staff running the small company's distribution network, while essential as part of an independent business, would become largely redundant when integrated into Wal-Mart.

After identifying the most essential groups of employees, the Buyer may try to identify particular individuals who are especially essential. These will tend to be staff with particularly unique expertise that the Buyer does not currently have and that may be difficult to replace. An excellent example would be a team that developed an in-house technology that the Buyer is planning on using. This is expertise that will be hard to duplicate, since this is a proprietary technology. The Buyer can also use information from the Seller to try to identify particular high performers. In some cases, the Buyer may get access to human resources' records, but, in many cases, this information will not be shared. The Buyer may be able to get more informal feedback during the due diligence process on key employees.

Once the Buyer has identified key groups of employees, and in some cases key individuals, it needs to assess the likelihood that it will be able to retain these individuals. It is important to note that, unlike other assets of a company that can be bought and sold, employees can walk out the door at any time. The first step in identifying retention issues is to assess the total compensation package that the employees currently receive, and to compare it to what the Buyer will be able to offer them. To the extent that the Buyer will not be able to offer similar levels of financial compensation and other benefits, there will be a retention risk. Beyond pure compensation, there are other reasons that an employee may not choose to stay with the business. It is important to understand these qualitative factors. Employees in smaller companies, particularly in start-ups, often feel a special affection for, or a loyalty to, the founders. After an acquisition, this loyalty will often disappear, and employees will be much more likely to consider making a move. Smaller companies also have unique cultures that are often hard to replicate in a big-company environment. For some employees, there is a strong allure to being in a more entrepreneurial "start-up" culture. After an acquisition, these employees will often feel stifled and uncomfortable in a large-company operation. Acquisitions often also create large wealth events for employees. If the acquisition itself causes a dramatic change in the employees' financial situation, retention may be a challenge. The recent Google IPO is a case in point. About 1,000 out of the 2,300 Google employees were made instant millionaires by the IPO.[2] This sudden wealth will create a temptation among many of the employees to retire, or at the very least could decrease their level of motivation. One moderating factor is that the initial founders have stayed on in management positions. When the sudden wealth effect is coupled with the removal of founders, as it often is in an acquisition, there can be a powerful dual incentive for employees to leave the company. Finally, employees may also have more direct career motivation to leave, after an acquisition. In many cases, an employee who had a fairly senior role in a smaller company will be relegated to a fairly junior position in the resulting larger company. This effective demotion may make the job far less appealing for many employees.

A Buyer can seek to mitigate all of these retention challenges. From strengthening financial compensation to trying to retain the small-company culture, a Buyer can take many steps to try to retain acquired employees. However, it is unlikely that the Buyer will be able to completely mitigate all these factors. When doing diligence on a potential acquisition, the Buyer needs to assess not only the value of the various employee groups but also the likely losses during the acquisition and integration process. These losses have to factor into the valuation of the business, as well as the core decision to do the acquisition. It is relatively rare that a Buyer will decide not to acquire a Target based purely on potential retention problems, but it does happen in some rare cases. The more central the employee base is to the success of a business, the more crucial the issue of employee retention becomes. For example, if a large consulting firm is considering acquisition of a smaller management consulting firm, employee retention is by far the most important issue. If the Buyer succeeds in acquiring the firm, only to lose the majority of the consultants, it will, in effect, have paid for an empty shell.

A Buyer can attempt to craft an acquisition to ensure retention particularly of key senior employees. The Buyer can require key employees to sign long-term employment agreements with very strict noncompetition clauses. While it is impossible to force people to continue their employment, a Buyer can create significant barriers to alternative employment for them, creating a powerful incentive for them to stay. On the positive side, the Buyer can create powerful financial incentives by either tying the financial gains an employee gets from the deal to continued employment, or creating new long-term financial incentives. However, it is important to remember that, at the end of the day, all employment is "at will," and there are very few measures that can keep employees who decide they want to leave. Thus, one of the key goals of employee due diligence should be to try to establish how likely employees are to be happy in their new roles and with their new company. In some cases, Buyers may want to make direct meetings with those key employees a condition of closing a deal. As will be discussed in Chapter 9, immediate focus on employee integration and retention after the deal is closed can be an essential element in retaining the value for which the Buyer has paid.

Customers

It is hard to find an acquisition where customers are not an important asset. Even if the Buyer is primarily concerned with acquiring technology, products, or other assets, customers and the revenue they generate are always valuable. In some cases, a Target company is at such an early stage that it has few customers and little revenue. In most cases, though, a significant part of the value proposition for buying a company is in the cash flow it already generates, even if the Buyer thinks it can enhance that cash flow substantially by integrating the Target into its own business. During due diligence, it is important for the Buyer to get an understanding of not only the revenue generated by a Target's customers but also the quality of those customer relationships and how easily they can be transferred during integration.

The first step in understanding a customer base is to review the core financial flows from those customers. The Buyer needs to review the revenue generated from customers, not only in the present period but also historically. The goal is to understand how stable those customer relationships are, and which customers are the most important. Data that will be useful in making this assessment includes:

- Dollar, volume, and unit volume for each customer.
- Longevity of each customer relationship—how long has the customer been purchasing?
- Volatility in customer purchases—does the size of the customer's orders vary from week to week and month to month?
- Customer concentration—how concentrated is the revenue in a small number of customers?[3]

This data will help the Buyer to understand how valuable the customer relationships are, and which customer relationships are most valuable. If revenue concentration is high among a small number of customers, the Buyer needs to focus its attention on those key, large customers. The loss of even one large customer can represent a significant loss of revenue to the company, and can often spell the difference between profitability and loss.

Complementing the quantitative analysis of customers will be a qualitative analysis. Through conversations with management and, if allowed, conversations directly with customers, the Buyer needs to assess the quality and strength of the relationship that the Seller has with its customers. The "stickier" the relationship with the customer is, the more valuable that relationship will be, if that stickiness can be retained during integration.

This brings us to the important point that customer relationships cannot be presumed to be easily transferred. Like employees, customers can choose to stay or leave. Once a Buyer has assessed the value of a Target's customer relationships, it needs to consider how easily those relationships will be transferred. Like employees, customers may have qualitative reasons to stay or leave, once the deal is done. For example, customers that like dealing with a small, focused business may not be inclined to continue doing business with the company once it is part of a large conglomerate. By contrast, customers may view the acquisition as a positive, to the extent that it makes the service provider part of a larger and more stable business.

One twist on customer retention that does not exist with employees is the matter of contractual relationships. As will be discussed shortly, in "Legal Issues," customers often have long-term contracts with suppliers. In predicting the level of customer retention that the Buyer will be able to achieve, it needs to review the customer contracts and understand whether the customers will have a legal obligation to stay, once the deal is done, or whether they will be free to take their business elsewhere.

Not all customers are created equal. When reviewing the customer base of the Target, the Buyer needs to consider the inherent value of each large customer, beyond the revenue it provides to the company. Different customers can have different levels of profitability. In some cases, a customer may provide a large amount of revenue but may do so at such low margins that it does not provide a great deal of profit to the company. While the Seller may attribute value to such large customers in helping it to achieve economies of scale, the Buyer may not attribute the same value to that low-margin volume. The Buyer also needs to consider the value of each customer in terms of potential synergies with its other businesses. Once the deal is complete, the Buyer may be able to leverage the acquired customer relationships to sell other products and services. For example, if Amazon.com were to acquire an online music store, it would not only consider the revenue generated by selling music to the customer base but also revenue it might be able to generate by selling books to those same customers.

As is true with employees, quick and effective action must be taken during the early stages of integration, to ensure that customer relationships are maintained and losses are minimized.

For particularly large and valuable customers, the Buyer may consider requiring the Seller to involve the customer in negotiations. The Buyer may demand that the customer approve the transfer of its contract to the Buyer, as part of the deal. Of course, this is only valuable if the contract with the customer is not easily terminable. In cases where a single customer represents a substantial portion of the total revenue of a company, the customer can actually become a material party in the negotiations, and wield a substantial amount of power. This is one of the reasons that getting an early read on customer concentration is an important part of due diligence that can actually affect the deal process.

Partners and Other Key Relationships

In some cases, a Target company will have valuable relationships with partners, suppliers, distributors, and other parties. As with customers, the Buyer needs to consider the value of each of these relationships, not only to the Target company but also in the context of an integrated business. In many cases, if these relationships are "arm's length," they will not have dramatic value, since the Buyer could easily replicate them. Even in these cases, there is a certain value attributable to having developed this network of relationships—having done the legwork. The Buyer can usually take some comfort in the fact that, if the relationships are profitable to partners and other parties, they will be willing to continue them after the deal is done. Nonetheless, the same factors that can cause customers to sour after the deal is completed can also put such other relationships in danger.

In the case of a particularly large and strategic relationship, the Buyer may want to consider making that party part of the deal. While the Seller may be reticent to get such parties involved, if the Buyer is very concerned about losing the relationship, it can demand that the Seller involve the counterparty. The Buyer can demand that the partner reaffirm its willingness to continue doing business, and even execute legal commitments to do so as part of the deal.

Products

The one thing a company is most likely to publicize is its products. In most cases, a company will provide substantial amounts of detail on the nature and features of its products and services to the market. As a result, this is the area where the Buyer is likely to have the most information prior to conducting due diligence. Nonetheless, it is important that the Buyer conduct thorough due diligence on the Seller's product line, particularly where products are a major asset and motivation for the deal.

The Buyer needs to begin by getting a complete picture of the full product line offered by the Seller. For each product and service, the Buyer needs to understand all the features and functionality, as well as the financial terms on which the product and service are offered. In some industries, the financial terms are highly variable, and the Buyer needs to understand not only the "quoted price," but the pricing structure that is actually used with customers.

The Buyer also needs to get a good assessment of the strengths and weaknesses of the products and services in comparison to comparable products and services in the market. In some cases, this information will be provided by the Seller, but, in many cases, the Buyer will need to do substantial market research to get this information, and, in any case, it will want to do enough market research to confirm any information the Seller may give it. Not only does the Buyer need to understand how the Seller's products compare to others in the market but also customer perceptions about those products. This is the area where brand, reputation, and features will blend together. For example, when assessing the Mercedes line of automobiles, a Buyer would want to consider not only the actual reliability statistics of the cars but also consumer impressions and perceptions of reliability.

When delving into the details of a Target's products and services, the Buyer also needs to consider how they will fit into its own product line. The Buyer needs to consider this fit from many angles, including technical integration, manufacturing, brand, customer perception, and economics.

Finance/Accounting Issues

The financial statements of a Target company are at once the clearest and most challenging parts of a due diligence process. At first blush, the neat rows and columns of numbers might seem to be nothing if not unambiguous. However, buried within those numbers can be the doom of a deal. At its core, a business is reflected in its financials. The final and central result of a business enterprise is the net income, revenue, or cash flow it generates, and its balances of assets and liabilities. The financials not only drive the valuation of a business, as will be discussed in Chapter 8 but also are the road map in understanding the nature of the business and its prospects in the future.

Financials and Finance/Accounting Staff

If financial statements were straightforward, clear, and unambiguous, there would be little need for accountants or finance professionals. Sadly, none of those things is true of financial statements. When conducting due diligence, it is essential for a Buyer to have finance and accounting staff involved, to review financial statements for both accuracy and accounting treatment. Since one of the first things usually provided to a Buyer in a transaction is the financial statements, it is important to line up finance and accounting expertise early in the process. In some rare cases, a quick review of the financials can even put an end to the deal.

The first step is to get the detailed financial statements of the company. It is common for a prospective Buyer to request historical financial statements going back at least three years, though the length of time will depend on the nature of the business and on how informative the older historical data will be about the future prospects of the business. In general, for more stable and slow-growing businesses, a longer tail of historical data will be useful. For high-growth or relatively young companies, the older financials may be less useful, or may not even be available. In particular, a Buyer will request a full balance sheet and a detailed P&L.

Eventually, the Buyer will want to get visibility into the details of each line item of the balance sheet and P&L. In most cases, at early stages in the negotiation, the Seller will be hesitant to provide such detail. Details of a P&L and balance sheet are more likely to provide competitive or sensitive information to the Buyer, and so are generally withheld until later in the process. Logistically, it also is usually impractical to provide that level of detail without substantial written or in-person explanation that the Seller will usually want to provide only once due diligence has begun in earnest. As a result, the Buyer's review of financial statements is usually an evolutionary process. The Buyer begins with a high-level set of financials and makes some general assumptions to reach an initial view of the business. As the deal progresses, and the parties enter due diligence, the Buyer will dig deeper into the financials to get a better understanding of the drivers of the numbers, and to confirm or disprove its initial assumptions.

In addition to providing the Buyer with an understanding of the Seller's financial performance and likely future performance, financials also often provide the Buyer with a clearer understanding of the business model and operations of the Seller. For instance, a detailed review of revenue can help the Buyer understand the nature of the Seller's customer base, including pricing, payment rates, and retention levels.

Audits/Audit Letters

One important question when a Buyer is handed financial statements is whether the numbers can be trusted. Whether because the Seller is actively seeking to deceive a potential Buyer or simply because the Seller may have made mistakes in the preparation of the statements, the Buyer cannot take the financials provided at face value. While a Buyer can try to test the validity of financial statements themselves by comparing historical data from different periods and questioning the Seller on underlying assumptions, the single most common way to get comfort with the accuracy of the financials is with the review and opinion of an auditor.

Publicly traded companies are required to have their financial statements audited by an independent accounting firm on regular intervals and those firms have to provide an opinion as to the accuracy of those financials. Most private companies will also choose to have their financials audited either in anticipation of this requirement when they sell the company or go public. They may also need to have financials audited if they are owned by multiple entities or individuals not involved in the day-to-day management of the business.

While scandals and lawsuits over the last few years should make it obvious, it is important to note that audited financials are not a guarantee of the accuracy of the financial statements. Auditors do not review every receipt or count every item in inventory. They still depend on management to provide them with most of the data that they use to construct the financial statements. Their primary focus is on ensuring that the raw data is reflected in financial statements in accordance with U.S. GAAP. A management team determined to falsify financials can often do so despite the best efforts of an auditor.

Accounting Standards

Outside the United States, it is common to find companies that do not conform their financial statements to U.S. GAAP. Similarly, some small privately owned companies may not have an auditor, and their financial statements may not comply with U.S. GAAP, even if they are U.S. companies. Thus, while an initial review of a company's financials may make it look like an attractive Target, those financials need to be converted to U.S.

GAAP (or whatever accounting standard the Buyer uses), to get a clear picture of how attractive the deal is.

At the end of the day, a Buyer wants to know not only what the financials of the company look like as it reports them to its shareholders but, perhaps more importantly, what those financial statements will look like when they become a part of the Buyer's business and the Buyer's financials. Before even building a pro forma model, as will be discussed in Chapter 8, it is important to adjust the financial statements of a Target to match the financial and accounting policies of the Buyer.

Projections

As will be discussed in Chapter 8, financial projections, rather than historical data, are the real driver to valuation of a deal. Along with historical financials, a Seller will almost always provide a Buyer with financial projections. The Seller recognizes that the true value of its business lies in its future performance, and thus has a powerful incentive to show strong future projections. One of the challenges to a Seller is to justify those projections, and one of the challenges to the Buyer is to validate how realistic those projections are.

During the due diligence process, the Buyer needs to dig deep into the assumptions that drive the financial projections, and try to correlate those assumptions to facts it discovers elsewhere in due diligence that either support or refute the accuracy of the projections. For example, if a Seller is projecting a sharp increase in sales, the Buyer can look to see if the Seller has made changes to its sales strategy, recently signed up marketing partners, introduced new products or features, or taken any other steps that would justify the increase.

Whenever possible, the Buyer will actually want to sit down with the Seller's management and go through the projections in detail. This not only gives the Buyer an opportunity to question the Seller on the justification for the key assumptions in the projections but also serves as a great platform on which to review the Seller's business and long-term strategy. By using the projections as a focal point, the conversation is anchored to specific facts. For example, rather than talking vaguely about new product roll-outs, the Buyer can ask the Seller to tie those plans to specific revenue numbers and dates.

In most cases, the financial projections provided by the Seller will serve as the foundation or starting point for the Buyer's own internal projections or pro forma financials that will justify the deal, as well as serve as the baseline expectations for the performance of the business once acquired (see Chapter 8).

Legal Issues

In some sense, a corporation is simply a complex set of legal relationships, a web of contracts. In that sense, legal due diligence is really the mirror image of the rest of the due diligence process. As a Buyer discovers the nature of a Target business, legal due diligence confirms, with a legal certainty, the impressions a Buyer receives from other parts of the due diligence process. Legal due diligence can also inform the Buyer as to the nature of the business, and often uncover substantial upsides—or, more commonly, downsides—that the Buyer had not yet discovered.

The other side of the coin is that a Buyer will usually step into the shoes of the Seller in all its legal obligations. In the case of a deal structured as an asset sale, a Buyer may be able to pick and choose the legal relationships it takes on, but certainly in a stock deal, the Buyer becomes the Seller for purposes of most, if not all, of the Seller's legal liabilities. Legal due diligence not only identifies the upside in terms of valuable legal rights but also the downside in terms of legal liabilities and obligations that will be taken over.

It bears repeating that it is essential for there to be an active interaction between legal and other due diligence processes. The business team cannot understand the Target without understanding the legal rights and agreements that make it up, and the legal team cannot differentiate between important and unimportant contracts and features thereof without understanding how the business operates and how the Buyer intends to use it. There is a range of different legal agreements and relationships that need to be covered during the course of legal due diligence, and these are reviewed in this section.

It is often impossible for a lawyer to scrutinize every page of every contract a company has, and certainly it would be impossible for a business professional to understand all that material, even if the lawyer could review it. This is why it is essential that the two work together to try to parse down the material to a subset of agreements and legal relationships that are material to the deal, and further trim the work to focus on the terms of those documents that can affect the terms of the deal or the Buyer's interest in doing it.

Contracts/Obligations

A Target will likely have a very large number of contracts with a variety of other parties. Almost every major relationship a company has is likely governed by a contract. These can include relationships with customers, suppliers, partners, vendors, and employees. The Buyer cannot understand these relationships without understanding the terms of the contracts that govern them.

Basic Features of Contracts

The structure and features of contracts can vary dramatically. Contracts can be as short as a page or as long as a book. One of the challenges during a due diligence process is to absorb thousands or tens of thousands of pages of contracts, and quickly identify both the important contracts and the important terms in each. It is always dangerous to make generalizations when talking about legal documents, but this section will try to identify some of the key contract terms that are likely to be particularly relevant during a due diligence process.

To the extent that the Buyer already has similar contracts in its current business, it should compare the terms of its own contracts to those of the Seller. Integrating these two sets of contracts will be part of the challenge of integration. For example, if the Buyer and Seller both offer customers a similar service but at a different price, once the deal is complete, the Buyer will have to rationalize its pricing structure or risk the wrath of customers bound by the higher price. On the positive side, if the Seller has a contract with the same supplier as the Buyer but on worse terms, the Buyer will likely be able to shift, at least over time, its entire supply to the better terms it receives under its own contract.

Nature of the Contract

The first and most important aspect of a contract is the most obvious question: What have the two parties agreed to do? For example, in a supply contract, the core purpose is for one party to supply a product or service to the other, in exchange for payment. In a marketing agreement, the core purpose may be for one party to provide access to its customers to the other party, in exchange for a share of any revenue generated. This is not necessarily a simple aspect to understand, since there can be a lot of nuance. The obligations of each party can be subject to standards and measures of performance, deadlines, and even remedies to failure. There is a huge difference between a contract to deliver 100 pounds of USDA prime beef, preground and packaged in one-pound units, exactly on February 3, and a contract to deliver 100 pounds of beef in bulk, sometime in the winter.

Pricing

Financial terms of a contract can also be complicated. Some contracts lay out pricing very simply, but in other contracts, the economics can be complex. It is important that the Buyer completely understand the financial terms of the contracts into which it is stepping. To the extent that they are particularly attractive, this is a benefit to the deal, although it should cause the Buyer to be more sensitive to the risk of losing the contracts. To the extent that they are on worse terms than the Buyer could get, the Buyer may view this is as a potential synergy that can improve the performance of the business postacquisition, but the Buyer needs to be sensitive to potential barriers to achieving that synergy.

Termination

An acquisition is a major event for the Buyer and Seller but also for the counterparties to all the Seller's contracts. Sometimes the counterparties will view the deal as a positive event, and sometimes as a negative. Similarly, as discussed above, sometimes the Buyer will be eager to inherit a contract, and sometimes will view it as a cost of doing the deal. Almost all contracts have embedded terms governing the termination of the contract and the relationship. Particularly during an acquisition, the Buyer needs to be sensitive to those terms and the likelihood that one or the other party will seek to make use of them to terminate the contract.

Almost all contracts have a specific term: a period of time after which they end. Beyond that, most contracts also have other mechanisms for early termination. Most contracts provide that either party can terminate, if the other breaches its obligations. Some contracts provide that either party can terminate on a particular period of notice. Contracts, particularly small ones, are often silent on what happens when one of the parties is sold. Some contracts specifically address the issue of transferability, either allowing or specifically disallowing the transfer of a contract—this would be the issue if the deal were a sale of assets, rather than of the stock of the Seller. In some cases, contracts have a "change in control" provision that either allows the contract to remain in force when a company is sold or allows for the contract to be terminated—this would be relevant in a stock deal.

The Buyer needs to have a clear understanding of its rights, and the rights of the counterparty, to terminate each of the material contracts it is acquiring as part of the deal. In some cases, this issue can actually affect the value of the overall deal and become a major issue and even a deal breaker. For example, if the Buyer is primarily interested in acquiring the Seller for its long-term customer contracts, if those contracts allow for immediate termination on the event of a change in control, the Buyer has substantial risk that most of the value of the deal will disappear.

Sifting the Chaff from the Wheat

Once the Buyer has established the basic terms of all the material contracts of the Seller, it needs to categorize these contracts. Some contracts will be valuable assets that the Buyer definitely wants to keep, and to which it attributes significant value. The focus here will be on how to best ensure that those contracts are not terminated. This can affect the structure of the deal, as well as the integration plan. Some contracts will be "nice to haves," meaning that the Buyer does not mind keeping them but would not be concerned if they were terminated. Common examples of this category include fairly standard supply contracts that are easily replaceable.

Some contracts the Buyer will actively want to avoid. In the case of an asset deal, the Buyer may be able to avoid taking them entirely, although, if the Seller is selling substantially all of its assets, it may be loath to keep a contract, or even unable to do so, if the contract requires actions using assets that are being sold in the deal. In the case of a stock deal, the Buyer will likely not be able to avoid taking these contracts. This is where the Buyer will turn to the termination language in the contracts and see how it can terminate the contract itself, once it becomes the counterparty in place of the Seller.

Assets

Seller assets can range from simple hard assets, such as desks, chairs, and cars, to real estate, to more ephemeral assets such as intellectual property. In most deals, at least some category of assets is a critical component of the deal. For a software company, the real estate may be of minor concern, but the intellectual property in the software code will be critical. For an oil company, real estate and refining facilities may represent most of the value. In each case, the Buyer needs to understand exactly what assets the Seller owns. For an asset sale, this is particularly critical, since there is less of a legal "catch-all," to include all the assets the company has, than in a stock sale. Once the Buyer has identified all the assets of the Seller, its lawyers need to make some judgments about the nature of the legal rights of the Seller in those assets. Those rights are not always straightforward.

Possession is not, in fact, nine-tenths of the law, and there is a big difference between saying one owns something and actually owning it. Strange as it may seem, a Buyer cannot assume that a Seller actually owns something, just because it tells the Buyer that it does. While an outright lie may be rare, exaggeration, or even a lack of understanding of its own company, can lead a Seller to purport to own things it does not. A Buyer's lawyers need to actually check and establish a Seller's ownership rights for major assets it is selling as part of a deal.

Ownership is often not a black-and-white issue. In many cases, multiple parties can have a claim to an asset. The Seller may have legal title to the asset, but it may still be encumbered by others who also have a claim to it. Any large or material assets may be subject to a mortgage or lien, in which another party has a right to repossess the asset if the Seller does not make payments, or otherwise uphold its obligations under an agreement. Like a house that comes with a large mortgage, an encumbered asset can be worth dramatically less. In many deals, the Buyer will make the removal of these kinds of liens a condition to closing, or structure the deal so a part of the purchase price goes directly to paying them off.

On rare occasions, there can also be other legal limitations on an asset that affect its value. Even if the Seller has full and clear title to the asset, it can have contracted, or have had imposed, limits on its fair use. Real estate is a good example. In major cities, a landowner can often sell her "air rights" to another party. In that situation, she has given away the right to build above a certain height on her property. This is often done so the other party can secure and ensure the views from its property. Clearly, a Buyer of a piece of land would want to be aware of such an agreement, since it can dramatically affect what it can do with the property.

Even where a Seller owns an asset free of any encumbrances or limits on use, the Buyer needs to assess the quality of the underlying asset. In many cases, this is not a legal exercise, but sometimes legal documentation can give the Buyer a clue as to the state of an asset.

Liabilities

The last section touched on the issue of negative contracts—those that bring costs rather than benefits to the Buyer. Why would any Buyer take on these obligations or liabilities? The answer is that, in some cases, they are a necessary component of the business that is being bought, and, in other cases, the Seller simply insists that they be part of the deal. An example of the former case would be warranty obligations on products already sold. It is hard to sever this obligation from the ongoing operation of the business, since that is where the capability to repair and refurbish products is. The Buyer also has an interest in keeping that customer relationship—potentially for sale of new products, upgrades, and accessories. Even if the Buyer does not want these obligations, a Seller probably does not want to keep them. As with contracts and assets, the key for a Buyer during due diligence is to get a clear and accurate view of the liabilities embedded in the Seller's business.

As with assets and contracts in general, the first step with liabilities is to get a handle on the nature of the obligation—what has been promised by whom. Liabilities can include obligations under contracts; financial obligations; and even potential but not certain obligations to pay.

Obligations under contracts are usually easy to analyze, and are the most likely to have an upside for the Buyer. Since they are usually integral to the operation of the business, while they are technically liabilities, they usually bring some benefit as well. A good example of a contract liability would be the obligation to service products already sold, or accounts payable to a supplier for products already delivered.

Financial liabilities are usually less tied to the business, and a Buyer is likely less eager to take these on. However, since they are usually easy to quantify, financial liabilities are fairly easy to value and reflect in the purchase price. A good example of a financial liability would be a bank line of credit that has been drawn down, or bonds that have been issued to investors.

Potential or uncertain liabilities are the most challenging for a Buyer. These are usually situations where the Seller may or may not have an obligation in the future, and the auditors have been forced to make a reasonable estimate of the potential exposure and book it. A good example here would be a lawsuit that has been filed and is being fought in court. This is a problem for the Buyer for several reasons. First, the uncertainty around the actual level of obligation creates an exposure to potential additional costs that the Buyer cannot factor into the purchase price. Effectively, the Buyer could discover, after the fact, that the deal cost it more than it expected. Second, these liabilities often also entail additional costs (such as attorneys' fees) and can be messy. The mess can include bad public relations impacts, conflict with counterparties, and distractions to management. Unfortunately, such liabilities are hard to sever from the core business, and usually travel with it. Avoiding these is one of the strongest motivators for doing an asset deal and trying to leave these uncertain obligations behind with the Seller.

As with other contracts, the Buyer also needs to consider the impact of the deal itself on these obligations. The sale of the business, either in an asset or stock sale, can trigger changes in these obligations that need to be factored in. For example, a sale of the business could trigger an acceleration of payments under the terms of a debt instrument, forcing the

Seller—or the Buyer, if it acquires the obligation—to make immediate payment of the full amount.

Ownership and Organization

As discussed in Chapter 2, a corporation is not a person but rather a set of legal relationships between investors and the people it hires to run the business. During due diligence, the lawyers representing the Buyer will review the ownership structure of the Seller and ensure, as with the assets, that the Buyer is getting what it thinks it is. Many of the documents that are executed as part of a sale are designed to ensure that the executives of the Seller completing the transaction have full authority to do so, and that they indeed act on behalf of the shareholders. Usually, this exercise is relatively invisible to the nonlawyers on a deal. However, in some cases, ownership structure and organization raise issues that merit involvement from business leaders in a deal.

Any time a company is owned by a number of shareholders—which is true for almost all companies—there is the potential for conflict between shareholders, particularly over something as important as the sale of the business. Buyers want to try to avoid getting embroiled in these conflicts, and certainly want to ensure that, when they reach a closing date, they are able to buy 100% of a company, and not a fraction less. Understanding who actually owns the Seller, and any dynamics between the owners, can be important to a Buyer. In particular, in situations where it is not clear that all the shareholders are supportive of a deal, the Buyer will want to understand any special rights that Seller shareholders may have.

To the extent that a Buyer is not buying 100% of a company, it will need to be well aware of who the other shareholders are. In a very real sense, the Buyer will be entering into a long-term relationship with its fellow shareholders. The Buyer needs to understand with whom it is getting into bed. For example, a Buyer of a minority stake in a company might want to be sure that none of the other stakes is being held by criminals, or, on a less melodramatic note, by direct competitors.

Similarly, to the extent the Buyer is paying with its own stock, it will want to have a clear understanding of who is receiving that stock, since, going forward, it will also have a relationship with these people. In particular, in a deal where the Seller shareholders are receiving a significant percent of the Buyer's stock, the Buyer will want to consider the effect of having these parties as major shareholders.

The Buyer will also want to understand whether any of the Seller's employees have significant stakes in the Seller. As discussed in this chapter, under "Employees," to the extent that the Buyer wants to retain these employees, the fact that they may be made suddenly and dramatically wealthy can have an effect on the Buyer's ability to retain them.

Intellectual Property

Intellectual property is one of the areas of due diligence where lawyers can make a huge difference. By definition, intellectual property is a legal right, and usually a fairly complex one, with inherent limitations and tight definitions. Since it can also be a source of huge value, it is particularly important that lawyers do a thorough review of any intellectual property that has substantial value to the business.

Broadly speaking, there are several large areas of intellectual property. Copyrights generally cover written materials, patents cover inventions and ideas, and trademarks cover brands and names. This is a dramatic oversimplification of the field of intellectual property.[4] For example, books, articles, and manuals all might be copyrighted; a software program or a piece of technology, such as an engine design, might be patented; a brand name like Nike™ would be trademarked, as would product names such as Doritos™ or Corvette™. There are some other assets that have an inherent intellectual property component, including domain names and toll-free (1-800) numbers. While these are assets based in a contract with the providers, they can be imbued with branding value beyond the value of the contract. For example, while it probably costs Amazon.com less than $30 per year to register the domain name *www.amazon.com,* it clearly has dramatically more value to the company, and it would not sell the right to that domain name for tens of millions of dollars.

The challenge with intellectual property is that the ownership right is based on a combination of use and legal documentation. Again, see more substantive texts to explore this interplay, but, in broad terms, a company's right to intellectual property is secured not only by filing a patent, trademark, or copyright but also by being the first to use it and, in some cases, by continuing to use it. Thus, it is important to have a lawyer specializing in intellectual property review not only the legal filings made but also the actual use of the property. Intellectual property gets even more complicated when one travels across national borders. Different countries and regions have different legal standards for intellectual property, and the fact that a trademark or patent has been filed in the United States does not necessarily provide protection in other countries. In the increasingly global market, it is important to consider intellectual property rights not only in one's home country but around the world.

In some cases, the intellectual property of the Seller may be a very valuable asset to the Buyer. For example, when Unilever bought Ben & Jerry's, no doubt a significant value was attributed to that name and trademark. Even when the Buyer does not plan to use the Seller's intellectual property in the long term, if the transition to the Buyer's brand or technology platform will not be instantaneous—as it rarely is—the Buyer needs to be able to make interim use of that intellectual property, to continue to operate the business. Whether this means acquiring the intellectual property or simply a license to use it for a period of time may be a matter of negotiation, and may depend on whether the Seller has any use for it apart from the business.

Other Audits

Depending on the nature of the Seller's business, there is a variety of other legal reviews and audits that may be merited. As a general matter, any area of the Seller's business that is subject to regulation, potential legal liability, or other legal obligation, requires some level of review by lawyers. Two of the most common areas are environmental issues and human resources.

Environmental

Environmental damage is an interesting liability, since it not only travels with the person or entity that committed the act but also with the real estate where it resides. When a company that owns real estate is acquired, the Buyer puts itself on the hook for environmental damage that emanates from the property, even if the pollution predates its involvement with the company. As a result, in any deal involving real estate assets, some level of environmental review is merited. In situations where there is some higher potential or concern about environmental damage, a fairly extensive review by an outside expert consultant, involving on-site visits and soil samples, is often necessary. These audits are designed not only to identify potential environmental liabilities but also to try to predict a cost associated with them. The Buyer may still go ahead with the deal, but it will be able to factor these potential costs into the purchase price.

Human Resources

When a business is acquired, the Buyer sometimes takes on, legally or at least by implication and expectation, the employee benefits and standards of the Seller. Even if the Buyer does not take on these obligations, and even if this is made clear to the Seller's employees, the Buyer still needs to understand these obligations well, since any decrease in these benefits or rights may trigger discontent and departure by Seller employees, after the deal is done.

The key areas to investigate include compensation, pension and other retirement plans, healthcare and other insurance plans, vacation, and severance. In many cases, there may be a two-tiered system, whereby some benefits are set out in detail and are an effective obligation of the company, while others are not a legal obligation but just a general policy that the company can change at will. Some employees, particularly at the executive level, may also have individual contracts with the company that create obligations around compensation and severance.

Regulatory Issues

Buying a business means buying into whatever regulatory regimes govern it. This is an important point that should not be lost on the Buyer, since it can have an impact above the level of the particular business, on the entire company. In a sense, once one operates within a regulator's purview, one's entire company is of potential interest and attention to the regulator. As part of due diligence, the Buyer needs to identify if and how the Seller is regulated, and also understand and get comfortable with the compliance obligations that are implied by that regulation, and how the Seller is complying.

Who Regulates the Seller?

In most cases, the Seller will be able to provide complete information on how it is regulated; however, the lawyers for the Buyer will likely double-check to make sure this is a complete view. Once the Buyer has identified all the regulators and regulatory regimes involved, it will need to take a crash course on them, to the extent they are not already familiar. In many cases, the Buyer will be in a similar industry and will already be familiar with the regulators. In some cases, particularly with a Buyer entering a new line of business by means of an acquisition, the regulators and requirements may be new to it. This is where lawyers' guidance can be essential in informing the Buyer of the requirements and costs associated with this new regulator. The Buyer needs to consider geographic region carefully, since the Seller can be regulated at the state, local, and federal level, as well as outside the United States.

Compliance

Once the Buyer has identified all the regulators that govern the Seller's business, it needs to get a good understanding of what is required to comply with all those regulations, and of how good a job the Seller is doing. Compliance can be an expensive exercise, and failure to comply can be even more expensive, in terms of fines, other regulator punishment, and bad press.

In recent years, there has been a huge increase in focus on the security of data, in particular customer data. For some businesses, the procedures and systems in place to control confidential data are regulated by various parts of the government and various laws. For such businesses, failure to have effective or compliant systems in place can create huge liabilities for a Buyer. In particular, when a large company is buying a small company, the increased scrutiny applied to a large company can make flaws that were ignored in a small company translate into huge and costly violations for the Buyer.

Finally, the Buyer also needs to consider how these regulatory regimes might impact the rest of its business, or how the acquisition might be viewed by the regulators. For example, if the Buyer is a foreign company, is it even allowed to own the Seller, and if so, will the regulator impose restrictions on its actions that might impinge on its other businesses and operations?

NOTES

1. This is also a potential source of synergies. In many cases, a Buyer will already have a license for a particular technology which will be sufficient to allow it to cancel the redundant license owned by the target and drive some incremental savings.
2. Bill Condie, "Party Time as Google Floats at Last," *Evening Standard* (August 20, 2004).
3. In many industries the rule of thumb is the "80-20 Rule." The assumption here is that 80% of the revenue is usually derived from 20% of the customers.
4. For a much more broad and complete discussion of intellectual property, see Donald Chisum and Michael A. Jacobs, *Understanding Intellectual Property Law* (New York: Matthew Bender, 2004).

CHAPTER 8

Valuation

The three most important things in real estate are location, location, and location. The same is true for Strategic Transactions: valuation, valuation, and valuation. While price may not be as complex a topic as integration planning, nor as sexy as strategic fit and vision, it is almost always the key driver of a deal. Too high a price, and even the best deal will end up costing money. Too low a price, and perhaps the Buyer is not getting what it thought it was. For the Seller, this is the culmination of all its work, the final assessment of its efforts, and the last and final payoff. Ironically, price terms usually make up a tiny fraction of the huge volume of legal documentation on a deal, and, in press reports of a deal, price is dwarfed by descriptions of strategies and synergies and plans. Like the trigger of a gun, or the cork of a bottle, price is the small but critical point through which all deals must flow. In a 100-page acquisition agreement, perhaps as little as one line of text will be devoted to price, but the work and analysis that go into that line are huge. At the end of the day, price is usually very simple and concrete: "$100 million for all the stock of the company." However, that simplicity masks a huge complexity in determining the price, and often gives the misleading impression that valuation is both easy and accurate. It is a cliché, but valuation, like so many other parts of a deal, is an art rather than a science.

The analysis, discussion, and negotiation that go into the valuation in an acquisition are usually highly confidential, but ample evidence can be found of the uncertainty of valuation exercises in the IPO process. When a company goes public, it usually attempts to price the securities to give the initial Buyers of the securities a first-day "bump." This rewards those initial Buyers, and allows the issuing company to be picky about who gets allocations, usually favoring the kind of investors that are likely to be long-term holders of the securities and thus reduce likely volatility in the stock price. However, any "bump" in price in the first day of trading effectively represents lost value to the issuing company—that is, they could have priced the shares higher. Thus, in pricing an IPO, the issuer will try to allow for a modest but not huge bump in the first day of trading. If the valuation of a company were an exact science, issuers could price their IPOs to provide a very specific bump, perhaps 5 or 10%. In point of fact, first-day trading in IPOs varies dramatically, and in some cases yields a huge bump of 20, 30, even 100%, whereas, in other cases, it actually yields a loss. On average, IPOs gain 15% in their first day of trading.[1] While some of this is an intentional effort by the issuer to reward Buyers in the IPO, the size of the average gain, as well as the volatility, suggests a lot of uncertainty in valuing a company, even one large enough to be going public.

In an acquisition, the effort is even more difficult. Often, the Target is a nonpublic company that may have less-detailed financial records and a shorter history of performance. In addition, the valuation of an acquisition has to consider not only the value of the business on its own but also the incremental value created through the acquisition, usually known as synergies. This is the exercise of adding one and one and getting three.

STANDARD VALUATION METHODS

While valuation may not be an exact science, there is a variety of tools that can be used to try to at least approximate a mathematical value. And by combining several methods, it may be possible to eliminate some of the uncertainty and get at least within "spitting distance" of the right value. Each of these tools has strengths and weaknesses, and each is more or less applicable to different companies. One of the arts of Strategic Transactions is knowing when and how to apply each.

Trading Comps

The public markets are a powerful surrogate for valuation exercises. Public companies are required to provide investors with a huge amount of information on their operations and financial performance. Entire areas of securities law are devoted to setting out in detail the amount, quality, and frequency of information that a public company must provide. The paramount concern of protecting small individual investors is addressed first and foremost through disclosure. While the SEC tries to ensure directly that investors are not cheated, it must draw the line at making investing decisions, and leave that to the individual investor. However, it can help the investor best by ensuring that he or she is provided with full and complete information on which to base investment choices. Thus, a public company's financials are supposed to be an open book. This information is analyzed in tremendous detail by an army of research analysts, financial journalists, and investors, producing a wealth of material on the performance of individual companies and industry sectors.

Some public companies are so small or obscure that, while they are technically public, they are rarely traded. However, most public companies are actively traded by a large number of investors, and thus, their pricing is a highly accurate representation of their current valuation in the eyes of this multitude of well-informed investors. This is not to say that public market valuations are always accurate. The accuracy of a stock price in the public markets is only as good as the quality of the information on which it is based, and that information, and its effect, can be swayed by a variety of factors. A company's valuation can be pulled up or down by events in its sector, even if it is not directly affected. A finding of accounting fraud in one company can create concern that similar behavior is common across the industry. Valuations can also be affected by false information, notably in the case of just such an accounting fraud. In recent years, the press has been full of stories of companies that manipulated their financial reports and accounting policies to boost their public market valuations, and when these manipulations were discovered, the valuations quickly, and dramatically, adjusted to the true information.[2] Nonetheless, most people would argue that, on average, and over a reasonable period of time, public market valuations tend to reflect the underlying valuations of the companies traded.[3] One common method of valuing both public and private companies is to look at trading comparables. This means comparing a variety of financial variables of the subject company to those of comparable publicly traded companies. Determining which variables to use, and which companies are in fact comparable, is itself a subjective exercise.

The first step is to determine which companies are comparable. Many variables must drive this analysis, and, inevitably, judgment calls must be made. Companies can be comparable based on the products they produce, the customers they sell to, or even where they operate. Recognizing these differences is important and can sway how relevant a company is as a "comp." For example, McDonalds and Smith & Wollensky are both restaurant chains that serve primarily beef. However, they are far from comparable. While McDonalds sells a high volume of very cheap meals, perhaps $3 to $6 per person, Smith & Wollensky serves a low volume of very expensive meals, $50 or more per person. They both serve beef, but their customer demographics, price points, and thus financial models and metrics, are incredibly different. Similarly, a bank in Brazil, where interest rates may reach well above 20%, and a bank in Japan, where interest rates may drop below 1%, may have identical products and even similar customers but totally different financials. When choosing comparable companies, it is important to choose companies that are comparable across a variety of variables that will determine their financial performance and metrics. It is therefore important to have an understanding of the underlying business models and industry trends that drive the companies that are being used as comparables. Since no company will be exactly comparable, it is also necessary to recognize those differences and factor them into the analysis. That is where the use of many financial variables may help to make an adjustment for such differences.

Once a set of comparable companies has been chosen, the Buyer must decide how to compare them to the company it is valuing. It needs to choose the financial metric that it will compare. Companies can be compared based on income statement items such as revenue, earnings before interest, taxes, depreciation, and amortization (EBITDA), or net income, or based on balance sheet items such as earning assets or book equity. In the simplest terms, valuing a business simply means saying that it is worth some multiple of some financial variable, so choosing which variable to use is as critical as choosing the comparables—even more so. Which variable the Buyer uses will depend in part on the nature of the business and business model. Companies that are primarily involved in lending, such as credit card or mortgage companies, may be valued as a premium to the lending assets on their books. High-growth companies, particularly those that are still losing money, may have to be valued on revenues, since net income and even EBITDA may be negative numbers.

While different industries use different variables to judge performance, there is rarely a single and exclusive variable. Rather, there are usually two or three different variables that give an accurate image of the relative performance of a company, and there is often interplay between them. Ideally, the combination of two different variables gives an even more accurate picture of the performance of a company. One good example is combining revenue with net income margin. The revenue metric shows strength and growth of sales to customers, while the margin measures the profitability of those sales. A company that is driving high sales growth through heavy discounting will have strong revenue but weak margins. By contrast, a company cutting costs heavily may show weakening revenue but strong margins. Even within a particular industry and set of comparable companies, there may be varying approaches to operation and strategy. Looking at multiple metrics will give the Buyer a better overall view of the company, and help compensate for different operating models.

There are no hard and fast rules on the choice of relevant variables, and there is a myriad of variations, based on the industry and the state of the market, but there are some general guidelines that may help the reader to understand how to think about this problem. As mentioned, high-growth pre-earnings companies will often be valued based on revenues, and also based on the growth rate of those revenues. The underlying assumption here is that the business model, once the company reaches a "steady state," is viable. The analysis assumes that the company will reach a point where it has a sustainable margin of profit, and it thus values the company based on how close it has come to that turning point and how fast it is approaching it. By contrast, a slow-growing, stable company is much more likely to be valued based on net income or EBITDA, a surrogate for cash flow. Each industry has its own quirks, which may be reflected in its financial reporting and thus in the choice of metric. For instance, in truck leasing and other transport sectors, companies often have the choice to finance vehicles with either a loan or a lease. Some companies will have a high interest expense, and others will have a high rent expense for lease payments. The choice between these two structures is a matter of legal liability and financial engineering, but often it has no impact on the financial performance of the company. As a result, in this industry, the relevant metric is earnings before interest, taxes, depreciation, amortization, and rents (EBITDAR), where both interest and rent are subtracted to get real effective cash flow. For example, consider two different trucking companies, one of which leases its fleet on long-term leases from a bank, while the other owns its fleet and pays interest on the debt. In theory, if the lease period of the first company equals the usable life of the trucks, then the lease looks exactly like a purchase with financing. The only difference is a technical one—whether the trucks are on the books of the bank or the trucking company. The cash flows will look identical. If an EBITDA multiple is used, the company that leases its trucks will look much worse, because rents are not subtracted from EBITDA, but interest is. Thus, EBITDAR will be a more accurate way of comparing these two companies, since the "R" and "I" are really interchangeable.

Using trading comparables is also subject to inherent volatility in the markets. Company stock prices fluctuate, not only with their individual performance but also as a result of trends in their industry, their region, their market, and the market as a whole. These changes can cause significant volatility in stock prices, and thus in the valuations they imply. One must distinguish here between long- and short-term trends. Long-term trends, such as a reduction in demand for a product in a certain industry, or an overall market decline in a recession, likely should not be factored out of a valuation. Unless one is willing to delay one's Strategic Transaction by a long period of time, these long-term trends are an accurate reflection of the value of companies in that market. By contrast, short-term trends probably need to be factored out. The fact that the market takes a short-term dip or rise is not relevant to the valuation of a company. One way of addressing this issue is to use an average value for the stock price of comparable companies over a period of time—for instance the average price over the past 30 days. In some cases, this will make little difference in the valuation, but for volatile sectors such as biotechnology—where individual companies, and the sector as a whole, make fairly dramatic daily moves in price—it can help "smooth" a valuation. For example, in the biotechnology sector, even on a day with little market volatility and no new developments on a company, it is not unusual to see a company's stock move up or down by 5 to 10%.

Once one has chosen the right comparables and the right metrics/variables to measure and adjust for other things—such as short-term market fluctuations that can bias the valuation—one will be left with a valuation range for the company. In most cases, there will be a range with some clear outliers and then a set of data in a tighter range. Most people will choose to remove the outliers and then look at averages and medians for the remaining dataset. There is no magic to this technique, other than the recognition that (1) no matter how carefully one selects comparables and variables, there will always be other influences on the dataset that will create aberrant results, and (2) removing the outliers will keep them from substantially biasing the results, pulling the average significantly down or up.

In the last decade, sources of detailed financial data have become plentiful and easy to access via the Internet. Basic financial data on public companies is available from all the large finance sites run by Internet portals such as Yahoo Finance and MSN Money. Even the most basic online brokerage sites, such as those run by Charles Schwab or Fidelity, will have detailed information. In most cases, these brokerage sites will actually provide basic comparables analyses on many companies. Beyond these sources, there are fee-based sites that provide more complex analytics and more complete data sets. The most expensive sites will actually run full comparables analyses, and even access databases on nonpublic deals that have been gathered through a variety of sources. This is one area where the value of an investment bank advisor has eroded. Today, almost anyone with a computer and a bit of time can develop a comparables valuation. The key to the continued value of investment bankers' work is partly the speed of instantly providing this analysis but much more the unique knowledge they have about these comparable companies and comparable transactions, which helps them sort, prioritize, and filter the data into a more accurate and relevant picture.

One final adjustment that needs to be considered with trading comparables is the control premium. Trading comparables represent the value assigned by the market to a small noncontrolling stake, a single share of stock in the company. In Strategic Transactions , the acquirer is either taking total control of the Target through an acquisition, or, at the very least, taking on some level of direct or indirect control through a large minority or even majority stake. This control almost always merits a premium over market valuation. Therefore, when using trading comparables to value a company for a Strategic Transaction, a Buyer needs to add some measure of value for the control premium.[4] While there is no clear rule or measurement of this value, some studies can provide guidance on historical trends. Exhibit 8.1 shows that, in recent years, the average control premium has ranged between 35 and 49%.[5]

However, it is important to note that these averages are strongly affected by sector upswings. For example, the higher control premiums in the late 1990s and 2000 are likely largely attributable to the frothy technology sector prior to the collapse of the bubble. When considering a control premium, one should examine the historical premiums paid in the particular sector, as well as recent market trends. This leads the discussion to the next valuation method, one that does inherently capture the value of the control premium transaction comparables.

Transaction Comps

A variation on the use of trading comparables is looking at transaction comparables. Here, rather than looking at the value assigned by the market to a set of comparable companies, the value assigned by acquirers is examined. The upside to this approach is that it directly mirrors the circumstances of the Buyer's deal. Transaction comparables are the values attached to comparable companies specifically when they are doing Strategic Transactions. They capture not only the generic control premium but also other variables that can affect the valuation of a company. For example, in an industry with a limited number of small players, and strong

EXHIBIT 8.1   Historical Control Premiums

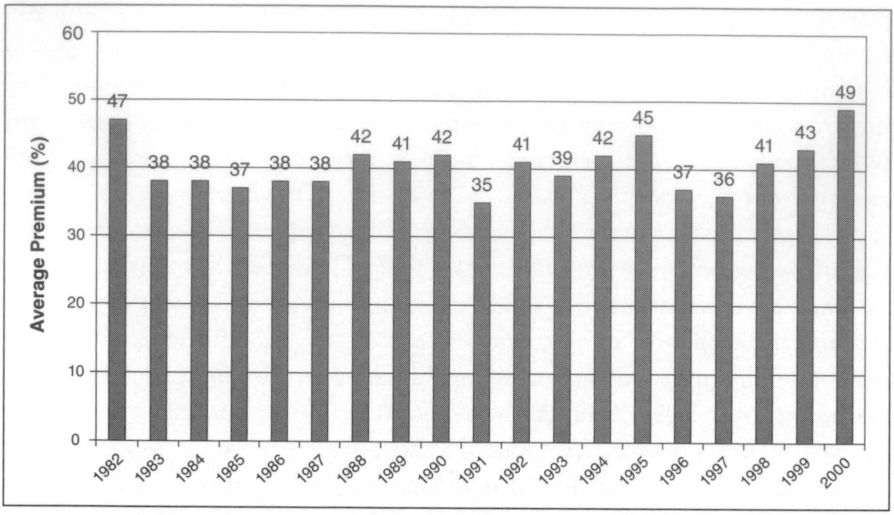

Source: Mergerstat Review 1995 and 2000 *(www.mergerstat.com).*

interest in entering the market by outside players, the premium that Buyers are willing to pay to gain a foothold in the industry can be high. One recent example can be found in the Brazilian banking industry. During the late 1990s, interest rates spiked, and consumer borrowing slowed. In the past few years, the trend has reversed, with interest rates dropping and consumer borrowing rising steeply. This trend—coupled with the introduction of a variety of new consumer finance products and the relatively new targeting of middle-class and lower-middle-class people for credit cards, home loans, auto loans, and other lending products—drove an interest, by both foreign and domestic banks, in acquisitions. These banks were looking either to get a foothold in the market or to buy a broader product range and customer base. The result was a flurry of Strategic Transactions and a sharp increase in the premiums paid for these companies. By late 2003, the number of available acquisition Targets had dwindled, as control premiums paid continued to rise. A combination of market trends making the business more attractive, and a limited number of midsized acquisition Targets, together drove up acquisition prices and multiples. It is likely that during periods of little change and an abundance of potential Targets, transaction comparables may not be substantially higher than trading comparables, but, during other periods, there can be a dramatic difference, as the value attributed to control of a particular type of company goes up well beyond its value as an investment.

The first step to developing transaction comparables is to identify the groups of potential comparable companies. By definition, there is usually a much smaller population of transaction comparables than of trading comparables. While trading comparables sometimes allow a Buyer to use privately held companies as data points, this is only when there is enough publicly available information about their financial performance and the purchase prices paid to develop multiples. In practice, many private company deals do not provide enough information. At the same time, the population of public companies that do Strategic Transactions is fairly small, by comparison to the total universe of publicly traded companies. There are some exceptional industry sectors and time periods, where so many deals are done that there is a rich population of highly relevant comparable transactions. Usually, though, the pickings are a bit slim. Thus, when finding comparable transactions, the Buyer usually needs to throw a wider net, in terms of its definition of a comparable company. The lessons discussed for correctly choosing a comparable company in trading comparables are even more essential where transaction comparables are concerned. Since the Buyer will have to look at a wider range of company types, with variations in product, customer, and business model, it needs to be more careful and analytical about choosing companies that are truly and reasonably comparable. An excellent example is the exercise of valuing an automobile manufacturer. This is an industry where Strategic Transactions are relatively rare. Developing a rich set of trading comparables will require the Buyer to look beyond the small set of directly comparable companies—other automobile manufacturers—to other sectors. One might consider manufacturers of other vehicle types, such as motorcycles or motorboats. One might also choose to look at manufacturers of other high-ticket consumer purchases, such as appliances or home electronics. In each case, it will be important to note, and try to compensate for, the differences. The Buyer may need to adjust implied valuations down, if the comparable company generates higher margins. It also may need to compensate for differences in market cycles; a low period for automakers may not be a particularly low period for refrigerator manufacturers.

Exhibit 8.2 is an example of a trading comps set of federal savings banks. In addition to the standard net income multiple, a return on equity and return on assets have been included, two metrics that are particularly relevant in the banking industry. There is a fair amount of consistency in the numbers, although there are some clear outliers. Here I have chosen to focus on net income and remove the high and low outliers. Every time a Buyer develops a comps list, it needs to make a judgment about what

EXHIBIT 8.2 Trading Comparables Example: Federal Savings Banks

Company Name	Market Cap ($ millions)	Revenue ($ millions)	Net Income ($ millions)	Market Cap/Net Income	Return on Equity (%)	Return on Assets %
ITLA Capital Corp.	$289.9	$ 94.4	$30.5	9.5x	16.18%	1.77%
Beverly Hills Bancorp Inc.	$219.6	$ 26.5	$19.7	11.2x	5.20%	0.61%
NASB Financial Inc.	$327.6	$ 73.1	$25.1	13.1x	19.60%	2.03%
Provident Financial Holdings Inc.	$204.0	$ 55.6	$15.1	13.5x	13.90%	1.17%
United PanAm Financial Corp.	$295.8	$ 78.6	$19.2	15.4x	18.48%	1.27%
First Financial Holdings Inc.	$394.2	$113.9	$25.2	15.6x	15.50%	1.07%
Horizon Financial Corp.	$202.5	$ 39.5	$12.8	15.8x	11.92%	1.51%
Heartland Financial USA Inc.	$299.4	$ 97.6	$18.6	16.1x	12.37%	0.86%
Flushing Financial Corp.	$376.2	$ 70.9	$22.7	16.6x	15.47%	1.17%
Southwest Bancorp Inc.	$268.2	$ 66.4	$16.2	16.6x	14.62%	0.98%
Coastal Financial Corp.	$231.2	$ 47.7	$13.8	16.8x	18.34%	1.14%
United Community Financial Corp.	$366.5	$107.0	$21.4	17.1x	8.23%	1.03%
OceanFirst Financial Corp.	$321.9	$ 74.9	$18.2	17.7x	13.45%	1.00%
Banner Corp.	$328.0	$ 98.9	$17.5	18.8x	8.80%	0.66%
BFC Financial Corp.	$226.7	$693.9	$10.9	20.8x	10.69%	0.18%
First Place Financial Corp.	$299.6	$ 65.8	$14.2	21.2x	6.97%	0.74%

EXHIBIT 8.2 Trading Comparables Example: Federal Savings Banks (*Continued*)

Company Name	Market Cap ($ millions)	Revenue ($ millions)	Net Income ($ millions)	Market Cap/Net Income	Return on Equity (%)	Return on Assets %
Berkshire Hills Bancorp Inc.	$222.5	$ 51.8	$10.3	21.5x	8.84%	0.88%
Center Financial Corp.	$315.6	$ 51.4	$12.6	25.1x	16.41%	1.21%
Sun Bancorp Inc. (NJ)	$380.1	$ 91.4	$14.9	25.5x	8.73%	0.62%
First Indiana Corp.	$315.3	$101.3	$ 9.9	31.8x	4.62%	0.45%
Westfield Financial Inc.	$239.3	$ 25.6	$ 5.8	41.5x	4.77%	0.72%
K-Fed Bancorp	$212.3	$ 15.2	$ 3.2	67.0x	5.09%	0.62%
Clifton Savings Bancorp Inc.	$359.0	$ 15.0	$ 3.6	100.0x	2.62%	0.53%
Average	$291.1	$ 93.7	$15.7	24.7x	11.34%	0.97%
Average without Clifton, K-Fed, Westfield, ITLA, and Beverly	$298.6	$110.0	$16.6	18.8x	12.61%	1.00%

the right metrics are and how to trim outliers to get the most accurate and relevant data.

Data on transaction comparables is also harder to get, and often more opaque. While public financial data sources do a fairly good job of reporting financial data and multiples in a fairly uniform way, the same is not true for the data needed for transaction comparables. Strategic Transactions are usually reported in much less detail, and the Buyer has to be careful to get an accurate assessment of the true purchase price. A purchase price can include many components, including cash, stock, deferred or contingent payments, and assumption of liabilities. All of these variables have to be factored into an accurate assessment of the real purchase price. In some cases, the companies involved will actively try to make these terms vague or unclear. A Seller may want to make the purchase price appear higher, to give shareholders comfort that they received fair value, and a Buyer may want to make the purchase price appear lower, to assure its shareholders that it did not overpay. Keep these machinations in mind, and read the public disclosures carefully and critically. When private company transactions are examined, both sides of the equation can become fuzzy. Not only can the purchase price be obscured but so can the financial variables against which it is measured. Private companies have no obligation to disclose financial performance, and, in most cases, neither do the acquiring companies. The same powerful incentives that can drive Buyers and Sellers to try to obscure the purchase price are in play on the financials of a private company, as well. Inflating the apparent financial performance of the Target allows a Buyer to make the Strategic Transaction look like a better deal. By contrast, reducing the apparent financial performance allows a Buyer to create a "hidden supply" of good financial performance that it can use in future periods. For example, consider a Target that generated $100 million in net income and is growing that net income stream at 20% annually. The Buyer can try to give the market the impression that the Target actually generated $80 million and is growing at 15%. If successful, the Buyer will leave the market, and Wall Street research analysts, assuming that the Target will contribute approximately $92 million to the Buyer's net income line next year, when in reality it will generate $120 million. If the "story" is accepted by the market, the Buyer will end up exceeding Wall Street expectations by $28 million. This kind of expectation management is common with public companies, and Strategic Transactions provide a unique opportunity, since they are large "chunky" financial events, and, when they involve a private company, there is little existing available information. As a result, when using transaction comparables involving a private company, it is important to delve deeply into the historical financials of the Target and be comfortable that they are accurate. One can often look at the financials of the Buyer in the period after the transaction, to assess the real financial performance of the Target but only if they are broken out in the Buyer's financials after the deal is done.

Discounted Cash Flows

The discounted cash flow (DCF) is another common method of valuing a business. This is an especially effective method for valuing more mature companies with stable and predictable cash flows. The basic premise of a DCF is that a company is worth the present value of the cash it will throw off in the foreseeable future, plus some premium for the residual value of the company in the longer term. The DCF thus has two components, the present value of a stream of cash flows plus a terminal value that the business has in the subsequent period. The DCF of a company is the combined value of these two components, keeping in mind that sometimes one component is actually a negative number driving down, rather than up, the value of the company. Each component will be discussed in turn.

The first component is the present value of cash flow generated by the company for a foreseeable period. How long into the future it is reasonable to predict cash flows will depend on the nature of the business and the company. In an extreme case, perhaps for a natural resource company such as a mine or oil well, one may be able to predict cash flows for a very long period of time. This would also be true for a company with a long-term guaranteed contract, perhaps a government-granted monopoly or contract with a highly creditworthy company. For these companies, it may be possible to roughly predict cash flows for perhaps 10 years. However, as a good rule of thumb, it is usually difficult to accurately predict cash flows for more than five years, and this is usually the standard used for a DCF. Once a stream of cash flows has been projected, it needs to be discounted back to produce a net present value of those cash flows. The premise of this exercise is that cash in the future is not worth as much as cash today. There are two reasons for this. First, there is the time value of money. In all but perhaps an exceedingly deflationary economy, money can be put to work to generate a positive return, even with zero risk. Thus, cash flow in the future must be discounted to produce a lower value today, which, if invested at some risk-free rate, would yield the same amount of cash at the same point in the future. However, using a risk-free rate assumes that the money for an acquisition is currently on hand and would otherwise be used to buy some kind of risk-free investment. In point of fact, companies always have alternative uses of capital for things like marketing, sales, research and development, and other avenues of organic growth, and any company can always choose to get more money by borrowing or issuing equity. At any point in time, a company always has access to more capital at some price. This cost of capital is a more reasonable measure of the time value of the money in an acquisition. The cost of capital is usually measured by looking at the cost of debt and the cost of equity, and producing a weighted average cost of capital (WACC). The cost of debt is the borrowing rate of the company, and the cost of equity is the return that will be expected by those making an equity investment in the company. The weighted average of the two is the cost of capital to the company.

Once a WACC is done, one can take the cash flows produced by a company and discount them back to a present value. What this means is that those cash flows are only worth as much money today as would be able to generate a similar rate of return as the WACC. There is a second component that must be considered before finalizing the discount rate, and that is risk. Any projection of future cash flows is an estimate but bears a certain amount of risk. The risk that the business will fall short of achieving those targets must be considered and should be reflected in the discount rate. The greater the risk that the business will miss these cash flow targets, the higher the discount rate should go. In the case of very volatile or unproven businesses, this risk variable will dwarf the WACC component of a discount rate. For example, a company like IBM might consider the acquisition of a tiny technology company. IBM may have a cost of capital of perhaps 5%, but, given the uncertainty around the acquisition and its performance, it may choose to use a discount rate of 25 to 30%. Here, the risk of the performance is the vast majority of the discount. Determining the risk component of a discount rate is an art, rather than a science, but over time various industries have started to develop standards. As the Buyer considers its valuation, it is useful to look to those standards, though it will have to make a case-by-case decision.

The result of this first part of a DCF is a value, or more likely a range of values, based on a range of projections and discount rates, which represents the present value of the first five years of the business. In a sense, this portion represents the value to an acquirer of a business, assuming that at the end of the initial period, the business ceases to exist and has no further value.[6]

This is a good point at which to note the inherent contradiction in the DCF. Many people take great comfort in the hard and fast quantitative nature of this valuation method. Since it is tied directly to the future cash flows of the Target, it feels more specific and accurate. However, this comfort is often an illusion. The key components of a DCF are estimates, rough approximations, and, in some cases, guesses. One theme that pervades the entire discussion of valuation is how uncertain these computations usually are, and this is just as true for a DCF. A DCF is driven by an estimate of financial performance, well into the future, an estimate of the risk of that financial performance, and finally by the terminal value of the business—all rough estimations.

This leads to the second component of a DCF—the terminal value. This is the more hypothetical and uncertain portion of the DCF, since it is driven by a combination of the financial performance of the company five or more years out, and the value of such a business at that distant point in the future. What this means is that, five years in the future, after reaping the benefits of the cash flow of the company, it can be sold or otherwise valued at a certain amount. That "terminal value" of the company is then discounted back and added to the discounted value of the cash flows during the first five years. In a sense, the Buyer is envisioning that, after milking the company for five years of cash flows, it will then sell the company and pocket the then-value. To establish a terminal value, one begins with the financial performance of the company in the last year of the DCF projections, typically year five. One then creates a hypothetical comparables valuation of that company at that time. Since comparables are, by definition, historical or present-time valuation multiples, certain assumptions must be made about the nature of the market in the future. The simplest assumption is to say that the market will value this company the same way, and at the same levels, in the future as it does in the present. If some clear trends for valuations in the industry can be established, the Buyer can try to adjust the comparables, but this is probably hard to do with any accuracy. Once the Buyer has decided on the comparables multiples it will be using, it applies them to the financial performance of the company that it has projected for year five. This gives it the value of the company at that terminal date. That value is then discounted backward to the present and added to the present value of the cash flows, to calculate the total present-day value of the company.

While failing to assign any terminal value to a business would clearly understate its valuation, any DCF that is driven predominantly by the terminal value is highly suspect. As a result, the greater the proportion of a DCF valuation that is driven by the terminal value, the less likely that the accuracy of that valuation will be dependable. In practice, DCF valuations are most useful and accurate when looking at companies with relatively stable and predictable financials, companies that have already achieved a steady state of profitability. The stability of financials allows us to have some confidence in the five-year projections of cash flow, and reaching steady state profitability means that a majority of the value is likely to be found in the cash flows rather than in the more hypothetical terminal value. Companies that generally do not lend themselves to DCF valuations include early-stage and/or high-growth companies, such as technology and biotechnology firms. When these companies are projected out, the present value of the first five years of cash flow usually represents a small, and sometime even negative, portion of total valuation. At this point, the Buyer is left valuing the company largely on the basis of its terminal value. In this case, it is likely to be far more accurate to look to a comparables valuation based on present-day financials. Companies that generally lend themselves well to the DCF will include established profitable manufacturing companies and other companies that have achieved a steady state of operation, likely with more stable and modest growth rates.

In the final analysis, like any other valuation method, the DCF is an inexact science. It is important not to be fooled by the apparent mathematical exactness of this method, just as for the others. Like any valuation method, the DCF only yields an exact result on the back of several very significant and very uncertain assumptions. The key to all these valuation methods is to take them with a grain of salt and use them as a general guide but never a hard and fast rule. This is also why using multiple methods is always helpful, as well as using multiple variables. In most cases, using several methods and basing valuations on several different financial metrics (revenues, EBITDA, net income, etc.) is likely to produce a "grouping" of close valuations, as well as several clear outliers. This richer approach is more likely to create a reasonable approximation of the value of the company.

Return on Equity and Other Internal Metrics

Different industries, and for that matter different companies, have different ways of judging financial performance. It is important to understand these in order to understand how to value a company (as an acquirer) or how one's company is being valued (as a Target). Which methods and metrics a company focuses on will depend on how its industry is judged, and, in some cases, even on its individual philosophy about how to drive its business. Some argue that certain metrics more effectively reflect real underlying and sustainable growth of a business, and thus use them to ensure that management's goals are more accurately aligned with those of shareholders. There is a rich literature devoted to a range of methods of judging financial performance, and so this area will not be covered in detail; however, a few examples will be provided to illustrate these methods and how they can affect valuation. Return on equity (ROE) is a common method of judging financial performance that is particularly valuable for companies and businesses that are able to borrow heavily to finance their operations. Businesses that are able to leverage up (i.e., fund themselves largely or in part through debt) need to differentiate the financial returns to debt (which are capped at the interest rate of the debt) and equity. In effect, when looking at a business that can be leveraged, a company will take the returns on the business, subtract the costs of borrowing, and then take the remaining returns and compare them to the equity investment they had to make. This is a more accurate way of looking at how the business performs. For instance, if a business can be levered at 9:1, this means that the purchase of a $1 billion business can be funded with $900 million in debt and only $100 million in equity. If the interest rate on the debt is assumed to be 10%, then the cost of financing the debt portion will be $90 million/year. If the business returns EBIT (earnings before interest and taxes) of $150 million, it subtracts the $90 million that will have to be paid to service the debt, and $60 million of pretax income is left that is attributable to the equityholders. After taxes, that is perhaps $36 million of net income—a 36% return on the $100 million equity investment. Thus, while the business only returned 10% (if one takes the $150 million and adjusts for taxes) on an unlevered basis (i.e., with no debt), once levered, the business returns more than three times as much to the equityholders. In this situation, ROE shows a much different return than simply looking at net income over total purchase price. Another example would be a company that focuses primarily on pretax income. Consider a company that, through historical losses, has accumulated a huge deferred tax loss. Such a company can offset any future income against those historical losses and not pay taxes. As a result, it will be focused primarily on pretax income, since it will assume that, when added to its business, that pretax income translates directly to net income (this kind of synergy upside will be discussed in "Pro Forma: Finding and Splitting the Upside," below). A similar example can be found with an acquirer that has a very low cost of capital. When acquiring a Target with debt, this acquirer will immediately swap out that debt for its own. Thus, if the Target has a high cost of capital, it will immediately be substituted for the acquirer's much lower cost of capital. In this situation, the acquirer will thus be likely to focus on EBIT and pro forma in its own interest cost and tax rate. An excellent example of this would be a bank that acquired a small technology company. While the technology company might be paying 10% or more on its debt, the cost of borrowing for the bank is likely to be more like 5%, or lower.[7] When considering the value of a company, it is important to consider not only the way the public market values the company but also the way a potential acquirer looks at the value. Appendix F provides an example of how a Buyer or Seller might review all of the different valuation methods just discussed.

Seller's Perspective on Valuation

First, however, consider the Seller's perspective on valuation. In Chapter 5, the process of making a company more "saleable" was discussed. When planning the sale of a business or company, it is important to look beyond standard comparables and DCF valuations to consider the value attributed to the business by specific Buyers, and how to maximize it. Certainly, the standard valuation methods are a starting point, since this is where the Buyers will also start their evaluation. It is key for a Seller to understand how its business will be valued by the market and the Buyer's financial advisors, using these standard tools. It may be possible to manage a business to maximize valuations, by recognizing the metrics that will be used. For example, in a relatively moribund industry sector with a lot of profitability but little growth, a premium may be paid for top-line growth rather than bottom-line margins. When considering a future sale to a Strategic Buyer in that industry sector, a potential Seller might choose to increase spending on research and development, sales, and marketing, even to the detriment of profitability. In some cases, potential Sellers will actually be able to identify specific potential Buyers. In those situations, gathering good intelligence about how these companies judge and evaluate acquisition Targets can help the Seller to craft a business that will garner a higher valuation. One important consideration is how the Buyer itself is valued in the marketplace. Companies will tend to evaluate an acquisition by the impact it will have, in both the long and short term, on its own financials. In simplest terms, whatever metrics drive the Buyers own stock price are likely to be the focus of their valuation of a Target. If a Seller knows that a potential Buyer's stock price is largely valued on revenues, it can maximize its valuation by focusing on driving up that metric in its own financials, perhaps increasing marketing spend or offering financial incentives to customers. Similarly, when considering a Buyer most focused on maintaining margin levels, a focus on cost cutting rather than growth may increase the Seller's effective valuation.

Now, clearly, this is a dangerous game to play. As discussed in Chapter 5, adapting one's business model to suit the needs of a potential Buyer can be damaging, if the net effect is to weaken the fundamentals of one's own business model, because, unless the Seller is successful in building its business, the Buyer will not even materialize, and the efforts to maximize the valuation will be moot. Job one must always be to make the business successful. That said, managing financial performance at the margins, to focus on the metrics that interest a Buyer, is a powerful tool in maximizing valuation for a Seller.

While this management of financials is most effective when it can be planned over long periods of time and crafted carefully, even in the short term, there are ways of maximizing one's valuation by making financial and operational choices. One powerful insight in this regard is that, while companies almost always get valued as a multiple of their income statement metrics (e.g., revenue, EBITDA, net income), they are usually given no incremental credit for assets on their balance sheet. In other words, an extra dollar of revenue translates into several dollars of total stock value, while an extra dollar of cash on the balance sheet is only worth a dollar in additional stock value (if that). The reason for this is simple: The market presumes that the income statement is a recurring event, and thus an extra dollar of revenue this year implies an additional dollar of revenue next year, and the year after that. The market will try to weed out non-recurring events (and companies are required to report them as such), but for the most part, revenue and profit are assumed to recur and usually grow. By contrast, cash is generally not given a premium; a dollar is worth a dollar. A Buyer should be willing to pay somewhere near, or even above, the incremental increase in market capitalization that the acquired company's financials will provide to it.

Here is an example of how an acquisition can enhance valuation. Assume a Buyer and Seller where the Seller is trading at lower revenue and net income multiples, and assume that the market will continue to give the Buyer the same multiples after an acquisition of the Seller.[8] When the Buyer acquires the Seller, even at a 25% premium, the resulting financials (at the Buyer's original market multiples) drive a higher valuation. In Exhibit 8.3, there is an example of such a valuation exercise.

EXHIBIT 8.3 Model Valuation Exercise

	Market Cap	Revenue	Net Income	Market Cap/ Revenue	Market Cap/ Net Income
Buyer	$13,000	$6,000	$335	2.2x	38.8x
Seller	$ 600	$ 500	$ 25	1.2x	24.0x
Purchase Price @ 25% Premium	$ 750				

	Market Cap	Revenue	Net Income	Market Cap/ Revenue	Market Cap/ Net Income	Market Cap/ Bump	Excess Over Purchase Price
Pro Forma Based on Net Income Multiple	$13,970	$6,500	$360	2.2x	38.8x	$ 970	$220
Pro Forma Based on Revenue Multiple	$14,083	$6,500	$360	2.2x	38.8x	$1,083	$333

This is certainly not a rule, but it is a useful guideline in judging the valuation that a Buyer will attribute to a Target. However, this and all the other valuation methods mentioned are much more a floor than a ceiling to valuation. With the exception of the last discussion about valuation based on incremental impact on the Buyer's valuation, all the methods discussed above are methods that would be used by financial Buyers such as private equity and leveraged buyout firms, to assess the value of a company. None of these methods takes into account the incremental benefits and synergies that will be derived by a Strategic Buyer, and this is the next topic.

PRO FORMA: FINDING AND SPLITTING THE UPSIDE

Financial Buyers generally purchase a company, try to make improvements in its operations, capitalization, management, and other areas, and then sell the business. By contrast, Strategic Buyers almost always seek to integrate an acquired business, to varying extents, with their existing business. Such integration can create synergies that make the combined entity more valuable—the old $1 + 1 = 3$ equation. Value in a transaction can be captured by either Buyer or Seller, or usually a combination of the two, by quantifying these expected benefits. In order to do this, it is necessary to develop a pro forma model. The antidrug ad campaigns of the 1980s provide a particularly apt analogy. In one of these ads, a single unbroken egg is shown, with a voice saying, "This is your brain." The screen then fills with the image of a cast-iron pan on a stove, filled with hot, sizzling oil, and the viewer watches as the egg is cracked into the pan, where it sizzles and fries, while the voice says, "This is your brain on drugs." While the message is negative, rather than positive, the analogy is a good one. A pro forma model says to the Buyer, "This is your company's financials," and then, "This is your company's financials after this acquisition." The pro forma is not a simple additive exercise combining the stand-alone financials of the two companies. Rather, it shows each company as a stand-alone, and then presents a column showing potential synergies, as well as incremental costs, of the combination. As one might imagine, for any deal that is at all attractive, the synergies and benefits far outweigh the incremental costs, except perhaps in the short term.

Before a pro forma model can be built, it is necessary to establish how a company is going to be integrated and operated, postacquisition. These concrete business plans will drive the numbers in a pro forma. In Chapter 9, integration planning will be discussed in detail; however, even the most well developed integration plan is only a general road map of how the Target company will be operated after it is acquired. As a result, a pro forma model is by definition an approximation, an estimate, of the results of that integration. These estimates are a crucial part of the deal process, since the synergies they project can make a dramatic difference in the effective valuation attributed to the Target company. As with most financial projections, the challenge is to find a balance between optimism and pessimism, and create a realistic and achievable model. It is not essential to project the smallest and most detailed items. Since a pro forma is by its nature a rough approximation, it is usually best to focus on the larger items that are likely to have the most impact on the financials. Which items are chosen will vary, according to the nature of the two companies and how they are going to be combined. For example, when Cingular acquired AT&T Wireless, there was likely a substantial overlap in their cellular networks. In areas where this created excess capacity, there would be a substantial savings in the shutdown of that excess capacity. Similarly, to the extent that the two companies had two billing facilities, and either one could be scaled up to take the volume of both, an obvious cost savings would be the shutdown of the other. Similar examples can be found on the revenue side. The merger of the Cosi sandwich chain and the Xando coffeehouse chain may have resulted in substantial revenue synergies, as each chain's locations began selling the other's products. The key to a pro forma is usually to focus on the largest potential synergies, and try to establish reasonable estimates. For groups of smaller synergies, a rough estimate is often done. A good example here is the Selling, General & Administrative (SG&A) line on the income statement. It is fairly intuitive to believe that two companies, when combined, will be able to make substantial reductions in their corporate overhead. For one, a CEO and a CFO, and the accompanying salaries, may often be eliminated. Thus, people will often make a simplifying assumption about the percentage of SG&A that can be eliminated in an acquisition.

Different parties have different incentives, when it comes to the numbers in the pro forma model, and it is important to keep these in mind as one gets input on the assumptions to be used in the model. Advocates of the transaction, notably the Seller but also including investment bankers and often the sponsoring business unit, will press for optimistic projections, to help justify the transaction or drive up the price the Buyer is willing to pay. By contrast, the in-house Corporate Development team, as well as senior management, is more likely to be skeptical of large projected synergies. Line management may also choose to be cautious, for, while an aggressive pro forma will help justify the acquisition, they will usually be held to those numbers for their own goals. The one party with an unambiguous incentive to drive up these numbers is the Seller, since it will reap at least some of the benefit of higher projections, and will "exit stage right" (unless bound by an earn-out or employment contract) before those goals have to be reached.

It is important to note that the development of an accurate pro forma model is dependent not only on making realistic assumptions but also upon the data on which those assumptions are based. Detailed and accurate due diligence is critical to developing an accurate pro forma. Thus, when doing due diligence on a Target, it is important to specifically keep both integration planning and the capture of cost and revenue synergies in mind. For example, understanding call volumes, frequencies, and maximum acceptable wait times will be critical in determining whether the customer service call center of a Target can be consolidated with that of an acquirer.

Revenue Synergies

Revenue synergies are one of the most common reasons for acquiring a company.[9] While cost savings through acquisition improve margin, revenue synergies grow the business overall, and this is often more attractive to an acquirer. The acquisition of a company can drive increased revenues in a variety of ways. The Buyer may be able to utilize the Target's channels to sell its products, or sell the Target's products through its own existing channels. The Cosi/Xando example is a good one here. Another would be if a large electronics retailer, such as Dell, acquired a small technology company with an attractive consumer electronics product. On its own, the small company might have had trouble developing the channels to sell its product, but when acquired by Dell, it would instantly get access to a huge customer base and marketing base. By combining products, the Buyer may also be able to create a new and better product that commands a premium. Many customers will pay a premium for a "one-stop-shop" source of multiple related products. One excellent example is the acquisition in 2004 of Kinko's by Federal Express, creating the literal one-stop-shop for small business.

Sharing branding is another example. If the Target has a good product but an unknown brand, simply rebranding it with the Buyer's well-known name can drive up sales substantially. And sometimes the reverse is true, as a high-quality brand is acquired by a Buyer and then used to heighten the appeal of its products. An excellent example of this is found in the fashion industry, where many well-known designers have sold their companies, and their names, to larger manufacturers, who then spread that brand and name across a broader range of products, capitalizing on the fame and cachet of the designer.

When projecting revenue synergies—and this is a theme that will repeat throughout this chapter—it is important to remember that it takes time to implement changes that drive those synergies. From training sales forces to reaching customers with a new marketing message, to integrating technologies and productizing them, it is likely that, in most cases, revenue synergies will not emerge immediately but rather over time. It is also important to remember that those changes come with a cost. General integration costs will be discussed shortly, but, in particular, it is important to keep in mind that taking advantage of revenue synergies often requires upfront investment.

While less common, negative revenue synergies—the loss of revenue as a result of a transaction—must also be considered. This effect is often overlooked and can have a substantial impact, particularly on near-term performance of the acquired business. There are many reasons that the transaction can drive down revenues. In some industries, customers have strong views and preferences as to service and product providers. If this is the case, the Target's customers may choose to abandon it after it takes on the guise of the acquirer. For example, if Starbucks acquires a small independent local coffeehouse, some of the patrons, who were there specifically because it was not a national chain, might flee the store after the Starbucks sign goes up over the door. Similarly, if some of the Target's customers, or channel partners, are competitors of the acquirer in other areas, they might choose to take their business elsewhere after the acquisition. A clear, though perhaps somewhat unlikely, example would be if Wal-Mart acquired an independent clothing manufacturer that had been selling both Wal-Mart and Kmart clothes. It is easy to imagine that Kmart would stop buying product from the company, once it was owned by a direct competitor.

After taking all these issues into account, the pro forma model will reflect not only the individual projected revenues of each company but also the incremental revenues that can be captured over time as a result of the merger of the two. Revenue synergies are often overstated, however. In one recent study, 70% of the deals surveyed failed to achieve the revenue synergies expected.[10] In most cases, companies will fail to achieve the revenue synergies they expect. Thus, it is important to be realistic, and even conservative, when making assumptions about revenue synergies, particularly in the first few years after a deal is closed.

Cost Synergies

As with revenue synergies, the key to understanding cost synergies is a deep understanding of each of the Target's and acquirer's business models and financials. As one considers the integration of the two businesses, one can determine if and which costs can be removed, and when. People often assume, incorrectly, that when two companies combine, most of the expenses of the smaller entity become redundant, since it will now sit within the larger company, which already covers such expenses. This is largely untrue, in most cases. Many times, the costs incurred by the two companies can be different, and thus not redundant at all. For example, if the acquirer markets its products through direct marketing and advertising to consumers, and the Target company exclusively markets through channel partners, there will be no overlap in spending on television ads.

Even when the two companies have a similar expense, it is by no means clear that one can simply zero out or substantially reduce one of those line items. One will have to consider capacity when combining resources and seeking to reduce costs. Even if the two companies have identical financial policies, it is not reasonable to assume that one entire finance staff can be eliminated. Most companies seek to minimize expenses, so most resources, where possible, are used to maximum capacity. As a result, when two companies are merged, even if they use identical resources, the expense on one side cannot simply be eliminated. Some incremental benefit can usually be realized through efficiencies. Perhaps if each company has 10 members of a finance staff, the combined company could be operated with a finance staff of 15, rather than 20. In most cases, the savings will come through a combination of economies of scale and the elimination of pieces of costs that are totally redundant. Any resources requiring a large initial investment, but with very low incremental cost for added capacity thereafter, are particularly good places to look for cost synergies. A good example here would be a software license, such as an enterprise email system. Usually, this kind of license has a minimum charge, but the incremental cost of adding "seats," particularly in large numbers, is fairly low. Replacing two email system licenses for 10,000 people each with a single license for 20,000 will usually be substantially cheaper.

Every line item of a profit and loss (P&L) is a potential source of cost synergies. However, given the limits of information and ability to think through the complexities of integration, it is probably best to focus on the largest areas of cost, since they are likely to yield the only material cost savings opportunities. Once the possibilities have been narrowed down to a limited number of cost line items, the key is to understand what those costs actually are, and compare the costs of each company. It will often be necessary to make simplifying assumptions, since, even in full-blown due diligence, one is not likely—nor would one have time—to get to per-contract or per-item levels of detail. If a similar set of costs between the two companies is established, it is common to make a simplifying assumption about the percentage savings.

The timing of cost savings is also important. As with revenue synergies, cost synergies will take time to be recognized, in most cases. It takes time to consolidate systems and staffs, and to change contracts and agreements with suppliers. In projecting cost synergies, it is important to take into account the integration plan and the time it will take to make those changes. In many cases, it takes a year or more to begin recognizing many cost synergies.

Other Synergies

There are other synergies that may not immediately or directly impact the P&L of a company but nonetheless have a material impact on the company and should be taken into account when considering and valuing an acquisition. In some cases, these synergies can be indirectly connected with cost or revenue synergies, but, in many cases, they are truly intangible benefits that clearly have value but a value that is not easy to calculate. As with revenue and cost synergies, this section will not try to catalog a complete list of possible other synergies but rather provide a few notable examples to be considered.

Balance Sheet

The potential synergies through access to a balance sheet are probably the closest thing to a quantifiable synergy. While, in theory, any company has access to capital at some price, in actuality, many companies, particularly small ones, find themselves capital constrained. It is a common plight of smaller start-up companies to find their growth constrained, not by product or technology but by capital. In the absence of a source of capital, such companies will usually have to grow at a more measured pace, constrained by their limited ability to spend on things like marketing, sales, customer service, and product development. If such a smaller company is acquired by a larger company with access to capital, it may be able to accelerate its growth and profitability. As a result, the synergies provided by a robust balance sheet can translate into revenue synergies, since the Target company will grow faster as part of the acquirer than it would on its own. It can also contribute to cost synergies, to the extent that the faster-growing company will achieve economies of scale faster, assuming that a significant percentage of its cost structure is attributable to fixed costs.

A strong balance sheet can also provide more indirect benefits. In many industries, a supplier of products or services needs to demonstrate an ability to compensate its customers for damages that might be caused by its failure to deliver those products and services correctly or in a timely manner. If a company is required to put up a bond, or demonstrate that it has a certain level of capital, in order to serve as a supplier for some of its customers, its ability to grow may be constrained by its weak balance sheet and its limited access to capital. Merging with a larger company can open up new revenue opportunities and new customers.

Regulatory

In addition to potential regulatory challenges to an acquisition, there are potential regulatory benefits to an acquisition. There are the direct cost synergies of consolidating regulatory reporting requirements, which can be substantial. There are also indirect benefits. Regulators are often concerned about the financial stability of companies that are given licenses and other rights to operate in regulated businesses. Smaller companies may have difficulty passing this test and receiving permission to operate in these sectors. Becoming part of a larger company may give a smaller player access to certain regulated businesses from which it was previously barred. One extreme example might be something very heavily regulated and safety-oriented, such as the operation of a nuclear plant. One can imagine that a small start-up with limited operating history would be an unattractive candidate to run a nuclear plant, even if it had superior capabilities and practices. Becoming part of a large and established Fortune 500 company might change that assessment. An even more concrete example concerns foreign versus U.S. ownership. Some businesses in the United States (as well as the European Union) are set aside, through regulation, for local companies. For example, a foreign-owned company is not allowed to own more than a 25% stake in any broadcast licensee (radio or television) or U.S.-based airline. In both cases, a foreign company acquired by a local company would suddenly have the ability to own and operate in businesses from which it was previously barred.[11]

Brand/Reputation/Credibility

Beyond specific balance sheet requirements, there are some broader brand and reputational synergies that can be achieved with a merger. Even if a customer does not require specific financial capacity, it is often concerned with the stability of a supplier. Customers do not want to risk having a supplier go out of business, or simply fail to deliver products or services. If the products or services become an integral part of the customer's business and/or require regular services, support, update, or parts, the customer is particularly likely to turn a critical eye to the long-term stability of the supplier. Thus, being part of a larger company may drive revenue synergies, simply by providing credibility and an impression of stability. A good example here might be a supplier to an automaker. Since automakers design new vehicles over a period of years, and will maintain a model for years, once it is launched, it is exceedingly important that any suppliers of parts that are designed into a new model are highly likely to continue to operate for the entire life of the model, and to be able to continue to supply replacement parts, adjustments and redesigns, and other support. Credibility and brand can also work in the opposite direction. The Target may have developed a brand or reputation, particularly in industries where nonconformist and antiestablishment images are popular. Through acquisition and maintenance of the brand, the acquiring company can benefit from the brand and reputation of the Target in ways that would be very hard to replicate organically. The music industry is a good example. Smaller alternative labels often attract cutting-edge acts that prefer them to the larger corporate labels. Similarly, customers may gravitate to these labels as a source of cutting-edge music. A large record company might acquire one of these labels as a way of accessing that alternative section of the market. Of course, the key here is to leverage that brand and reputation, rather than destroy it. That large record company can be expected to try to keep that alternative brand isolated and "true to its roots." When Viacom acquired Black Entertainment Television (BET), it certainly did not rebrand BET, nor even make it particularly obvious that it was now a subsidiary of Viacom. Presumably, it was seeking to maintain the viewer base that came to BET not only for its unique content but also because it was an independent, minority-owned business. So brand, reputation, and credibility can work in both directions, and may lend additional value to both the acquirer's and Target's businesses.

Costs of Synergies

Synergies are usually a positive, but they are by no means manna from heaven. It takes time, effort, and investment to achieve most synergies. When developing a pro forma, it is essential to properly account for these costs. The challenge is that, prior to completing an acquisition, the Buyer usually does not have a fully developed integration plan in place, on which to base detailed cost estimates. As a result, costs of synergies are usually a rough estimate. While most people doing deals capture the base costs of immediate integration and costs at the corporate level (where these deal-makers usually sit), they often neglect to include longer-term costs and those that are incurred at the business-unit level. Legal and investment banker fees are always included in a pro forma, but costs like termination fees on supplier contracts and new signage for stores often are not. It is important that those developing the pro forma have detailed discussions with line management and the team responsible for integration planning, to make sure that a complete estimate of costs is included.

There is as wide a variety of costs of synergies as of synergies themselves. There are several broad categories that most of these costs can be broken into.

This section begins with the costs of closing the deal itself. This category will include such items as the allocated costs of an internal Corporate Development team, as well as the fees of lawyers, investment bankers, accountants, and other outside specialists. These are the easiest costs to estimate, since most will be incurred at or directly after closing.[12]

There is the broad category of people costs. This will include the cost to terminate employees, either immediately following the acquisition or in the months and even years following. If one of the major cost synergies being projected is a reduction in headcount, remember that for each reduction in headcount there will be an upfront cost to termination, including severance and perhaps extended benefits and outplacement (depending on the terms of the employee's contract). Another broad category is technology and infrastructure. Similarly, if one is consolidating locations, there will often be moving and other expenses during the process of relocating employees.

When systems and operations are consolidated, one must devote either internal or external manpower to making the transition, and it is often necessary to build new systems or infrastructure to support the transfer. A simple example here would be that, if one is consolidating two facilities, one will, at a minimum, have to pay a moving company to move equipment from one building to another.

Marketing and branding is another potential source of costs of synergies. The process of rebranding products or marketing new ones can be very expensive. Before one can take advantage of a newly acquired product, one must take the time and spend the money to introduce it to one's sales channel. The cost of rebranding a business should also not be underestimated. Between signage, stationery, marketing material, and all the other places where branding is positioned, rebranding a Target company to match the Buyer's brand can be expensive and time-consuming.

Finally, there are customers. Communicating with customers of both the Target and Buyer is often the most important element in recognizing revenue synergies but also often the most delicate. If the Buyer does not communicate effectively with the Target's customers, they may leave, and if the Buyer does not communicate the benefits of the new products or services it has acquired from the Target, then it is unlikely to see the leverage of its sales channel yield much incremental revenue.

Studies suggest that companies are somewhat more effective at achieving cost synergies than they are at hitting their goals for revenue synergies. In one study, fully 60% of the companies largely achieved their expected cost synergies.[13] However, in the same study, almost 25% of the companies did not achieve expected cost synergies. Thus, it is important, as with revenue synergies, to be conservative and realistic when projecting cost synergies, particularly the timing of achieving these savings.

Who Gets the Gravy?

When a pro forma model is completed, it should show an incremental benefit from the transaction—the $1 + 1 = 3$ effect—net, of course, of the associated costs. In most transactions, this will be a substantially positive amount, and often can be a significant portion of the total value of the transaction. This incremental benefit can be thought of as value created by the transaction itself. The question then arises: Who is entitled to this benefit? This upside is created by the combination of the Buyer and the Seller, and each will want to claim it. The Seller will want to add the effective current value—the net present value, perhaps—to the purchase price, while the Buyer will want to pay no more than the stand-alone value of the Seller, keeping the upside for itself. The answer is usually a split between the two parties, though the level and nature of the split will, of course, be the subject of aggressive negotiation.

The best demonstration of how this upside gets split is found in the difference between the price paid for acquisitions by Strategic and financial Buyers. Financial Buyers cannot attribute substantial synergies to an acquisition, since they have no operations, customers, or products of their own to contribute. The notable exception here is for financial Buyers with a portfolio of companies, which, like the Japanese *Keiretsu*,[14] leverage their network of investments to their mutual benefit. By contrast, Strategic Buyers usually find substantial synergies in an acquisition. As a result, and, again, as a broad generalization, Strategic Buyers can usually afford to pay higher prices and premiums for acquisitions than financial Buyers. The difference between the two, where it exists, is largely due to synergies. In one study, financial Buyers were found to be materially less aggressive in valuation than Strategic Buyers, paying 5 to 20% lower valuations.[15] This is, of course, a generalization. In specific situations, a financial Buyer may be able to offer a higher valuation, particularly where there are actually negative synergies for a Strategic Buyer, such as overlaps between the two businesses that will actually reduce combined revenues.

Buyers will always consider synergies when negotiating an acquisition, but it is equally important for Sellers to do so. By understanding the potential synergies, a Seller will be in a better position to estimate the value of the deal to the Buyer, and thus the likely best price it can extract.

GETTING THE VALUATION AND PRO FORMA DONE

Both the Buyer and Seller will need to do a valuation, and, as discussed, while the Buyer will likely have more details to do a pro forma, the Seller should also attempt a rough one, to try to get an idea of the incremental value the Buyer is attributing to synergies. This is a crucial exercise for both parties, since it will frame the most important discussion in the negotiation: price.

It is important that the person doing the valuation and pro forma have not only good financial modeling skills but also a good understanding of the transaction—the business and the industry. While all financial models are driven by assumptions, the valuation and pro forma are more assumption-driven than most, and those assumptions are unusually rough. As any financial planning and analysis (FP&A) professional, or line manager, for that matter, can attest, projecting future performance is challenging. The pro forma is far more challenging, since one must not only project financial performance for two different entities but then take a crack at the differences in performance resulting from the combination of the two. Whoever builds these models needs to work very closely with the due diligence and integration teams in developing his or her assumptions.

The valuation is inextricably bound to the pro forma, since it is these numbers that will serve as the base inputs. There are different approaches to developing these models. In most companies, the Corporate Development team will take responsibility for a valuation model. In some companies, they will also own the pro forma. Another model, particularly in larger companies with a deep pool of finance talent, is to have the finance staff build a pro forma model. In addition to their expertise in modeling, the finance staff brings two additional capabilities to bear. The finance staff has a detailed understanding of the way a company runs its accounting and the assumptions it makes concerning things like the cost of capital. The finance staff is also more familiar with the exercise of projecting performance of businesses. If the finance staff does the pro forma, it is crucial that they work closely with the Corporate Development staff in linking those projections to the valuation work.

Sellers will often not have as deep a set of skills in this area, and even some smaller Buyers may not. In some cases, an investment banker will be hired as an advisor and can provide modeling expertise, but it is crucial that a critical eye be focused on the work of investment bankers. As discussed, investment bankers have an adverse incentive to drive the completion of a deal. There is a powerful incentive to be overly optimistic about a deal. Investment bankers are also not particularly expert at planning integration or predicting the costs and challenges of driving synergies. They may tend to assume that synergies are quick and easy to achieve. Using bankers to provide expertise is good, but, at the end of the day, a Buyer must take responsibility for the projections that drive a deal, since it will have to deal with them and live up to them in years to come. Similarly, a Seller is responsible to shareholders for delivering the best value for the business.

In companies where deals are done repeatedly, establishing procedures for developing these models, identifying staff that will do them on a regular basis, and even developing a standard model that is the basis for these exercises, can make doing deals easier and more streamlined.

Never forget that these modeling exercises are driven by many simplifying assumptions, and are by no means to be taken as fact but more as educated guesses. An apt analogy can be made to political polls, which might say, for example, that a candidate has a 3% lead, with a margin of error of 4%. All too often, a model is developed quickly and then set in stone. There is an understandable temptation for people to try to reach a definitive "right answer," but, in the case of valuation and pro forma models, the best one can hope for is something that is reasonable and roughly accurate. If one finds oneself negotiating the last $10 million gap in a $1 billion deal, it is helpful to remember that the model that allowed the deal to be valued at $990 million, rather than at $1 billion, likely has a margin of error of $100 million.

At the end of the day, valuation is at best an educated guess. This is a huge decision to be made on the basis of a rough estimate. Investment bankers are arguably the most valuable outside advisors for purposes of providing "cover" to executive management and the board of directors on the issue of valuation. For particularly impactful Strategic Transactions, and the vast majority of sales, the board of directors will likely seek a "fairness opinion" from an investment bank, to support the terms of the transaction. Again, in the most general terms, a fairness opinion is a legal document provided by an investment bank, opining to the fairness and reasonableness of the financial terms of a transaction. In effect, the investment bank is providing an opinion that the board has made a wise decision, or at least has not made an unwise decision, in doing the deal. While it is highly uncertain how much legal protection from shareholder liability lawsuits a fairness opinion provides to the board of directors, it is clearly seen as a powerful "optic" to demonstrate to shareholders and the public that the board of directors has done everything it can to ensure it is making a wise decision. My personal view is that the fairness opinion is a document with dubious value. Investment banks are rarely held liable for their work in developing a fairness opinion; it is largely a symbolic document that allows a board of directors to justify their decision on a deal.[16]

Currency and Payment

Cash is not the only currency that can be used to pay for an acquisition, and the question of currency is tied inextricably to that of price. In simplest terms, there are two currencies of payment: (1) cash and (2) other.

Cash is a fairly simple exercise, although in cross-border transactions, one cannot assume the U.S. dollar as the de facto national currency of payment. In these transactions, which currency is used for payment can be a significant source of discussion. This is particularly true when dealing with companies in countries where currency is not freely exchangeable, or where there is significant volatility in valuation. In some countries, currency is not freely and easily exchangeable. As a result, if payment is made in local currency, it will be hard, time-consuming, or expensive to repatriate that money back to one's home currency. The Seller may be forced to effectively make a long-term investment in that country's economy, as it slowly retrieves its purchase price back to its home country. Similarly, some Sellers will seek to be paid in a currency outside their home country, to avoid such restrictions. A Seller of a Chinese company, for instance, might well seek to be paid to an offshore account in a more liquid and stable currency, such as the dollar or euro. Even when a currency is freely tradeable, if there is significant volatility in the value of the currency, there may be a risk of losing money during a delay in payment. For example, if the Seller of a Latin America–based company signs an agreement to sell that company, and the deal is denominated in the local currency, a devaluation of that currency between signing and closing of the deal will effectively reduce the purchase price, often substantially. The converse would be true if the local currency appreciated, giving the Seller a windfall and the Buyer a higher purchase price. There are ways to protect oneself from such currency fluctuations, which include defining purchase price in terms of a more stable currency, such as the euro, or simply entering into a simultaneous hedge transaction with a bank, to lock in the value of the payment in the future. Whenever one is doing a Strategic Transaction involving assets, businesses, or companies in different countries, it is important to consider the impact of currency fluctuations, as well as restrictions on exchange, and plan for them.

The more complex currency of payment is the "other" category. Broadly speaking, this can be thought of as some form of security equity or debt, or some variation thereof. There are as many forms of noncash payment as there are forms of equity and debt securities. Every variation will not be covered here, but a general discussion about these two categories and their implications will be provided. Equity is a very common currency in Strategic Transactions, particularly where the Target is very large, or where the selling parties who own the Target are going to continue to be involved with the business after the deal. In basic terms, what happens is that, rather than paying cash at the closing, the Buyer will pay some combination of cash and stock (or entirely stock) to the selling shareholders. Each shareholder of the Seller will generally receive a pro rata share of the purchase price, in the form of stock in the Buyer.

In some cases, the selling shareholders receive unrestricted and liquid stock, and are immediately able to sell it on the open market. In other cases, the Buyer may put restrictions on the sale of this stock. Usually, these restrictions involve a lock-up period, like that found in most initial public offerings, where the selling shareholders must hold the stock for a period of time before they are permitted to sell it. Similarly, in some situations, the selling shareholders will receive unregistered stock (i.e., stock that has not been registered with the SEC and is not freely saleable). In these situations, there is usually a registration rights agreement, which requires the Buyer to register the stock, at some point in the future, and allow the selling shareholders to sell it. The use of unregistered stock is more common in transactions where a large portion of the Buyer's stock is being transferred to the selling shareholders, and the Buyer may not want a huge flood of additional stock entering the market at the same time, impacting its stock price. The concern here is that a flood of stock into the market directly after the deal closes will push down the stock price of the Buyer, by effectively creating a short-term imbalance between supply and demand. The Buyer will seek to avoid this by putting limits on how the selling shareholders can sell their Buyer-stock into the market. Often, the selling shareholders will be limited to "trickling" the stock into the market over time. A common mechanism is to limit daily or weekly sales to a small percentage of the average daily volume of trading in the Buyer's stock. For example, if a Buyer whose stock usually trades about 2 million shares per day paid for an acquisition with 1 million shares of its stock, it might limit the selling shareholders who receive that stock to dumping no more than 1% of the average daily volume on any given day. As a result, the selling shareholders could sell a maximum of 20,000 shares a day. In this situation, a selling shareholder who did not want to hold Buyer stock would often set up a standing order with a broker to regularly sell shares into the market, trickling them in until the stake is completely sold.

In addition to managing the impact of its public stock price, the Buyer may have other reasons for restricting the sale of the stock it uses to purchase a company. If the selling shareholders will not be involved in the business after purchase, the Buyer has little interest in incentivizing them. A good example here would be financial Sellers such as venture capital and private equity firms. When the deal closes, they will generally walk away from the table and cease all involvement with the company. However, in many cases, some of the selling shareholders will continue to be involved in the operation of the business. Notably, if management of the Seller has agreed to stay in place for a period of time following the closing, the Buyer wants to create strong incentives for good performance. One way of doing this is to pay these particular selling shareholders in Buyer stock, thus tying their financial fortunes to those of the Buyers stockholders. Even when the selling shareholders will not continue to be involved, a Buyer might want to create this same tying effect. This is an indirect way to ensure that the Seller is providing accurate information on the business being sold. The implication is that if the Seller misled the Buyer, and the business purchased underperforms, the stock of the Buyer will suffer, and the selling shareholders will share in that pain. Keep in mind that the connection between Buyer stock price and the performance of the sold business is a function, at least in part, of the relative sizes of the two businesses. The larger the proportion of the Buyer's business that will be represented by the Seller's business, once incorporated, the more direct and effective this linkage will be. If General Motors (GM) buys Ford, the performance of GM stock will be strongly and directly affected by the performance of the Ford business. By contrast, if GM buys a $25 million, family-owned parts business, it is unlikely that even a complete collapse of that purchased business will have any material impact on GM's stock price.

Less common than an equity component in a purchase price is a debt component. The Buyer may offer to pay part of the purchase price with a debt instrument, or some hybrid, such as convertible debt. This is highly uncommon, since it is likely to be an inefficient method of funding a transaction. It is rare that the selling shareholders are professional lenders. The Buyer can usually go to a bank or to the financial markets to borrow funds to make an acquisition, and usually get better terms for the debt. However, in some rare cases, the selling shareholder will be willing to effectively lend the Buyer part of the purchase price, and get paid over time. A hybrid that allows the selling shareholder to participate in some of the upside of the business may also be attractive here. This is probably most common in smaller transactions, where the Buyer may not have access to the capital markets or other lending sources. One example would be the sale of a medical practice by an older retiring doctor to a young protégé. The younger doctor might not be able to fund the entire purchase price, and might offer part of the price in the form of a debt instrument and IOU.

Setting aside the mechanics of, and reasons for, paying in a noncash currency, it is important to note how different this is from getting paid in cash. First, there is the basic time value of money. Rather than getting the cash purchase price on the day of closing, the Seller will have to wait weeks, months, or even years to receive its full purchase price. But far more important is the inherent risk of taking noncash currency. In effect, the Seller is making a forced investment in a new security, trading the risk of its business for the risk of an equity or debt security. Sellers will, understandably, discount the value of a purchase price made in part or in whole with noncash currency, to account for the inherent risk. To the extent the Seller is particularly risk averse, the discount can be fairly severe. A good example is the financial or family Seller. A financial investor, like a venture capital firm, needs to show financial returns to its investor and will be hesitant to take anything other than cash, since it can neither dividend the rewards of a successful investment to its limited partners, nor reinvest the returns in a new investment vehicle. Similarly, a family Seller that is selling a business to lock in a pool of cash for future generations may be similarly nervous about "rolling over" into another risky venture, and one in which it has no control. While the transaction was less a sale than a merger of equals, certainly Time Warner had this experience when merging with AOL. In retrospect, the Time Warner employees and shareholders likely regret the merger, after which they were pulled into the dot-com collapse.

Earn-Outs and Contingent Payments

Noncash payments have been discussed as a way of indirectly tying the effective purchase price to the performance of the sold business; however, there are more direct ways of tying these two together. In most acquisitions, future performance of the business is a primary driver to valuation, and usually also the key point of dispute between the parties. A business is not acquired for what it has done in the past but for what it will deliver in the future. Whether a business is being valued based on cash flow, net income, or revenue, it is being judged based on what it will produce after it is acquired. In this sense, historical performance is only relevant to the extent that it helps a Buyer predict future performance. But since historical performance is fact, and future performance is prediction, the Buyer will tend to try to lean on historical data as much as possible, anchoring itself to the one set of financial facts that can be confirmed.

In the case of low-growth and stable businesses, future performance is easier to predict and more certain. If a business has a long history of producing certain levels of financial performance, in the absence of any significant changes in the business or the economic environment, similar performance can be expected in the future. The extreme example would be a business with a large diversified portfolio of long-term contracts—a commercial real estate or ship-leasing business, for example. In this case, while there are some variables that will affect future performance, they are mostly economic factors such as the price of fuel or real estate price levels. Similarly, any business with an established brand and customer base and a modest growth rate is probably easier to project into the future. Higher-growth businesses and those at an earlier stage of development are much harder to project, since their future performance depends not only on assumptions about the economic environment but also on predictions of the success of the business itself in developing things like new technologies, additional customers, or new product offerings.

By their nature, Buyers will tend to be pessimistic, and Sellers will tend to be optimistic about future performance. Each side has a bias to project performance to affect the purchase price. Sellers get more when there is high growth projected, and Buyers pay less when weak performance is projected. Beyond these biases, there are more inherent biases at work. A Seller is judging itself when it projects future performance. Has it built a successful business? In the absence of a sale, would it be able to deliver on its own promises and plans? Thus, a Seller's projections are a judgment on its own management and vision. A Buyer, by contrast, is considering worst-case scenarios as it peers into the unknown, not only of future events but also of the effects of acquiring a new business with new products and customers. In the face of these unknowns, a Buyer is naturally skeptical of optimistic projections.

These differences, and the crucial importance of future performance in the valuation of a business, will tend to create a substantial gap in implied value between the Buyer and Seller. As discussed in Chapter 3, some of this gap may be taken up by synergies that a Buyer believes it will be able to realize by integrating the acquired business with its own. Sometimes this gap will be filled by a combination of compromises on both sides of the table, but there is almost always a substantial difference of opinion to overcome. It can be particularly hard to find a compromise when dealing with privately held Sellers, where the people negotiating the sale have a personal interest in the valuation, as a direct judgment on the success of their efforts over past years or decades. The higher the projected growth in a business, the greater this gap will tend to be. Usually, the valuation gap is tighter with slower-growth, more established companies, and it is thus easier to overcome through compromise. Similarly, publicly traded companies come with their own starting point for valuation, the public market price, making a very large valuation gap between Buyer and Seller fairly unlikely. However, for privately held earlier-stage companies where the Sellers have aggressive, or optimistic, projections for future growth, the gap between Buyer and Seller valuations can be huge.

In these situations, a contingent payment structure can help bridge the gap between Buyer and Seller. The basic premise of a contingent payment, or "earn-out," structure is the Missouri motto: "Show me." Part of the purchase price is set aside and is contingent on the future performance of the business. In effect, the Buyer is saying, "I will pay you x for your company, but if your projections, which I consider optimistic, turn out to be accurate, I will pay you an additional y." One example of a very simple contingent payment would be one based on revenues. A Buyer might stipulate that, at the end of the second year following the acquisition, the Buyer will pay the Seller 10% of any revenues the purchased company produces, above some target level established by the two parties.

On its face, this would seem like a neat and seamless solution to the gap in valuation. Since future performance is hard to predict, but historical performance is certain, why not just wait until future performance becomes historical, and then judge it? Whoever was right about how the story turns out will get the money. As with most things, the devil here is in the details. The certainty that a contingent payment structure purports to offer is only as good as the certainty of details, terms, and measurements of the structure. Crafting an effective contingent payment can help make a deal happen, but crafting a bad one can cause more problems than it solves. Effectively, a contingent payment is a "punt," where the parties agree to disagree on valuation but set the rules for the eventual determination of who was right. If these rules are not clear, easy to execute, and totally unambiguous, the parties can find themselves in a much more difficult position in the future, having completed a deal without really having an agreement, and then fighting, ex post, about the terms of the deal.

In many cases, contingent payment terms end up being litigated in the courts. This is not only time-consuming but also costly and distracting. Contingent payment terms are seductively attractive, since they allow both sides to walk away from the initial deal believing, and saying publicly, that they got the deal done on the valuation they viewed as accurately reflecting the future performance of the company. Unfortunately, this tends to drive parties to rush too quickly toward contingent payment structures, and, even worse, toward badly thought out and planned structures. The cost and pain of these mistakes are not felt for months or years, but when these chickens come home to roost, they can be very painful and expensive.

There are two common drivers to conflict over contingent payments: uncertainty about terms and metrics, and disagreement over responsibility for performance. Uncertainty about terms is probably the easier of the two to fix. As with any legal document, when a contingent payment structure is set up, it is critical to try to craft an agreement that predicts all the potential outcomes and makes the terms of the agreement clear under all those situations. In the case of contingent payments, methods of calculation and sources of data will be particularly critical to clarify. A well-structured earn-out provision identifies clearly how the earn-out will be calculated, where the data for those calculations will come from, and under what circumstances an earn-out is payable. In most cases, a contingent payment is made payable based on a financial performance trigger, such as reaching a certain level of revenue or net income. The first step is to make any such metrics and triggers clear and unambiguous. For example, the specific measure and time period in which it is being measured should be laid out clearly. It is also important to carefully choose the metrics to be used. A company may grow revenue dramatically but remain unprofitable, or become highly profitable but slow its top-line growth. Choosing metrics to match goals and expectations is important. When crafting a contingent payment structure, it is important to consider all these variable carefully. While lawyers will take the lead in crafting the language, the business leader for the deal will be responsible for choosing variables that match the underlying goals of the Buyer and choosing variables that can be measured and calculated accurately, and without debate when the earn-out is being determined in the future. Among the variables that need to be chosen will be the amount of the earn-out, the metrics that are being measured to determine if the earn-out will be paid, how those metrics are measured, when they are measured and over what period of time, who does the measuring, how the earn-out will be paid, and whether partial payments or sliding scales will be used.

Here is an example of the key terms of a basic earn-out. Any final earn-out would be a much more detailed legal document, but this would be an example of the key business terms.

- Initial Purchase Price: $10.0 million
- Earn-Out Amount: $3.0 million
- Earn-Out Triggered by:
  - Net Income Hits $1.0 million
  - Measurement Period: 12-Month Period Following Closing
  - Measurement Method: GAAP
  - Measuring Party: Buyer Auditor
- Dispute Resolution Mechanism
  - Independent Auditor (Predetermined in the Agreement) Makes Final Assessment
  - Decision Binding

Even a well thought out earn-out provision does not guarantee a painless transaction. A huge challenge in any contingent payment provision is the issue of control. As a general matter, after the completion of an acquisition, the Buyer will have complete control over an acquired company, and the Seller will generally lose all control over operations. This means that the Seller will be depending on the management and control of the Buyer to determine the performance that drives the payment, or nonpayment, of the earn-out. First, there is an adverse incentive problem. Since the Buyer is on the hook for payments under the earn-out, the Buyer has an incentive to try to manage performance of the acquired business to avoid paying the earn-out. This adverse incentive is usually balanced or eliminated by the interest of the Buyer in seeing the acquired business perform well. However, it is important to keep it in mind. If an earn-out is large enough, it can create an incentive for the Buyer to damage performance of the business, to avoid paying it. A more likely adverse incentive scenario has the Buyer manipulating the operation to shift the financials away from paying an earn-out. If an earn-out is driven by net income, a Buyer could invest heavily in marketing and/or research and development during the earn-out period, resulting in an artificial and temporary reduction in net income. Even if the adverse incentive problem can be avoided, there is still a potential for conflict over the management of the business. If the triggers for an earn-out are not met, the Seller will be likely to question the management skills or choices of the Buyer, and argue that under the Seller's control the business would have hit its targets. A potential solution to this issue is to either allow the Seller to retain some control over the business or try to set parameters under which the business will run. Both are challenging to put in place effectively. If the Sellers are members of the management team who will stay on after the acquisition, the Buyer may be able to address some of their perceived or real concerns over the management of the business during the earn-out period by leaving it in their hands. Alternatively, the Seller may be able to put constraints on the Buyer that govern its operation of the business, such as minimum expenditures for sales and marketing, or commitments not to make material changes to the business model. Each of these brings its own complexities, since the Buyer will be hesitant to accept any limitations on how it runs the business, particularly if it is planning to integrate it with other operations.

In the final analysis, contingent payment structures are sometimes the only way to make a deal happen, by bridging a large gap in perceived valuation between Buyer and Seller. In that sense, they can add huge value by making a deal happen. However, it is crucial to remember that they are complex, hard to manage, and likely to lead to conflict and disagreement. It is rare to find an earn-out that is not eventually debated, argued, and even litigated. One general counsel used to argue that, as a Buyer, one needs to assume that one will always end up paying off an earn-out, regardless of performance, and get comfortable with those terms. While that may be an overly pessimistic approach, it is important to understand the minefield created by crafting and executing a contingent payment structure, and to view it as a last resort, rather than an easy fix for a difference in valuation between Buyer and Seller.

NOTES

1. One study of IPOs from 1960 to 1996 found an average gain of approximately 15% in first-day trading. See Philip D. Drake and Michael R. Vetsuypens, "IPO Underpricing and Insurance against Legal Liability—Initial Public Offerings," *Financial Management* (Spring 1993).

2. One study found that, for announcements of class actions in the *Wall Street Journal* (approximately 60% of class actions relate to accounting fraud), companies experienced an average 10% price decline on the day of the announcement. See Paul A. Griffin, Joseph A. Grundfest, and Michael A. Perino, *Stock Price Response to News of Securities Fraud Litigation: Market Efficiency and the Slow Diffusion of Costly Information,* Working Paper No. 208, John M. Olin Program in Law and Economics, Stanford Law School (November 2000).

3. This is commonly known as the Efficient Market Theory. For a review of efficient market theories, see Richard Brealey and Stewart Myers, *Principles of Corporate Finance* (London: McGraw-Hill, 1991), p. 290.

4. For a detailed discussion of various premium and discount theories, see Shannon Pratt, *Business Valuation Discounts and Premiums* (Hoboken, NJ: John Wiley & Sons, 2001).

5. There are many studies of control premiums. One of the definitive sources is the *Mergerstat Review,* published annually by Mergerstat, an affiliate of Los Angeles–based investment bank Houlihan, Lokey, Howard & Zukin (available at *www.mergerstat.com*).

6. As a side note, there are some businesses that inherently lend themselves to such a valuation, since they are in fact likely to cease at the end of the initial period. One good example is exclusive contracts. The issuers of private-label credit cards typically have contracts to provide this service to a retailer for a particular period of time, with the contract being renewable at the end of the period. In actuality, the contract is likely to go up for competitive bid, so a private-label credit card company will usually assume the contract to have no terminal value, since retailers effectively have to recompete for the next period. Another good example is monopoly government contracts. The contract that VeriSign Inc. has with the U.S. Department of Commerce to operate the dot-com global registry (the registry that keeps track of all dot-com domain names) is at a fixed price per name and extends to 2009.

7. For a discussion of other metrics of performance, notably Return on Investment, see *Principles of Corporate Finance,* Richard A. Brealey and Stewart Myers (London: McGraw-Hill, 1991).

8. This is, of course, not always true. If the acquisition is particularly large, or if it brings the Buyer into a market space or new business that the market values on lower multiples, the acquisition can cause the market to reduce the multiples it applies to the Buyer's financial performance.

9. Growth was the stated objective in three out of four mergers, in a recent study. See Matthias M. Bekier, Anna J. Bogardus, and Timothy Oldham, *Mastering Revenue Growth in M&A* (McKinsey & Co., 2002).

10. Scott A. Christofferson, Robert S. McNish, and Diane L. Sias, *Where Mergers Go Wrong, The McKinsey Quarterly,* no. 2 (McKinsey & Co., 2004).

11. It is important to note that this works in the opposite direction as well, and the acquisition of a U.S. company by a foreign company will eliminate rights only available to U.S. companies.

12. These costs, investment bankers in particular, are in some ways akin to paying a real estate broker, when buying or selling a home. This suggests that a Seller might be able to negotiate a higher price, if she is able to connect directly with a Buyer, without the intervening services of an investment banker. While this makes logical sense, in practice, Buyers tend to think of those fees separately, as a cost of doing business, and value a target on its own merits, regardless of whether such fees are going to be incurred.

13. Scott A. Christofferson, Robert S. McNish, and Diane L. Sias, "Where Mergers Go Wrong," *The McKinsey Quarterly,* no. 2 (McKinsey & Co., 2004).

14. A Japanese term describing a loose conglomeration of companies organized around a single bank, for their mutual benefit. The companies sometimes, but not always, own equity in each other. Source: *www.investorwords.com.*

15. Lakshmi Nambiar, M&A Trends: *Increasing Prevalence of Financial Buyers* (*www.merger.com,* 2003).

16. For a discussion of the value of a fairness opinion, see Paul Sweeney, "Who Says It's a Fair Deal?" *Journal of Accountancy,* vol. 188, issue 2 (August 1999), pp. 6, 44.

CHAPTER 9

Integration Planning

The key issues surrounding integration planning have been touched on in the previous chapters, particularly Chapter 7. However, at the risk of being repetitive, it is important to review the key challenges of integration planning directly. Integration is often cited as the single greatest determinant of success or failure in a Strategic Transaction. In my experience, it is also the least understood or established within most Buyer organizations. The modest effort necessary to develop a basic integration plan prior to closing can yield substantial rewards in terms of the ease of integrating a new acquisition and the performance, particularly in the first year, that it produces.

While integration planning does not have to begin at the start of the deal process, it is important that some integration planning work be done before a final decision to do a deal is made. This is the case because integration costs and benefits need to be factored into that decision. The cost of integrating a new business, and the synergies that can be achieved as a result, can often be key components in the decision to do a deal. Specific timing will vary from deal to deal, but a general rule is that by the time due diligence is in full swing, it is a good idea to have some integration planning begun, at least at a high level. By the time a final decision is made to sign a purchase agreement, the high-level integration plan should have been completed and reviewed.

Accurately predicting costs and benefits is key to an effective set of financial projections for a deal. Since the deal team will tend to be advocates for the deal, there is a strong tendency to overplay the potential synergies and underestimate the associated costs. Part of effective integration planning is to generate realistic expectations on both sides of the equation. For example, deal makers may be quick to recognize the potential for a revenue synergy from cross-selling customers but slow to identify the cost of consolidating databases and mining them for relevant information. Integration costs will include both the costs of doing the basic work of integration and the investment necessary to realize potential synergies. As synergy opportunities are discussed in this chapter, keep in mind that realizing them will usually require an upfront investment.

One very notable exception is found with financial Buyers. Private equity and LBO firms that are acquiring a business will sometimes integrate the Seller into another portfolio company but will often buy a business and continue to run it as a stand-alone entity. In these situations, many, but not all, of the challenges of integration go away. Even with a financial Buyer, it is necessary to consider some aspects of integration, including the impact on employees, customers, and suppliers, as well as regulatory requirements that may result from a change in ownership to a private investor.

DEDICATING RESOURCES

The first challenge in integration planning is getting resources dedicated. The problem is that, in the absence of a closed deal, integration planning is a project with a significant likelihood of being irrelevant. Doing work that no one ever uses is not generally a career booster. Similarly, until a deal is closed, the relevant line manager will not create full-time positions and hire permanent employees to devote to integrating and running the business. Therefore, employees doing integration planning usually have full-time day jobs, which are, at least until the deal closes, the real metric on which their career and compensation will be based.

In theory, one path is to have the Corporate Development team develop the integration plan. While some companies may have the deal team do initial integration planning, this approach is fundamentally flawed. Since the Corporate Development team will not have a significant hand in running the business after closing, and generally is not very familiar with the deep details of how the business unit is run, it will be difficult for the Corporate Development team to craft a realistic integration plan, and even harder to get the line management team to embrace it. There are some rare exceptions where this dynamic will not play out, but, in general, integration planning needs to be done, and owned, largely by the relevant line unit. The notable exception here is for acquisitions that will stand on their own, as a new business unit, and not be integrated into an existing business. Here the Corporate Development team may well take the lead in integration planning, but this is a much lighter level of integration, largely focused on imposing corporate standards and procedures on the new business unit and integrating staff functions, such as human resources and finance.

As a result of these forces, there are two paths to finding the resources to develop an effective integration plan. The first method is to leverage the resources provided by the line unit for due diligence. The advantage here is that the staff involved are already the deepest pools of knowledge on the Target company. The challenge is to ensure that they have enough time to do both due diligence and integration planning. The second challenge is that, in an ideal world, the people who do integration planning would also be the people to execute on that plan. This requires the happy coincidence that the people who are available to do due diligence can also be devoted to a long-term integration exercise, in the event of a closed deal. The second alternative is to press line management for a separate or overlapping set of resources to begin integration planning. As with due diligence, it is often difficult to get these resources devoted from their operating roles, and equally difficult to motivate them. However, unlike the due diligence function, there is one powerful motivator to use with integration planning. In the event that the deal closes, those who craft the integration plan will be the best qualified to take a leadership role in the integration, and potentially take a new role within the new business. Strategic Transactions often create opportunities for promotion, as staff members are plucked from their role in the business unit to be inserted into the newly acquired business.

LINKING DUE DILIGENCE TO INTEGRATION PLANNING AND EXECUTION

Once resources have been assigned to begin integration planning, it is important to create a link between the integration plan and the due diligence process. This should be a virtual feedback loop, where information gleaned in due diligence is fed to the integration team for consideration in their plans, and the integration team sends questions and clarifications back to the due diligence team. If there is substantial overlap between the people working on both efforts, or at least they are close and friendly colleagues from the business unit, this information flow can be fairly seamless. A failure to foster this kind of communication can mean that the integration plan ignores some major challenges, and the due diligence team fails to ask the right questions. For example, consider the case of a large manufacturer with a unionized employee base, buying a smaller manufacturer with a nonunionized workforce. If the integration team did not know that the Target's employment policies effectively violated their union contract, they would not be able to factor resources into the integration plan for raising the Target employee base up to their union-level standards of compensation and benefits. If the integration team did not identify this as an issue for the due diligence team, they might not delve into the details of the Target's benefits program, to discover how dramatic the difference between the two benefits packages was. The result would be that a substantial cost would not be considered in measuring the value of the deal. Furthermore, rather than be able to plan for a smooth transition and communicate in advance to the union, the Buyer would be faced with a sudden realization upon closing, and likely a hostile reaction from the surprised union.

KEY INTEGRATION ISSUES

The first step in integration planning is to scope out the nature of both businesses, and identify where and how they will need to be integrated. This comes in two distinct steps. First, the integration team needs to understand each business, how it works, and what its key components are. Then they need to decide how to integrate the two businesses. In some cases, they may choose to leave certain components separate, while integrating others. For example, when integrating businesses that run their software on two different platforms, it may be far more costly to try to convert one system over than to just continue to run two different systems. This will be particularly true where each business is large enough to reach critical mass in terms of efficiency of running different systems, and where the conversion costs would be substantial and could include buying new hardware and new software licenses, and hiring new employees or substantially retraining existing employees.

For components or areas that are chosen for integration, planners need to determine how that integration will take place and, where there is redundancy, which side will be eliminated. For example, if two manufacturing facilities will be integrated by closing one, the Buyer must decide which facility will be a better long-term platform for both businesses. While the Buyer may have a preference for its own facilities, systems, employees, and methodologies, it is important for the Buyer to take an unbiased look at each component and make a business judgment about whether to eliminate its own or the Seller's facilities, systems, employees, or methodologies. One of the valuable synergies that a Buyer can get from an acquisition is not just a reduction in cost by integrating two components but an increase in quality, efficiency, or other metrics of performance from adopting a superior approach or platform from the Seller. In many cases, the Seller's products, employees, systems, infrastructure, or facilities may be superior and should be the "winner" in an integration decision.

The important or relevant integration issues will vary from deal to deal, and from business to business. However, certain issues tend to be important in most integration planning efforts. Some of the most common integration issues and efforts will be discussed in this section.

People

As discussed in Chapter 3, for some businesses, people are one of the key assets that a Buyer is seeking to acquire. While law firms and consulting firms are extreme examples, where nearly all the value is embedded in the employees, for almost all acquisitions, people represent a significant source of value and knowledge. The sale of a business is a traumatic event for Seller employees. While both Buyer and Seller employees in the relevant units will have a sense of uncertainty, and dread the potential results of an integration, this is more likely to impact Seller employees, since they understand that there will be a natural preference for retention of Buyer employees by the Buyer. When developing an integration plan for employees, it is important for the Buyer to act quickly and clearly.

Some areas of integration can be allowed to progress slowly, but a failure to develop a clear integration plan for employees, either before or directly after a deal is done, can be very damaging. Employees left in a state of limbo and uncertainty are much more likely to leave for other jobs, and those who remain are likely to be distracted and perform badly. Ideally, an integration plan will establish a fast process for identifying both the employees who will be laid off and also the responsibilities and management structure for the remaining employees, as quickly as possible.

There is often a huge gap between the way a Buyer needs to deal with management and rank-and-file employees. In most cases, Seller management realizes a financial windfall on the sale of their company. In some cases, the Buyer will be able to negotiate terms that require the Seller management team to stay with the company for a period of time, to get their full payout. In the absence of such terms, the Buyer needs to expect that, armed with a large payout and likely chafing under the management of Buyer executives, Seller executives will often depart soon after a deal is done. To the extent that the Buyer wants to retain any of these executives, it will have to consider not only creating an attractive role for them in the Buyer's organization but also mitigating the impact of the financial windfall. Buyers usually do not lay off their own executives as part of an acquisition, but, to the extent Seller executives are being retained, the Buyer needs to consider whether any of its own management is redundant or needs to be repositioned into a new role.

By contrast to executives, Seller employees usually do not reap a huge financial windfall and still need to work for a living. That said, the uncertainty created by a sale of their business will usually drive Seller employees to consider a job search. To the extent they have not been assured of a job in the new organization, this is a totally reasonable reaction. Even when they have been assured of continued employment, the change in culture or organization may make the job less attractive, and drive them to consider leaving. One major integration planning challenge is to quickly review the employee base of the Seller, and try to identify key employees whom the Buyer wants to retain, as well as employees it will actively seek to discard. Seller executives can be critical to this review, since they have a deep knowledge of their own employee base. For Seller employees whom the Buyer wants to retain, the Buyer needs to act quickly, both to confirm that the employee will be offered continued employment and to set out terms of their new role that are attractive enough to retain them. For Buyer employees who may be made redundant as a result of the integration, the Buyer has to be sensitive to the cultural impact of laying off some of "its own." For some companies, where the culture creates an expectation of loyalty to the employees, this process can be a difficult one and can impact morale for the remaining employees.

There are a variety of regulatory and other legal issues that need to be considered, when planning people integration. In addition to the employee benefits policies of both the Seller and the Buyer, there may be union contracts on one or both sides, as well as state and federal regulations governing layoffs. This is one reason that it is important to involve human resources and legal staff in this and other portions of the integration planning process.

In some relatively rare cases, a Buyer will acquire a business and do little integration of people, keeping the two platforms largely separate. In this case, it is possible to avoid many of the issues of people integration but rarely to avoid them entirely. Even when a Buyer is keeping two entirely separate workforces, issues such as corporate culture and employee benefits will usually bleed across from one organization to the other.

Integration of people is likely the most complex and treacherous area of integration. The single most important lesson is that early planning, particularly in this area, can be the difference between success and failure. While computer systems can be run separately for months, and multiple buildings can be leased for years, failure to quickly develop and initiate people integration can lead to an immediate degradation in performance. In deals where there is a gap between signing and closing, the Buyer would be well served by sitting down with Seller management and doing the work of people integration planning, so that the plans can be announced at, or shortly following, the closing of the deal.[1]

Technology

For businesses with a heavy technology component, integration of hardware, software, and systems can be a significant issue. Integration of technology can often be a substantial source of costs or of savings, and needs to be considered, at least at a high level, as part of the valuation of the business. Unlike people integration, technology often allows the Buyer the luxury of waiting before completely integrating two businesses, with less chance of degradation. The counterweight against the luxury of time is the singular risk involved. For businesses where technology is a core element, a shift or transition holds substantial risk of damage to the business. Imagine the damage to a software maker from the release of a product with a major bug, or to a television network from a system failure that took it off the air for minutes or even hours. Integrating technology is an effort in which exceedingly careful and well thought out planning is hugely important. The key issues to consider in a technology integration plan will vary, based on the types of technology involved and the nature of the business, but this section will discuss some overarching themes that usually apply.

The Buyer needs to compare both hardware and software platforms used by itself and the Seller, and decide whether a single platform can effectively support both organizations. Usually one starts by considering the software component and comparing capabilities. Consideration must be given not only to the current needs and products of each organization but also to future plans. For example, if one software system offers flexibility to create new products, it may be preferable, even if such new products are only on the drawing board right now. The Buyer needs to try to choose the "best in class" solution for the combined organization. In theory, a migration to the best platform should create greater efficiency and/or capabilities. When calculating these benefits, the Buyer needs to include all the costs of accomplishing such an integration, as well as needs that go beyond efficiency and product capabilities.

One area of concern is compatibility. Not only must the integrated system be compatible with the internal systems of both businesses, but it must be compatible with external systems with which it needs to interact. The technology platform adopted needs to continue to be able to interact with the systems of counterparties such as suppliers, partners, and, most importantly, customers. The cost of bridging any such compatibility gaps has to be factored into the integration plan. In particular, the integration plan needs to consider the fully loaded cost of integration, including the more qualitative issues such as pain and hassle to the customer. If an integrated system generates 1% more efficiency but leads to the loss of 5% of the customer base, it is unlikely to be viewed as a win.

Security and reliability are also important issues, in the context of technology. As was discussed in Chapter 5, high levels of security and data integrity are required in many areas, not only by customers but also, in some cases, by law. To the extent that the Seller's systems do not meet the Buyer's internal standards, they will have to be brought into compliance very quickly. To the extent the Buyer is entering a more regulated space through the acquisition of the Seller, the deal may actually create higher standards for the Buyer itself. Similarly, there will be expectations for reliability embedded in customer contracts and, potentially, in regulatory requirements. If one set of systems does not meet these requirements, it will quickly need to be upgraded. In some cases, the deal itself will create new standards for one side. For example, if the Seller is a small company, it may be able to formally or informally avoid the requirement that it maintain fully redundant backup systems, but, once acquired by a large public Buyer, it would become subject to those requirements.

Scalability can be both a benefit and a curse. To the extent that systems can be integrated, and a single platform can support more volume, the Buyer can usually generate economies of scale. However, the integration can trigger a need to upgrade systems to support the new scale. While this may lead to long-term efficiencies, it will generate a short-term cost.

Products

When a Buyer uses an acquisition to enter an entirely new business or space, there may be absolutely no overlap between the product sets of Buyer and Seller. However, in most cases, acquisitions involve at least some overlap or connection. The integration plan needs to address how the conflicts, as well as the synergies, between products are going to be managed, resolved, and/or exploited. This effort is particularly important, since it has an impact on customers, and, if managed badly, can lead to alienation and loss of customers or a degradation of the brand or reputation of the Buyer or Seller business.

While the Buyer cannot expect to immediately integrate two product sets, it is important to act quickly to rationalize the combined offering. The goal is to ensure a unified offering of products that maximizes the value of the whole business. There are a variety of variables at play in this exercise. Three broad areas will be highlighted here, although, depending on the type of product, market, and customer, other issues can arise.

When Buyer and Seller products overlap, the integration plan needs to address how they are going to be blended into a unified product line. In some cases, a Buyer may choose to maintain two similar products, particularly where they have subtle differences in terms of pricing, branding, or customer focus. For example, when Daimler and Chrysler merged, each company had a midsized sedan, but they did not eliminate one, since each product appealed to a different price point and type of customer. By contrast, if Dell and Gateway were to merge, one might imagine that many of their product lines would be consolidated, since they are much more similar. Therefore, when comparing product lines, the Buyer needs to look not only at the product functionality but also at the marketing. Even similar products can have different price points, quality levels, or branding strategies. The integration plan needs to identify all these issues and come to a conclusion about which product lines will be maintained and which will be merged. If separate product lines are maintained, the Buyer needs to be sensitive to price compatibility issues. While there is no rule that says the same product cannot be sold at different prices, once the product lines are part of one company, it becomes harder to maintain that price difference. At the very least, it requires a more careful segmentation and differentiation between the product lines.

To the extent separate product lines are maintained, they may have to be adjusted, to minimize the level of cannibalization between them. Between two different companies, cannibalization is not just accepted but encouraged. Take the example of Kentucky Fried Chicken (KFC) and Friday's restaurants. KFC (the down-market player of the two) has actually made an advertising push noting the similarity in product but difference in price between KFC and chains like Friday's—attempting to cannibalize on the competition's customers by offering a supposedly identical product at a much lower price. If KFC and Friday's were under the same ownership, they might not consolidate the two brands, since they target different price points and demographics, but they would likely make an effort to avoid cannibalizing each other.

In some cases, products do not overlap but can interact in a positive way. Separate product lines can often provide synergies to each other, when owned by a single company. The integration plan should also address the potential for synergies between different product lines and the path to achieving them. These efforts could include bundling complementary products together, leveraging each other's manufacturing or marketing channels, or cross-selling existing customers. For example, if a big credit card issuer acquired an auto loan company, it might use the credit information it already had on its customers to preapprove them for auto loans, and send out offers. Similarly, if two clothing retailers merged, they might consolidate their offshore manufacturing agreements, leveraging greater combined volume to get better terms from their suppliers. An excellent example of bundling, though not through an acquisition, is the integration of Starbucks stores into Barnes & Noble locations.

Operations

Integration of operations is usually viewed as a source of synergies through cost savings, but it can also be a source of best practices and improvements to efficiency. However, this needs to be balanced against the cost of achieving these benefits. Generally speaking, integration of operations is done at a slower and more methodical pace. While practices and procedures may need to be standardized quickly after closing, particularly where there are legal or regulatory requirements to do so, actual integration of operations and facilities usually takes months or years. Nonetheless, the integration plan should be able to lay out a base case for integrating operations, and a general timeline for doing so.

The challenge in integrating operations is to balance cost savings, cost of integration, and impact on business results. Any integration of operations will likely create some pain for the business that is being serviced. The key is to be able to balance that pain against the benefits received. For example, if the Buyer and Seller both have a call center with staff that are expert in their particular products, part of the pain of integration will be in cross-training the remaining call center staff in the other group of products. If the training is fairly quick and easy, the pain to the other business will be short-lived and likely worth it. However, if the single call center staff will be incapable of providing high-quality responses to the new set of customers—for example, if the new products are much more complex, and the staff is not well educated enough to master them—the pain may be substantial and do long-term damage to one customer base.

Call centers are a common area of integration savings. The key challenge is to try to minimize disruption to customers, and ensure the same level of service to each of the integrated customer bases. The Buyer needs to consider not only the capabilities of the call center staff but also the operation of the call center. Such issues include the technology infrastructure of the center, and its ability not only to take calls but also to provide service over the Internet; the hours of operation of the call center; and the scalability of the center, to grow in terms of physical facilities and access to additional staff from the local population. For example, some particularly scalable call centers are located in rural areas near state universities or vocational schools, giving them low-cost real estate and a low-cost but well-educated workforce on which to draw.

There is a similar set of concerns with integration of manufacturing facilities. The Buyer needs to consider whether a single facility can accommodate the requirements of each product line. To the extent that the facility will need to be adapted, the Buyer must decide whether the changes are so costly and dramatic that it is more efficient to maintain two facilities. The line must be drawn between reasonable costs to make slight adjustments, and an effort to create a "Frankenstein monster" of a facility that tries to be all things to all businesses.

Technology infrastructure is usually held to a higher standard, since it is harder to operate parallel technology platforms, and the benefits from integrating information systems are usually greater. In the long term, most companies will seek to integrate their core information systems. This is particularly true for systems that provide reporting that eventually gets centralized, including financial reporting and any regulatory compliance reporting. Systems that hold and utilize highly sensitive and confidential data will also be strong candidates for integration. A good general rule is that any time data interacts throughout the company, or is held to high standards of security and integrity, the Buyer will likely want to integrate systems. The Buyer will also want to integrate information systems where it can achieve economies of scale and efficiencies, or take advantage of best practices. These are also fairly common in information technology, where infrastructure often runs with a lot of excess capacity. Since a lot of information technology is licensed rather than owned, there are also obvious efficiencies from operating under a single larger software license. In deals where the Buyer is much larger and more sophisticated than the Seller, it is likely that the Buyer will want to migrate many of the Sellers information technology systems onto the Buyer's existing platforms, for all these reasons.

More generally, there is usually an option to do some "rooftop consolidation," where the Buyer and Seller consolidate locations and reduce the total number of buildings, or "rooftops." The benefits to such integration include the cost savings from fewer building leases or mortgages, as well as the cultural integration that comes with blending staff in a single building. However, there are substantial costs to rooftop consolidation. There is the cost of breaking leases, selling buildings, and moving people and material. There is also the impact on employees, since moving location can have a substantial effect on commute time and convenience for employees. In some cases, rooftop consolidation will actually require a company to lay off some employees and refill the positions in the new location. All these costs have to be balanced against the benefits of a smaller number of buildings.

Brand

Brand integration, almost as much as employee integration issues, can stir strong emotions. More than with physical facilities, particular product lines, or technology platforms, companies often associate themselves strongly with their brand. While brand can feel "intangible," it often has huge value. The process of integrating two brands or transitioning one business onto another's brand can be delicate and complex and the opportunity for value destruction is substantial.

Customers

To begin with a stark reality: the average merging company loses 2 to 5% of the combined customer base during the course of a merger, with some losing more than 30%.[2] More than most other areas of integration planning, customers are a place where there is a substantial potential for damage, as well as benefit, from an acquisition or merger. Like employees, customers can react quickly to the announcement of an acquisition, and thus, it is important that the integration plan for customers be well thought out early in the process.

The integration plan needs to begin with an analysis of the Seller customer base and a decision about the value of different groups of customers.

In some cases, customers will be highly attractive and key assets of the Seller. In some cases, a group of customers will be attractive, but not crucial, to the value of the business. In some cases, a group of customers may even be unattractive to the Buyer. This view of the customers may be based on the volume of their purchases or on their own characteristics, including, notably, their creditworthiness and payment history.

Once the Buyer has assessed the relative value of different groups of Seller customers, it needs to assess the likely reaction of those customers, as well as its own, to the announcement of the deal. As was discussed in more detail in Chapter 2, customers can have a range of reactions to the announcement of a deal. In some cases, the deal may be viewed as a positive event by customers, creating a financially stronger supplier with a wider range of products. In other cases, it may be viewed as a negative, creating a company where the customers' particular needs are not a core focus, or a company with a bad reputation for other reasons.

The integration plan needs to determine which customers are highly valued, and then predict their likely concerns about a deal. The integration plan then needs to identify a path to address those concerns. For customers that are highly unattractive, the integration plan may also want to address whether there is any way to eliminate those customer relationships, within the terms of any legal agreements or commitments.

Legal terms can be an important component of the analysis of customers in an integration plan. Depending on the structure of the deal (stock or asset purchase), and the terms of the customer contract, it may be possible to transfer the relationship on the same terms, or it may be necessary to get some sort of consent from the customer. Many customer relationships are either terminable at will, terminable on a change in control—such as a Strategic Transaction—or, in many cases, not even governed by a contract but maintained on a transaction-by-transaction basis. For example, customers at a restaurant do not sign a contract committing them to eat a certain number of meals there per year but simply purchase services—in this case, a nice bowl of soup and a salad, perhaps—one at a time. This is a good example of the need for interaction between members of the due diligence and integration teams. The lawyers reviewing the terms of the customer contracts need to communicate these terms to the integration team, which then needs to plan appropriately. Even if there is a contract in place, and it is transferable, the Buyer may still need to take certain actions, such as sending out a notification, to complete the transfer.

In many cases, the key focus of a customer integration plan will be on communication. By quickly reaching out to customers, after a deal is announced, a Buyer can try to allay concerns and woo Seller customers, seeking to minimize any breakage during the integration.

Another potential negative impact of a deal is customer overlap. To the extent that both Buyer and Seller are competing for the same set of customers, the integration plan needs to start to address how that competition is going to be eliminated. The challenge here is to eliminate damaging intracompany competition, and apportion the customers to the right businesses to most effectively compete against outside businesses. There is usually a strong political component to this exercise, as each of the two relevant business unit managers will want to keep as large a portion of the customer base as possible.

The integration plan should also try to start to address the positive synergies of acquiring a new customer base. Unlike the remediation of breakage, positive synergies will usually take longer, and they are less critical during the early months after a deal closes. However, they are often a significant benefit identified to justify a deal, and so they need to be considered and analyzed early, even if it will take time to execute on plans to realize them. Cross-sell is an obvious potential synergy, where the customer bases of the Seller and Buyer are cross-sold the products of the other party. Customer overlap can also have a positive impact to the extent that the two businesses can consolidate the costs associated with servicing a single customer. For example, if the two businesses can consolidate their billing to a customer, or move to a single sales representative calling on the customer, they can generate cost savings, while keeping the standard of service to the customer the same, or even improving it.

Suppliers and Partners

Since suppliers and partners generally benefit from their relationship with the Buyer or Seller, and they are usually larger businesses, more comfortable with Strategic Transactions, there is likely to be less need for urgent action than in the case of customers. Nonetheless, it is important for the integration plan to consider these relationships and the impact that the deal will have on them.

As with customers, the first step is to review the supplier and partner relationships, and determine their relative value. This review has to be done in the context of the combined business, and must consider redundancy and overlap with the Buyer's existing supplier and partner relationships. As with technology, this should be an exercise in best practices, where the Buyer tries to choose the set of optimal supplier and partner relationships from those of both the Buyer and Seller.

For those relationships that the Buyer does not want to maintain, it needs to work with its lawyers to determine what steps are necessary, and what costs will be incurred, to terminate them. For those that are highly valuable, the Buyer will need to consider the terms of the contract between the supplier or partner and the Seller. Supplier and partner relationships are far more likely to be governed by an ongoing contract than are customer relationships. The first step is to review these contracts and see whether the relationships are transferable, and, if so, what steps the Buyer will need to take to effectuate the transfer.

Where the contracts are not transferable but are highly valued, the Buyer will have to put a plan in place to negotiate new terms with the supplier or partner. To the extent that the original relationship with the Seller was attractive to the supplier or partner, it is likely that, barring some particular problem with the Buyer, the counterparty will be willing to continue the relationship on the same terms. In some cases, the deal will be a positive event for the supplier or partner, since it creates a relationship with a larger entity. In those cases, the Buyer may even be able to negotiate better terms than the original agreement contained.

NOTES

1. Note that, in some cases, antitrust regulations will put some limits on how companies that have entered into a purchase agreement but are awaiting regulatory approval can work together. For deals that are subject to this regulation, this can limit any execution of integration planning but usually still allows the planning process and information sharing to take place. For a detailed discussion of this issue, see Robert Pitofsky, Harvey Goldschmid, and Diane Wood, *Trade Regulation Cases and Materials,* 5th ed. (New York: Foundation Press, 2003).
2. Scott Christofferson, Robert McNish, and Diane Sias, "Where Mergers Go Wrong," *The McKinsey Quarterly,* no. 2 (McKinsey & Co., 2004).

CHAPTER 10

Financing Issues

It sounds obvious, but any deal, whether a full acquisition or an equity investment, involves a purchase price that must be paid. The Buyer has to come up with a purchase price. As discussed in Chapter 8, the purchase price can be paid in a variety of currencies and, in some cases, over time. In some cases, the Buyer can use cash, stock, or other assets it has on hand, and in other cases, it must go to outside sources. Where, how, and even if the Buyer can come up with the purchase price are important considerations for both sides in a deal.

COST OF CAPITAL

For the Buyer, opportunity cost is an important and often overlooked part of the equation in any acquisition or equity investment. When analyzing a deal, it is crucial to factor in the path not taken. When a company or an equity interest is acquired, the capital used always has a cost, regardless of how it is financed or what currency is used to pay. If the capital is borrowed, there is an explicit cost, and if it is cash or stock on hand, the lost opportunity cost of not being able to use it for another deal or other purpose must be considered. Determining the value or attractiveness of a deal has to include the cost of whatever capital is used in the acquisition. If you do not factor in the inherent cost of the purchase price, you can substantially overestimate the value of an acquisition or investment.

Cash Financing Sources

If the purchase price must be paid in cash, a Buyer may have sufficient cash on hand or may have to borrow. However, just because a Buyer has the cash on hand does not mean that it is a costless exercise to make payment.

In a theoretical sense, a company can always borrow more money at some rate. Thus, there is an inherent cost of capital for any company. For purposes of this chapter, I will dramatically oversimplify the principles of calculating cost of capital, but there are many books that explain how to calculate cost of capital in much greater detail and specificity. They generally calculate the weighted average cost of capital to take into account the variety of different capital sources, both equity and debt, of a company.[1] Let us begin by considering the various sources of capital.

Raising Capital

Larger companies can access the public markets by selling securities. They can sell debt securities or sell stock. Similarly, companies can sell equity or debt to private investors. Debt is usually "sold" to banks, in the form of loans, or to large investors, such as pension funds, in the form of privately placed bonds (usually similar in form to public debt but sold only to a small number of large investors). The choice of whether to use public or private markets will depend on the rates charged in each. In most cases, public markets will offer lower rates, but only some companies can access those markets, and they usually need to borrow in a large enough amount to create a liquid market in the security. A company borrowing $5 million will usually be better off going to a private investor or a bank, while a company seeking $1 billion in financing will often get a lower rate by going to the public markets.

For the sale of additional equity, public companies have to consider the impact of that sale on the broader market in their stock. If the company believes that there is little appetite in the market for more shares, it may shy away from issuing equity for fear that it will push down the price of its stock. One can imagine a situation in which the negative impact on the overall market capitalization of the company exceeds the amount actually financed. For instance, a company with a $1 billion market capitalization issues an additional $20 million in stock, but there is so little demand for the stock that the sale pushes the stock price down by 4%. Effectively, in financing $20 million with stock, the company has reduced the total value of its equity by $40 million. For a private company, the issuance of equity may be logistically challenging. There are significant regulatory limits on the ability of a private company to sell securities. Generally, it is limited to selling to very large investors, and, even then, a relatively small number of them. A private company is far more likely than a public company to encounter a limit in the appetite for equity given the much smaller universe of potential Buyers.

Public companies, or private companies that have made the necessary regulatory filings, can sell debt securities, effectively borrowing from the public market. As with equity, it usually does not make sense to issue debt securities unless one is talking about a reasonably large amount. For smaller amounts, and companies that do not want to make the necessary filings, private borrowing is often an attractive alternative. Companies can borrow from banks, but they can also access a large population of other institutions that make large private loans or participate in syndicated private loans, including insurance companies, pension funds, and other large investors.

Then, there is the choice of equity versus debt, which will depend on a variety of factors. First, the company will have a view on whether its stock is currently over- or undervalued in the market. If it believes the stock is overvalued (i.e., the market thinks a share of stock is worth more than the company's management really believes it is worth) there is an incentive to sell more stock into the market. However, in practice, it is pretty rare to find managers who think their stock is overvalued. By definition, a management team tends to be optimistic about their company's prospects, and most management teams spend their time trying to sell their vision and optimistic views to the market with less than total success. This would suggest that companies will prefer to finance an acquisition, or any other need for capital, with the issuance of debt. In a sense, this belief is driven by their optimism about the prospects of the company. If one believes that the company's business model is good, one has an interest in putting more capital behind that model by borrowing. To use a blackjack term, managers will usually want to "double-down" on their business model. However, there is a countervailing market force that limits a manager's ability to lever up her company (i.e., increase borrowing to fund growth). The market will only lend to a company to the extent that it has a reasonable expectation of being paid back. As that expectation goes down, the interest rate that the market will charge the company will go up. High interest–rate, or "junk," bonds are debt securities offered to the market by companies where there is a greater risk of default.

While the cost of debt is an actual number, the cost of equity is more ambiguous. As a general matter, the return on equity expected by the market on the company's stock is a good shorthand for the cost of equity. That is, if the market expects the company's stock to appreciate by 10% per year, this is a good estimate of the cost of equity, since, theoretically, that gain would have been "kept" by the company if the equity had not been issued.

The cost of either equity or debt is also affected by the market as a whole. The rate of return expected for equity, and the interest charged for debt, is really a combination of the base market rate and a risk premium associated with the particular company. Therefore, as interest rates rise and fall, and as market expectations of return on equity change, the cost of equity or debt for a particular company will move in sync. Similarly, market expectations for a particular industry can affect the cost of debt or equity. Separate from the risk of the issuing company, a market perception of changes in the risk of the sector can cause it to charge an issuer in that sector more or less for equity or debt financing.

All of the financing tools discussed apply not only to acquisitions but also to a company's capital needs. From investment in technology to building new plants, a company's operations are, by definition, either funded from cash the company has on hand or from some form of equity or debt financing. As a result, it is silly to consider acquisition financing in a vacuum. This would be like thinking of the money in your left pocket as separate from the money in your right pocket. It is all your money, and you can move it from pocket to pocket at will. Instead, a company looks at its overall capital needs and capital sources. As a result, when considering the financing of an acquisition, a Buyer should factor in the general cost of capital for the company. And any acquisition or investment's performance must net out the cost of capital applied to that deal.

Since a company is funded by a combination of equity and debt, a company's cost of capital will be a weighted average of its cost of equity and its cost of debt. For example, if a company has gotten $100 million in equity (i.e., shares of stock purchased by investors) and $900 million in debt (i.e., loans taken from either the market or private entities, such as banks), the company's cost of capital will be the 0.9 times the interest rate on the debt plus 0.1 times the rate of return that is expected on the stock. If the Buyer uses cash on hand to finance a transaction, it clearly needs to use the overall cost of capital to assess the transaction. If a Buyer issues equity or debt specifically to finance a deal, one might argue that it should use that specific financing cost in reviewing the deal. However, it can be argued that, in a theoretical sense, this is inaccurate, since it is simply taking money from one pocket and transferring it to the other, and that the overall company cost of capital is still the right metric to use when considering the opportunity cost of the deal. One exception is found when a deal is so large that it actually changes the cost of capital of a company. For example, if a company goes from having no debt, to having a massive debt burden as a result of buying another company of about the same size, its cost of capital could increase dramatically as a result of the deal itself. However, even in this situation, it can be argued that the new, revised overall cost of capital of the company is the right metric to use for opportunity cost.

In addition to the actual cost of equity or debt financing, there is a related opportunity cost related to the fundamental inelasticity of the market. In a theoretical economic sense, there should be no limit to the amount of equity or debt that a company can issue, just a steadily increasing cost as the risk of default for debt or the risk of underperformance for equity, rises. However, in practice, this is not a smooth curve. There is only a certain finite appetite for equity or debt of a particular company, and as the company approaches that limit, there will be a sudden and dramatic increase in the cost of that financing source. Since an acquisition or equity investment usually requires a single large "slug" of financing, one has to consider the short-term impact of "dumping" such a large slug of equity or debt into the market. Particularly in the case of equity, the introduction of a large amount into the market where there is no appetite for additional investment in the company can cause a drop in the stock price. In theory, if the acquired assets will drive growth and earnings at an equal or higher rate to the predeal company, there should be no drop in stock price. However, the market is usually skeptical of such performance and may take a wait and see approach, punishing the stock price in the short term and rewarding it only after such performance is realized. This will often shape the choice of equity versus debt for a Buyer. In more than one instance, I have seen the financing choice determined not by the long-term cost of capital but by an aversion on the part of senior management to enduring a short-term hit to the stock price, preferring instead to seek higher-cost debt alternatives. At the very least, a Buyer who is issuing equity to finance a transaction will become particularly sensitive to the public relations and investor relations efforts that come with the transaction and will make a significant effort to ensure that the market understands the benefits of the deal clearly, in an effort to buffer the negative effect of the additional equity.

A company can also choose to sell equity or debt privately to large investors or institutions. These transactions raise the same issues of opportunity cost discussed in Chapter 8, but there are some key differences. A private transaction is much simpler and usually subject to a lot less regulation. However, large institutions may demand better terms than the public markets would, so the financing may be more expensive. For equity financing, the likely Buyers are going to be private equity and other financial investors. If the Buyer is a private company, it can tap current investors or use this as an opportunity to widen its investor base. The challenge here is that a round of equity funding will precipitate a valuation of the Buyer's business, and depending on a variety of factors, including recent company performance and the state of the industry and the market, this could be a good or bad time for the Buyer to have its business valued. The timing of the Strategic Transaction may not coincide with the best time to sell additional equity in the company. The Buyer may be able to alleviate this by tapping its existing investors so that no one is diluted in their ownership and the valuation of the company can be maintained; however, this assumes that the current investors are interested in putting more money into the company, which is not always the case. A public Buyer can also choose to place equity privately in a PIPEs transaction (as discussed earlier), where stock in a public company is sold to a single or small number of large investors in a private transaction. PIPEs deals have some inherent regulatory complexities. They also require a Buyer who is willing to buy a chunk of a public company and usually to be locked up and required to hold that stock for a period of time.

The Buyer can also choose to issue debt privately. In its simplest form, this can simply be a bank loan from a large lending institution. Bank loans or lines of credit are most likely to be available to larger companies with solid credit and assets that can be secured to support the debt. However, even for a larger company, financing a Strategic Transaction with bank debt can be difficult. Unless the Target company is dramatically smaller than the Buyer, the Buyer may not have good enough credit or a large enough pool of assets to secure a basic bank loan. More importantly, most banks will be hesitant to take that much risk on a single company. Another alternative is to issue a private debt security. The Buyers for this debt will be institutional investors and private equity funds specializing in debt rather than equity. The Buyer may pay a higher rate on this debt, but the use of a debt security allows a company to effectively borrow from a larger number of institutions, who individually might not be willing to take such a large risk on a single company but collectively can do so. The same effect might sometimes be accomplished by a syndicate of banks.

Debt obligations of any sort will include terms and conditions called covenants that encumber the issuing company and whose breach can trigger a number of unpleasant events. These conditions can include limitations on the ability of the company to issue additional debt or take other actions, and triggers that require immediate repayment, such as minimum cash flow and debt level ratios. It is crucial that the Buyer consider these triggers and limitations carefully. For long-term debt, these are obligations and barriers that the Buyer may have to live with for years. Putting in place the wrong limits can stymie the growth of a business, and breaching these covenants and obligations can have even more devastating effects. Breaching key covenants in a debt instrument can result in an obligation to make immediate payment. This, in and of itself, can drive many companies into bankruptcy or the need to sell off chunks of the business.

The term of the debt is also an important factor. The Buyer has to project its cash flow effectively and determine how quickly it can pay back the debt and on what schedule. The Buyer needs to build in enough flexibility to account for unexpected changes in its business and the market in general. Defaulting on debt financing can be damaging or even fatal to a company. Nonbank debt may allow the Buyer to negotiate a longer payment period and, in some cases, a structure where interest payments are deferred or even paid in one lump sum with the principle at the end of the term of the debt.

The Buyer may also factor in the nature of its relationship with different lenders. If the Buyer has a strong business relationship with a bank (for instance, if the Buyer also does credit card processing or payroll there), it may be able to leverage this relationship into better terms. Similarly, if one of the Buyer's investors also offers debt financing as well as equity, its familiarity with the Buyer and its desire to see its equity investment appreciate could make it the best choice for borrowing. In choosing the type of debt and lender, the Buyer will have to balance a variety of factors, including the interest rate charged, the term of the debt, the conditions and commitments it must make, and sometimes even the nature of the lender.

Borrowing or issuing equity to a private investor has timing advantages. Since the regulatory requirements are far lower, and the investor base is sophisticated and used to doing such deals, and since the number of counterparties and involved parties in general, is much smaller, private financing can usually be accomplished much faster. This is very important, since a Strategic Transaction usually takes place quickly, and a Seller is unlikely to want to stall the process to wait for financing to be completed (see also the "Financing Contingency: 'Bird in the Hand'" section below).

Even private financing will take some time and require documentation and negotiation. It is important to recognize and plan for this when embarking on a Strategic Transaction. This can be challenging, since the Buyer can end up in simultaneous negotiation with both the Seller and the Buyer's financing source. The contingent nature of the financing negotiation is also challenging. Usually, when a company seeks to borrow money the use of funds is already established and fairly certain (e.g., building a factory, expanding operations, funding research). In most cases, when a Buyer is negotiating funding for a Strategic Transaction, there is a significant chance that the deal will never close and the financing will not be needed. However, financing sources, particularly those that provide deal financing on a regular basis, are used to this uncertainty.

Paying in Equity

One variation on financing a deal with equity is actually paying the purchase price in stock. There are several advantages to this approach. First, the Buyer can limit the market impact of issuing a large chunk of equity. By putting limits on when, how, and in what quantities a Seller can sell its shares into the market, the Buyer can manage any impact on its stock price. However, Sellers are likely to resist such constraints, since they limit the immediate liquidity of the Seller and also introduce new risks. Instead of getting cash, the Seller has taken a significant position in the Buyer's stock and the effective purchase price it ends up receiving could be substantially different if the Buyer's stock price fluctuates.[2] These limits can also serve business purposes. To the extent that some of the Seller's shareholders are going to remain involved in the business after the transaction, requiring them to continue to hold their portion of the purchase price in Buyer's stock ties their incentives to those of the Buyer. The best example of this is the case of a Seller where the management team owns a substantial portion of the stock and is being required to stay on in a management role for a period after the completion of the transaction. Particularly when the Seller's company is going to be a substantial portion of the resulting merged entity, linking the eventual value received in purchase price by the management team to the performance of the Buyer's stock creates a powerful incentive for that management team to drive performance even postacquisition.

Using equity for a purchase price does create some potential pitfalls for the Buyer. If the purchase price represents a significant portion of the total value of the Seller, paying in equity will change the character of the Seller's shareholder base. In some cases, this may not be of particular concern. If both are large public companies with diverse shareholder bases, the combination is less likely to have a material impact. However, if the Seller's stock is concentrated in a small number of holders, the result could be a new and fairly powerful shareholder in the Buyer. Some recent examples of this include Ted Turner's sale of his network to Time Warner and Craig McCaw's sale of his telecom business to AT&T, which made him one of AT&T's largest shareholders. An activistic and disgruntled large shareholder can be a real frustration to a Buyer's management, and it may choose to pay in cash to avoid the potential for this.

Payment in equity can also be a matter of optics and public relations. If two companies both have overvalued stock, it may be hard for a Buyer to agree to pay cash but easier for it to agree to pay the same amount in equity. Similarly, paying in equity provides the Buyer with a better argument to shareholders that the Seller is participating in the risk of the deal. In practice, this is not necessarily the case to the extent that Seller shareholders are allowed to quickly sell the equity, or even to the extent that they are not barred from constructing hedging positions to offset the risk of the Buyer's stock. Optically, however, paying in stock may help a Buyer's management to fend off criticism from the market that they have overpaid for an acquisition.

If the Buyer is a private company, paying in equity creates a lot of additional complexity for both parties. The result will be a private company with new and likely significant shareholders who, unless the Seller's shareholders remain employed by the Buyer, have no real interest in the company. Few Sellers are likely to accept an illiquid security in payment, unless it is a situation in which the selling shareholders are planning a long continued involvement with the Buyer. The most likely situation is in the purchase of a smaller private business, where the Seller's shareholders are also employees and plan to continue employment with the Buyer. Even in this case, unless they are going to exercise substantial management control, they will likely be reticent to accept stock in payment.

It is also important to remember that paying in stock creates a number of significant additional legal and regulatory requirements. For a public company Buyer, it will require public filings with the SEC and likely a follow-on registration of the securities to allow the Seller's shareholders to sell them. These requirements can cost a Buyer hundreds of thousands of dollars in legal fees alone. Even for a private Buyer, the inclusion of additional shareholders will create additional obligations under state corporations law. All things being equal, paying in cash is easier and less expensive.

Having said that, if a Buyer is seriously concerned about market impact from doing an equity or debt offering to finance an acquisition or investment, paying in equity may be an attractive alternative to consider. If a Buyer is planning to retain key employees who are significant shareholders, paying them in equity helps to align their incentives and keep them focused after the transaction is complete. In practice, this is often a challenge when senior managers are suddenly paid millions or tens of millions of dollars for their shares. The temptation to chuck it all and retire is strong. This, of course, is an additional tool above and beyond the more direct contingent payment and earn-out methods discussed in Chapter 8.

Paying in Assets

In relatively rare cases, a Buyer may pay a purchase price in assets. This situation is rare because it would require the Seller to happen to be the most appropriate Buyer of those particular assets—the party who attributes the most value to those assets. In any other case, the Buyer could recognize more value by selling the assets to some other Buyer and then using the proceeds to pay the Seller. Of course, in most cases, it also presupposes that the Seller is selling less than all its assets, or that it wants to "swap" the business it is selling for one owned by the Buyer. The chances that each party in a Strategic Transaction will be the most enthusiastic Buyer for the other party's asset are fairly slim. When this does occur, it can be economically efficient, since it eliminates one separate sale process and many of the costs that go along with it.

I served as the financial advisor for one such transaction in the mid-1990s. Rollins Truck Leasing, a truck leasing company, had a small logistics subsidiary that it wanted to divest. One of the most logical Buyers, United Parcel Service, had a small truck leasing business that it also considered to be nonstrategic. Initially, a basic sales negotiation was developed around the Buyer acquiring Rollins' logistics business, but as the discussions progressed we realized that the truck leasing business would be of interest to Rollins as well. In the end, we were able to negotiate effectively a swap of the two businesses, with the negotiated difference in value being made up by a cash payment to my client. Both parties accomplished two transactions in a single negotiation.

While there were still two sets of due diligence, it was a single negotiation with a single set of advisors, and since the transactions were closed simultaneously, the need to temporarily finance one transaction, while waiting for the second to close was eliminated. This transaction is an example of a particularly synergistic swap of assets. Each party traded a noncore business for an addition to a more strategic offering and in the process removed one significant competitor from its space. Setting aside, but recognizing, the potential antitrust implications of such a deal, it is one of those rare cases where a payment in assets is the optimal result for both parties.

LOST OPPORTUNITIES

In addition to limits on capital, there are other constraints or opportunity costs to doing a Strategic Transaction. As discussed, a Strategic Transaction requires a lot of resources to negotiate, close, and integrate. In particular, it requires a lot of attention from senior management. Since senior management's time is a limited resource, which cannot easily be expanded and must always be rationed and spread between any Strategic Transaction and the day-to-day management of the business, there is a limit to how many Strategic Transactions a company can effectively do in a given period. The high failure rate for Strategic Transactions is usually attributed to weak integration, and at least part of the key to effective integration is sustained senior management involvement and focus. Some companies have become particularly adept at doing Strategic Transactions, but even companies like Cisco and Cendant have limits to the volume of large deals they can do.

Strategic Transactions also put a strain on other resources. Line management teams that have to be dedicated to due diligence and integration are pulled from their regular duties. While more resources can be hired, the need for a detailed knowledge and familiarity with the current business limits a company's ability to "backfill" additional new resources. Bringing in new people without that familiarity can cause a company to suffer from diminishing returns because the new team members need to be brought up to speed and managed more carefully.

In theory, financial, legal, and other outside advisors are an unlimited resource. However, in practice, even these can be constrained. Most companies have preferred relationships with one or two firms in each of these areas. The team dedicated to, and familiar with, the company, can have its own resource constraints. For example, while a large accounting firm can pull resources from other projects or even other offices, the team dedicated to a company and most familiar with its financials, and its industry, may be limited.

Finally, there is also a theoretical limit to the public markets' tolerance for Strategic Transactions. Each new large transaction requires a certain education of shareholders, because the strategy and logic behind the deal has to be explained in order to spin the deal as a positive, or at least as not a negative. If a series of Strategic Transactions share a common theme and strategy, it is easier to spin a series of deals, but, even then, one has to allay market fears about the ability of the company to accomplish a number of overlapping integrations. To the extent that each Strategic Transaction is driven by a different story or strategy, the ability of the market to absorb different stories without getting confused, or losing confidence in management and its overall strategy, is limited. Thus, even market perception can limit the volume of Strategic Transactions that a company can do.

All these constraints, ensure that companies that do not do Strategic Transactions regularly are likely to find it difficult to do more than one a year and, even then, can expect it to put a strain on senior management and other resources. Even companies with deep expertise in doing deals will find the potential volume of Strategic Transactions constrained by these factors. As a result, when evaluating a Strategic Transaction, a Buyer needs to consider the opportunity cost of making use of limited resources which would otherwise be available to do other deals in the future.

FINANCING CONTINGENCY: "BIRD IN THE HAND"

Strategic transactions require a large influx of capital, and, in many cases, this is capital that the Buyer does not have readily available. While it is very common for a Buyer to finance an acquisition, it is important to recognize that this is more than just a matter of paperwork and logistics. Financing introduces a new party and a new level of uncertainty into the transaction. There are different levels of financing commitment that a Buyer can get. In some cases, a Buyer can get a fairly firm and irrevocable commitment from a bank or other source of capital. In other cases, the financing will be subject to the whims of the market, as it will be with a public offering of equity or debt securities.

A Buyer will often try to sign a purchase agreement before actually executing the transactions necessary to finance the closing of the deal. This is usually a far more cost-effective approach, since the financing transaction will cost money and once done will burden the Buyer with the cost of servicing that obligation. Thus, the Buyer will tend to want the financing to close at or very shortly before the closing of the strategic transaction itself.

However, this leaves the Seller in a dilemma. Unless the signing and closing are simultaneous, the Seller is left to sign an agreement that is subject to obtaining successful financing to close. In most such cases, the Buyer will have to have a financing contingency added to the agreement that, in effect, says that its obligation to close is subject to a successful financing transaction.

In this situation, the Seller must weigh the risk of a failed closing against the value of the bid from the Buyer. In theory, the greater the risk that the

Buyer's financing will fail, the greater the discount that the Seller should apply to the Buyer's bid. The steepness of this discount curve will also depend on how much damage the Seller thinks will be done to its company, or how difficult it will be to reapproach other bidders, should the financing fail and the deal fail to close.

NOTE

1. The details of a weighted average cost of capital (WACC) calculation are laid out in Richard A. Brealey and Stewart Myers, *Principles of Corporate Finance* (London: McGraw-Hill, 1991), p. 407.
2. For an example of this effect, see Michael E. S. Frankel, *Deal Teams* (Boston: Aspatore 2003), p. 17.

CHAPTER 11

Closing the Deal and After

For many business professionals, the signing and closing of a deal are somewhat mysterious waypoints in the transition from making an acquisition to integration. While each is a single point in time, and sometimes they are simultaneous, technically speaking, the signing and closing are the actual events to which all the effort, negotiation, planning, and analysis are devoted. Until a deal is signed and then closed, it is still possible for either side to walk away and abandon the agreement. And while a term sheet may lay out the general outline of an agreement, and a historical financial statement may give a good indication of the financial state of a company at a future date, only the definitive legal documents set out the true and full terms of the agreement, and only the closing balance sheet sets down the exact financial balances that are being bought and sold.

HOW IS A DEAL CLOSED?

There is no one standard structure and timeline to the closing process, and details will vary and must be adapted to the nature of the business being sold, the needs of the parties, and often the regulations that apply. There are some key steps that are fairly standard in any Strategic Transaction and provide a good outline of the mechanics of closing a deal.

There is often a significant difference between signing and closing a deal. Signing a deal means that the two parties execute a binding agreement to do the deal, subject to certain closing conditions. Closing a deal is the act of executing the final documentation that causes the deal to take effect. In simple terms, signing a deal means signing an agreement to sell a company, while closing a deal means actually completing the sale. When a deal is signed, the two parties then take whatever steps are necessary to satisfy the conditions to closing. Once those conditions are satisfied, the parties will choose a date to execute final and definitive documents to close the deal. In most cases, the gap between signing and closing is created to allow the parties to comply with regulatory requirements, but in some cases, it is used to allow the Buyer time to finalize financing or to allow the Seller to make certain changes to the business. The agreement executed at the signing is designed to make it fairly difficult for either of the parties to walk away from the deal, but it allows them to do so if the conditions to closing are not met. In addition to required regulatory filings and approvals, the conditions to closing may often include a requirement that the Seller's business has not had a "material adverse change." Generally, this means that the Seller's business has not been substantially damaged during the period between signing and closing. The conditions to closing will be hotly negotiated as each party tries to create exceptions to its own obligations to close and tighten the exceptions to the other parties obligation.

At the signing, the two parties will generally sign a purchase agreement (also termed a merger agreement or a stock purchase agreement, depending on the nature of the deal). In addition to the conditions to closing, the purchase agreement will set out the detailed terms of the agreement, including the purchase price and method of payment, as well as representations and warranties made by both sides and the terms of indemnification. Representations and warranties are basically promises made by both sides as to the key facts of their business. In the case of the Buyer, the representations and warranties will usually focus on its ability to pay the purchase price and its authorization by relevant parties (board of directors or shareholders) to do the deal. The Seller's representations and warranties are usually much more extensive and will cover the key facts of the business being sold that the Seller is attesting to be true. Seller representations and warranties will usually include references to financial statements, key agreements, and contracts as well as other important facts about the business. Indemnification is basically the obligation (and limits thereto) of each party to cover the costs to the other party of certain events, including the failure of their own representations and warranties to be true. For example, if the Buyer is taking on contracts, it will often agree to indemnify the Seller for obligations under those contracts going forward. Similarly, if the Seller has represented, for example, that there are no accounts payable owing from the business, it will often indemnify the Buyer for any undisclosed accounts payable or other liabilities. Usually indemnification includes both a cap (a maximum dollar amount) and a basket (an amount under which indemnification will not apply).

After the deal is signed, the two parties will usually proceed to closing as quickly as possible. For each party, the period between signing and closing holds a lot of uncertainty, and, in most cases, both sides will be eager to close as soon as possible. The gap between signing and closing will vary based on the external factors that required the gap in the first place. The most common, and usually the longest, source of delay is the requirement for regulatory approval. For businesses that are heavily regulated, there are usually requirements that the sale of the business, and sometimes the purchase of a large new business, receive approval from the relevant regulator.

Once all the closing conditions have been met, the parties will arrange a closing. The closing usually involves much more documentation than a signing. Most of the documents are legal forms used to transfer ownership and rights to assets and securities. The lawyers will usually also require legal documents demonstrating the authority of the signing parties. The representations and warranties in the original purchase agreement will often be "brought down" to the closing date. Effectively, this means that the parties attest that the facts in the representations and warranties continue to be true at the date of closing.

When all these documents have been signed, the purchase price will be formally transferred, as will, when relevant, any securities held by trust institutions. This can be as simple as making a phone call and authorizing a wire transfer but can also involve executing a transfer of securities through holding agencies, such as the Depository Trust Corporation, or releasing funds held in escrow by a bank. All these transactions need to be well planned and documented in advance so that all but the last step has already been taken. Generally, the group in the closing room will actually wait around to make sure that funds and/or securities have been transferred, and the lawyers will not release the executed documents to the other side until the transfer has been confirmed.

In terms of logistics, the signing and the closing will usually take place at the offices of either the Buyer's or Seller's lawyers. Technically, a faxed signature page is legally valid, but most parties will prefer an original ink copy. Also, given the significance of the transaction, senior executives from each side will often choose to attend the event in person rather than simply sending signed documents to the lawyers by courier. The closing is often a celebratory event. Setting aside any animosity of the negotiation, both parties generally are pleased with the result and usually enjoy the signing process and then go out to celebrate the deal. The closing is such a positive event that both sides usually arrange a closing dinner weeks, or sometimes months, later to celebrate the completion of the deal.

After the deal is done, the integration team generally takes center stage and begins the process of refining and executing the integration plan.

However, the lawyers and finance team usually have some clean-up work to do in the weeks and months after the closing. The lawyers will likely have some postclosing paperwork and often regulatory filings to complete.

The finance team usually has a more substantial project. Financial statements are a reflection of a business at a given point in time. Of course, it takes time to gather the data and come to those final numbers, so, by definition, financial statements are always a look backward. This is why companies report their financial results to the market weeks after the end of the relevant period. It takes that long for them to gather data, have it reviewed by their auditors, and come to a final set of financial statements. As a result, it is impossible to close a deal knowing exactly the financial state of the business at that date and time. At best, the Seller can provide an estimate of those financial statements based on historical trends and projections.

Lawyers have devised a basic mechanism, and many variations on it, to deal with this problem. In most deals, there is a postclosing adjustment to the purchase price to reflect the difference between the estimated and actual financial performance through the date of closing. During the period directly after closing, the finance staff of both the Buyer and the Seller, and usually the auditors of the Seller and sometimes those of the Buyer, will work to create a final set of financials for the Seller's business. This can be a bit challenging, since, while the Seller ran the business through closing, as of the date of closing, the business and all the accompanying financial reporting mechanisms are usually owned and run by the Buyer. Through a variety of different mechanisms, which can include reviews by outside auditors, the finance teams will reach a final set of financial statements, and one party or the other will pay an adjustment to the purchase price based on a predetermined calculation driven by the final financial statements. These calculations can be as simple as an adjustment based on total cash on the balance sheet but are often far more complicated. In most cases, the postclosing adjustment is completed in a matter of one or two months but for businesses where it takes a long time to resolve financial balances and accounts, the "tail" on this calculation can go much longer.

OTHER SIGNING AND CLOSING EVENTS

At and directly after both signing and closing, there are a variety of potential interactions with internal and external parties that the deal team must consider having. Broadly speaking, they can be categorized into public statements, private statements, and legal actions. Which of these are required and when will depend on the nature of the deal, the businesses involved, and the details of the integration plan. Whether these things are done at both the signing and the closing or just at the closing will depend on how public the signing is. In some deals, the signing will be made public by either necessity or choice. For some companies, the fact of a signing is an event that must be made public by law. Some regulators require public filings as part of the approval process. For companies that are publicly held and governed by the Securities and Exchange Commission (SEC), material transactions are usually required to be disclosed to shareholders. As a result, almost any agreement to sell a public company will need to be publicly disclosed by the Seller, and the purchase of a business (even a privately held one) that represents a material portion of the Buyer business may also be required to be disclosed.

Planning the full message that will be communicated once a deal is announced is important. Since messages to both employees and the outside world need to be carefully crafted and usually vetted with a variety of people, it is not the kind of thing that can be done quickly. In most cases, a variety of people, including public relations, human resources, legal, and financial staff, as well as executive management and, in some cases, the board of directors, will need to be involved in crafting the language used to discuss a deal.

Public Statements

Public statements have to be crafted carefully and universally. Unlike private messages, in which one may (though not always) expect a certain level of discretion, one needs to assume that public statements are read by everyone. As a result, it is hard to tailor public statements to specific audiences, since each statement would tend to bleed between different audiences and be read by all. Lawyers often call this the "*Wall Street Journal* Test," and it says that you should not make any statement or write any document that you would not want published on the front page of the *Wall Street Journal*. In the context of public statements regarding a Strategic Transaction, this means that you need to consider not only your targeted audience but also all other audiences. Any public statement is likely to be read by shareholders, employees, regulators, and competitors. This is not to say that public statements cannot be crafted to address all these different groups but just that you have to assume that everyone will get a blended message. As a result public statements about a Strategic Transaction tend to take a lowest common denominator approach, whereby they try to minimize anything that would offend or trouble any constituent group. This makes the crafting of public statements a delicate art, and, thus, this is usually reserved for public relations professionals, who have experience with such carefully worded statements.

Beyond fulfilling any regulatory requirement, the goal of a public statement about a Strategic Transaction is to put a positive spin on the deal and create a positive perception among the key constituent groups. The press and the community of research analysts that provide coverage and research on publicly traded companies are channels through which the public statements can be funneled to reach the key constituents of a company. The challenge is to try to simultaneously send several messages though these channels. Generally, both the Buyer and the Seller will seek to allay fears of employees that the deal will translate into layoffs and pay cuts. Clearly, one does not want to lie when such actions are planned, but the companies can still do a lot to moderate these concerns. For example, to the extent that the Buyer is only contemplating a small number of layoffs, making that clear in the public statements will calm employees by lowering the chance that they will be affected.

To the extent that the Seller is publicly traded, an announcement about a Strategic Transaction can have a substantial impact on the stock price of the Buyer and cause a dramatic shift in the stock price of the Seller. The latter shift is hard to control, since it will simply reflect the market adjusting to the announced value of the deal. However, the impact on the Buyer's stock price is based on the market's perceptions of the deal and can be impacted by the way the deal is portrayed to the market. Public statements by a Buyer should be crafted to send a clear message to the investor base about the value and benefits of the deal and should seek to address and allay concerns that the investors are likely to have. For example, if a Buyer is acquiring a business in a wholly different field, the public announcement of the deal may try to explain how the new business will leverage the existing business and create synergies and competitive advantages.

Public statements also have an impact on the perception of regulators. To the extent that a transaction requires regulatory approval, regulators will read the public statements about a deal with interest, and such statements can cause increased concern or suspicion, or help to allay it. For example, if a company is entering the market in a new state through acquisition of a local business, state regulators will be focused on how much attention this out of state parent will pay to in-state customers and perhaps on whether the parent plans to lay off any in-state workers. Affirmatively announcing plans not to lay off local workers, or to invest in infrastructure to support local customers, can help address regulators' concerns in this case.

Even parties that may receive some sort of private and direct statement from the Buyer or Seller will be impacted by public statements. Employees, customers, partners, and even competitors will read public statements with interest and draw conclusions about the impact of the deal on them. This is one of the reasons that the parties to a Strategic Transaction will try to make private statements to key groups and constituencies either prior to, or at the same time as, public statements about the deal.

Private Statements

The parties to a Strategic Transaction are sometimes able to communicate privately with key constituent groups before a deal becomes public. In other cases, notably where regulations require a public statement at the time a deal is signed or closed, these private statements will happen simultaneously or shortly after a public statement. The goal of these private communications is to directly address the concerns and interests of key constituent groups and sometimes to sway their view of a deal.

Private communications to employees are often made at the time of a deal. In some cases, the Buyer will communicate with its employees, and, in almost all cases, the Seller will reach out to its employee base. The goal of these communications is to allay unreasonable concerns and dispel rumors. In most cases, when a deal is announced employees, particularly those of the Seller, will expect the worst. By communicating plans for integration, at least at a high level, the Buyer is often able to at least somewhat allay concerns of the Seller employee base. The communication can also be used to put a positive spin on the deal as a potential opportunity. For example, a Seller might announce a deal and tell employees that, while there may be some layoffs, it expects most employees to keep their jobs and, in turn, get a better benefit package and more career stability within the larger Buyer's organization.

Private communications may be made to key counterparties, such as suppliers, partners, and large customers. Again the goal is to allay any concerns the deal may raise and highlight the benefits of the deal. For example, the communication might emphasize to a customer of the Seller that the Buyer is committed to continuing to provide the Seller's products and, in fact, will be able to offer a range of complementary products.

It is important to remember that just as it is hard to keep the recipients of private statements from being influenced by the public statements made, it is often hard to keep private statements confidential, and they often leak into the public domain. While a conversation with a single large supplier may be kept secret, a mass email to thousands of employees will usually find its way into the hands of the press.

POSTCLOSING ISSUES

During and after the closing of a Strategic Transaction, the lawyers involved will complete the legal mechanical process of combining the two businesses. While the technical merger of entities occurs at or shortly after closing, there can be a long legal "tail" to the process. In many cases, particularly with a company whose customers are individual consumers, there are regulatory requirements that customers be notified of the transaction, whether or not they are required to consent. There may be other regulatory filings that need to be completed over the weeks and months after the deal is done as well.

Contracts, licenses, leases, and titles may all need to be assigned or changed. In some cases, filings are required to make these changes effective. In the case of contracts and other agreements with counterparties, the Buyer may need to get their approval for the assignment or at least provide them with notification. The process of obtaining approval to assignment is sometimes painless and mechanical. However, in some cases, it can be a challenging process when it is not clear that customers will want to accept the assignment. In situations where some group of contracts represent a material asset of the Seller, the companies will want to expend substantial effort to ensure that these assignments are given. In some cases, getting approval to assignment from some specified percentage of a group of contracts may either be a condition to closing or may drive a mechanism for a postclosing adjustment of the price.

INTEGRATION AND LOOK BACK (THE POSTMORTEM)

When the dust settles on a closing, everyone usually celebrates, but, as discussed in Chapter 9, the closing is only a waypoint in the process of making a deal successful for a Buyer. In most cases, a Seller will leave a closing with the purchase price in hand and little concern about what happens next. The notable exception being a deal where part of the purchase price is linked to postclosing results through an earn-out. However, in every deal, the closing marks the formal start of the integration process, which may go on for months or even years.

One of the keys to doing a successful acquisition, and to running a successful corporate development effort, is to monitor the performance of a deal after it is completed. Not only does this monitoring process help to identify where a deal is failing to live up to expectations in time to change course and correct any problems, but it also serves as a powerful cautionary tale so that the promises and commitments made in the heat of a deal will be remembered and enforced. The temptation to make rosy projections and develop aggressive integration plans, in order to spur support and approval for a deal, is very strong. Business unit managers will see an acquisition as a way to quickly and substantially enlarge their responsibilities and will have an incentive to promise the moon in order to get approval and funding. The key countermeasure to this incentive is to monitor the success of a deal and measure it against the promises, projections, and predictions made during the approval process. The advancement and compensation of key leaders who architected and championed a deal need to be impacted by the performance of the deal. This is particularly true for business managers that have the day-to-day responsibility for managing the acquired business.

There are a variety of ways to create these ongoing incentives and monitor the performance of deals. One simple method is to set regular status checks and require standardized performance reports on every deal. The status checks will force the integration team leader and the business unit owner to carefully monitor the progress of the deal and report the results to company executives.

Another powerful tool is to tie specific metrics of performance to the leaders responsible for them. For the business unit leader, the easiest method is to force her to sign up to any projections made during the approval of the deal. The manager will be expected to ensure that the business meets the performance metrics that justified the investment. For the integration manager, it is useful to set out key goals along a timeline during the integration planning phase and then periodically check on how the integration plan is progressing and whether the milestones are being hit. It is harder to link the performance of a deal to staff functions, such as corporate development, but certainly at a high level, the general performance of a portfolio of deals is a good metric of the performance of corporate development staff. While a shortfall on any one deal may not be within the control of the corporate development team, a pattern of unrealistic expectations going unmet suggests that the team is being too aggressive in promoting deals and not critical enough of the merits of the deals—acting as advocates of the deals rather than of the company and shareholders.

At the end of the day, there is no magic solution to ensure a successful Strategic Transaction, but managing the process effectively, staffing with talented and smart people, and creating the right incentives for the team will go a long way to ensuring that the right deals are chosen and then executed well.

Standard Form Deliverables During a Strategic Transaction Example

Document	Responsible Party
List of Potential Acquisition Targets	Business Unit Manager/Corporate Development
Memo Summarizing Specific Opportunity	Business Unit
P&L Impact Model	Corporate Finance/Business Unit Finance
Business Unit Budget	Business Unit
Valuation Analysis	Corporate Development
Senior Management Presentations	Business Unit/Corporate Development
Term Sheet	Corporate Development/Legal
Due Diligence Report	Due Diligence Team
Definitive Documents	Legal/Corporate Development
Integration Plan	Business Unit Manager
Postclosing Integration Reports	Business Unit Manager

Due Diligence Report
Table of Contents

Standard Deal Process Checklist Example

1. **Identify candidate company and make a preliminary evaluation.**
   - ❑ Business unit drafts one page memo outlining strategic rationale for acquisition and reviews with Corporate Development.
   - ❑ Corporate Development enters deal into internal tracking database.

2. **Hold initial meetings with company to determine mutual interest in acquisition/investment.**
   - ❑ Approval from Business Unit general manager and involvement/approval of Corporate Development necessary for acquisition/investment discussion.

3. **Begin formal acquisition/investment process.**
   - ❑ Corporate Development leads process with assistance from Legal and Finance/Accounting.
     - ☐ Negotiate term sheet—Corporate Development/Legal.
     - ☐ Perform valuation analysis—Corporate Development.
     - ☐ Build initial model to determine pro forma P&L impact—Finance/Accounting.

4. **Obtain approval to proceed to diligence stage.**
   - ❑ Make presentation to Business Unit SVP/EVP and Corporate Development EVP (3–5 pages).
   - ❑ Business Unit SVP/EVP and Corporate Development EVP to sign approval form.

❑ Provide initial notice to corporate groups (HR, IT, Facilities, PR, and Policy—if appropriate).

5. **Complete prediligence activities.**

❑ Finalize term sheet, LOI, and/or no-shop as appropriate.

6. **Perform due diligence.**

❑ Business Unit leads the diligence and integration process with support from Corporate Development.

❑ Form due diligence team and conduct due diligence.

❑ Engage members from all relevant functional groups.

◻ Business diligence—Business Unit

◻ Financial diligence

A. Historical—Corporate Finance and Accounting

B. Projected P&L Impact—BU Finance, Corporate Finance and Accounting

◻ Legal Diligence—Legal

◻ Human Resources Diligence—Human Resources

◻ IT and Facilities Diligence—IT/Facilities

❑ Draft due diligence report for distribution to Business Unit SVP/EVP and Corporate Development EVP.

❑ Develop integration plan for distribution to Business Unit SVP/EVP and Corporate Development EVP.

7. **Approval to sign/close.**

❑ Make presentation to Business Unit SVP/EVP and Corporate Development EVP on transaction and integration plan (10–12 pages).

❑ Business Unit SVP/EVP and Corporate Development EVP to sign approval form.

8. **Close transaction.**

❑ Complete negotiation of definitive documents.

❑ Begin integration implementation planning.

9. **Provide postclosing integration reports to Senior Management at 30, 60, and 90 days.**

Standard Approval Process Example

This is one example of the key steps and kind of approval that might be required by a company during a Strategic Transaction. Each company will have its own standards, procedures, and required approvals. However, nearly all companies will require formal approval for the steps shaded.

Deal Stage	Approval Sought	Approver
Broad M&A strategy	Pursue initial strategy and use resources	Head of Corporate Development and/or GM of relevant unit
First contact	Initiate contact and begin discussions	Head of Corporate Development
Confidentiality agreement	Execute confidentiality agreement on behalf of the company	Head of Corporate Development and legal
Due diligence	Assemble team and conduct full due diligence review of Target	CEO and GM of relevant unit
LOI	Sign nonbinding letter of intent with specific deal terms	CEO, legal and GM of relevant unit
Definitive agreement	Execute binding acquisition agreement	Board, CEO, legal and other key areas, including risk and finance

Approval of a Strategic Transaction: Key Topics in Presentation

Strategic Plan/Basis for Transaction. This section will give the approvers a review of the initial M&A strategy that led to considering this transaction and help them view the deal in the context of the company's overall business.

Overview of New Region and/or Industry Sector. To the extent that the Target company is in a region or industry where the Buyer is not already heavily positioned, this material will provide the approver with a background in the relevant industry or region. This section will discuss such topics as the competitive landscape, growth characteristics of the relevant industry or region, and risks or concerns of entering the industry or region.

Overview of Target Business. This section will discuss the Target business. It will explain the business model of the Target and likely discuss such topics as the product line, major operations, key assets, and competitive advantages of the Target.

Results of Due Diligence Review. This section will review the key findings of the due diligence effort, both positive and negative. To the extent that the deal is still being advocated, this section will also note any key problems and propose mitigants or solutions that prevent them from being "deal breakers."

Financial Pro Forma. Here, a summary of the financial pro forma will be presented. This will be a summary set of financial projections showing how the acquisition will impact the financial performance of the acquiring company or division. The section will also identify key assumptions made in the pro forma, including synergies.

Key Deal Terms. This section will summarize the most important terms of the transaction, including price, payment terms, and any conditions or post-closing obligations.

Initial Integration Plans. The deal team will provide a high level summary of integration plans, which hopefully correlate to the synergy assumptions in the pro forma. Ideally, this section will be drafted and presented by the same leaders who will undertake the actual integration.

Path to Closing. This section, often called "next steps," outlines the key actions and the timing to complete the transaction.

Generic Valuation Exercise

This is an example of a valuation review that might be conducted for a potential acquisition. The chart presents the valuation ranges resulting from an analysis of trading comparables, an analysis of transaction comparables, a discounted cash flow analysis, and a measure of the buyers internal return-on-equity targets or thresholds. The point of this presentation is to allow the reader to review all the different analyses and try to come to some view on the likely market valuation for a Target company.

EXHIBIT F.1 Generic Valuation Exercise

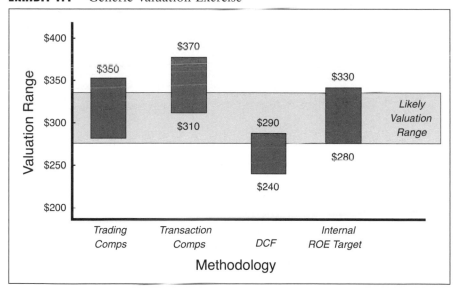

Generic Acquisition Term Sheet for Acquisition by Public Buyer of Privately Held Target

Structure

- Stock-for-stock merger
- Purchase of interests accounting treatment
- Tax-free reorganization with Buyer shares to be issued to Target stockholders in an unregistered private placement.

Economics

- $[   ] of Buyer common stock (number of shares and options issued calculated based on Buyer average stock price over last 10 trading days before signing the definitive agreement) and $[   ] in cash for all outstanding shares of Target capital stock on a fully diluted basis (including common shares, preferred shares, warrants, and options).

- Included in consideration described above, Buyer will assume all outstanding options of Target. Prior to closing, Target shall grant [   ] Target options to its nonexecutive employees, which will be mutually agreed upon by Buyer.

- All Target warrants will be exercised for Target common stock prior to closing, and all Series A preferred stock will be converted into Target common stock prior to closing.

- Pending execution of a definitive agreement, no issuance of securities by Target other than upon exercise of then outstanding stock options.

■ Assumes audited financial statements do not materially differ from those previously given to Buyer, no convertible debt or other securities outstanding other than as set forth in the capitalization table dated [December 31, 2004] provided by Target, and no shareholder distributions pending execution of a definitive agreement.

Posttransaction Management Structure

■ It is anticipated that principal employees will enter into employee agreements on a basis to be discussed.

■ Principal employees will place Buyer shares representing [50]% of their Target common stock ownership in escrow for two years, with 25% released at the end of year one and 25% released at the end of year two. In the event of termination for cause to be defined narrowly or voluntary termination by employee, employee will forfeit shares in escrow. In all other events of termination of employment, (i) all shares in escrow will be released to employee or estate. The principal employees of Target will enter into two-year noncompetition/nonsolicitation agreements without additional compensation.

■ All retained employees will receive cash compensation in line with comparable Buyer employees. Upon closing, Buyer will grant [50,000] options at fair market value to Target employees.

Employee Stock Options

■ To be assumed by Buyer with an appropriate adjustment to exercise price and share numbers, based on the exchange ratio.

■ No new acceleration of vesting other than as previously provided.

Loan

■ Upon execution of this term sheet, Target shall have an option to require Buyer to make a loan of up to $[12] million to Target. Such loan shall be at an interest rate of [6]% and shall be repaid in full on or before [June 30, 2006].

Representations and Warranties

■ Customary representations and warranties.

Conditions to Closing

■ Regulatory approvals, no injunction action, etc.

■ Target shareholder approval.

- No material adverse change in Target.

- 4Q2004 results will be provided prior to closing.

- Receipt of tax opinions regarding tax-free nature of transaction.

- No breach of representations.

- Compliance with preclosing covenants.

- All required third-party consents.

- Other customary conditions.

Termination Rights

- Illegality, material adverse change in Target, breach of representations, warranties or covenants, failure to close by [December 31, 2005].

No-Shop

- Target and its officers, directors, and agents will not directly or indirectly solicit, encourage, facilitate, discuss, negotiate, or accept any offer or proposal from any third party for the acquisition of all or any part of the business, assets, or securities of Target during the term of the merger agreement except for [the investment/loan described above]. Target will immediately notify Buyer of any such offer or proposal, including the terms and parties involved.

- Period of no-shop to begin upon acceptance of these terms in a separate no-shop letter and expire on [June 30, 20X5].

Shareholder Meeting

- Target's board of directors will call a shareholder vote on the merger and recommend a vote in favor of the merger.

- At the time of the signing of the definitive merger agreement, the principal shareholders of Target, who collectively can ensure approval of the merger, will agree to vote and execute irrevocable proxies in favor of the merger.

Indemnification and Escrow

- Shares representing [10]% of the total consideration issuable in merger will be held in escrow until one year after closing to cover undisclosed liabilities and breaches of representations and warranties. This is a subset of the shares held in escrow as outlined in Posttransaction Management Structure provided that if such shares are forfeited to Buyer due to the principal employees terminating, either voluntarily or for cause, the principal shareholders will continue to indemnify Buyer up to a total cap of [10]% of total consideration payable in the merger on a pro rata basis.

- Escrowed shares will be valued at closing stock price for indemnification purposes.

- Representations of the parties shall survive for one year after closing provided that Target's representations as to taxes, capitalization, and title to shares will survive for the applicable statute of limitations.

- The liability of the Target shareholders for indemnification shall not exceed the shares placed in escrow.

Preclosing Covenants

- If practicable the transaction will be simultaneously signed and closed. If not practicable, both parties will use best efforts to close as quickly as possible.

- Target to operate in the ordinary course between signing of definitive agreements and closing of the transaction (e.g., no dividends, incurrence of debt or other liabilities, equity issuances, acquisitions or dispositions, etc. without prior consent of Buyer)

- Target to preserve and maintain customer relationships.

- Target and Buyer will use reasonable best efforts to cause the conditions to closing to be satisfied.

- Other customary covenants.

Fees and Expenses

- Each party will be solely responsible for any fees and expenses it incurs through the use of legal, accounting, financial, and other professional services, including investment banking fees.

Timing

- Upon acceptance of these terms, Buyer, its legal advisors and accounting and financial advisors are prepared to commence expeditiously their due diligence review of Target, as well as the drafting and negotiation of definitive agreements.

Nonbinding

- Except with respect to the sections entitled "Investment," "No-Shop," "Fees and Expenses," and "Confidentiality," no agreement providing for the proposal discussed herein shall be deemed to exist unless and until a final definitive agreement has been executed, delivered, and approved by the respective board of directors, and neither Buyer nor Target nor any other party will have any liability or obligation under the proposed terms contained herein. Both acknowledge that these proposed terms are subject to changes, additions, and deletions prior to the execution of a definitive agreement. In addition, this proposal is subject to satisfactory completion of due diligence.

Confidentiality

- Buyer and Target each agrees to use its best efforts to prevent the unauthorized use or disclosure of any confidential information concerning the other party that has been disclosed to it previously or is disclosed during the course of the negotiation and investigation contemplated by this proposal. The parties also agree to maintain the confidentiality of this proposal and any negotiations between the parties. This obligation shall survive even if a definitive agreement is not reached. The proposed transaction is subject to the terms of our Nondisclosure Agreement.

Generic Investment Term Sheet

Structure	■ Investment for Series [C] preferred stock.
Economics	■ $[ ] cash for [ ]% of all outstanding shares of Target capital stock on a fully diluted basis (including common shares, preferred shares, warrants, and options).
	■ Implied valuation of $[ ] postmoney.
Representations and Warranties	■ Customary representations and warranties.
Conditions to Closing	■ Regulatory approvals, no injunction action, etc.
	■ Target shareholder approval
	■ No material adverse change in Moon.
	■ 4Q2004 results will be provided prior to closing,
	■ Receipt of tax opinions regarding tax-free nature of transaction.
	■ No breach of representations.
	■ Compliance with preclosing covenants.
	■ All required third-party consents.
	■ Other customary conditions.
Termination Rights	■ Illegality, material adverse change in Moon, breach of representations, warranties or covenants, failure to close by [July 31, 2005].

Preclosing Covenants	▪ Target and Investor will use reasonable best efforts to cause the conditions to closing to be satisfied.
	▪ Other customary covenants.
Fees and Expenses	▪ Each party will pay the fees and expenses of its legal, accounting, financial, and other professional services.
Timing	▪ Upon acceptance of these terms, Investor, its legal advisors, and its accounting and financial advisors are prepared to commence expeditiously their due diligence review of Target as well as the drafting and negotiation of definitive agreements.
Nonbinding	▪ Except with respect to the section entitled "Investment," "No-Shop," "Fees and Expenses," and "Confidentiality," no agreement providing for the proposal discussed herein shall be deemed to exist unless and until a final definitive agreement has been executed, delivered, and approved by the respective board of directors, and neither Investor nor Target nor any other party will have any liability or obligation under the proposed terms contained herein. This is intended to define the provisions of an equitable agreement that may be deemed acceptable to both parties. Both acknowledge that these proposed terms are subject to changes, additions, and deletions prior to the execution of a definitive agreement. In addition, this proposal is subject to satisfactory completion of due diligence.
Confidentiality	▪ Investor and Target each agrees to use its best efforts to prevent the unauthorized use or disclosure of any confidential information concerning the other party that has been disclosed to it previously or is disclosed during the course of the negotiation and investigation contemplated by this proposal. The parties also agree to maintain the confidentiality of this proposal and any negotiations between the parties. This obligation shall survive even if a definitive agreement is not reached. The proposed transaction is subject to the terms of our Nondisclosure Agreement.